Bullying in Popular Culture

Bullying in Popular Culture

Essays on Film, Television and Novels

Edited by ABIGAIL G. SCHEG

McFarland & Company, Inc., Publishers
Jefferson, North Carolina

LIBRARY OF CONGRESS CATALOGUING-IN-PUBLICATION DATA

Bullying in popular culture : essays on film, television and novels / edited by Abigail G. Scheg.
    p.   cm.
Includes bibliographical references and index.

ISBN 978-0-7864-9629-7 (softcover : acid free paper) ∞
ISBN 978-1-4766-2100-5 (ebook)

1. Bullies in mass media.   2. Bullying in popular culture.
3. Bullying—Social aspects.   I. Scheg, Abigail G., 1986– editor.
P96.B85B87 2015
302.34'3—dc23   2015013126

BRITISH LIBRARY CATALOGUING DATA ARE AVAILABLE

© 2015 Abigail G. Scheg. All rights reserved

No part of this book may be reproduced or transmitted in any form or by any means, electronic or mechanical, including photocopying or recording, or by any information storage and retrieval system, without permission in writing from the publisher.

Front cover image © 2015 Stockbyte/Thinkstock

Printed in the United States of America

McFarland & Company, Inc., Publishers
  Box 611, Jefferson, North Carolina 28640
    www.mcfarlandpub.com

Table of Contents

Introduction—Abigail G. Scheg	1
The Changing Faces of Bullying in Popular Culture: An Historical Account of Research in Bullying—Kulwinder P. Kaur	13
Bullying Boundaries: How Are Reality Television Programs and School Policies Shaping Youth Perceptions of Acceptable Aggressive Behaviors?—Tamara Girardi	29
Bullying Bullies: Narratives of Territoriality in American Popular Culture—Eduardo Barros-Grela	40
The Chocolate War and Anti-Bullying Novels in Popular Culture—Nina Marie Bone	55
The Power of Praise—Mary-Lynn Chambers	65
Not Just for the Kids: Parents Who Cyberbully—Abigail G. Scheg	82
"Fire is catching!" and So Is Bullying: *The Hunger Games*—Katherine Lashley	91
Queerness and Bullying in Popular Culture—Kylo-Patrick R. Hart	103
Swatch Dogs and Plastics: The Codification of Female Bullying—Kasey Butcher	117
It Gets Better (When You Come Back from the Grave and Kill Them All): Bullying and the Horror Film and the Indeterminacy of the Monster—Fernando Gabriel Pagnoni Berns, Mariana S. Zárate and Canela Ailen Rodriguez Fontao	130

Bullying, Quidditch and the Golden Snitch: *Harry Potter and the Philosopher's Stone*—CHANTELLE MACPHEE 144

"Carrie White burns in hell": Re-Evaluating *Carrie* in the Post-Columbine Era—DON TRESCA 152

Dauntless Bullying in Veronica Roth's *Divergent*— KATHERINE LASHLEY 164

The Post–9/11 John Wayne vs. Bullying: A Tale of a Schadenfreude Obsessed Culture—KELLY F. FRANKLIN 176

About the Contributors 189
Index 193

Introduction

Abigail G. Scheg

Bullying has gained tremendous cultural awareness in recent years. Identifying it as an element of explanation in tragedies such as school shootings has shed light on the need for more critical analysis of interpersonal relationships and the dynamics that establish a bullying situation. Also, bullying has moved from being solely associated with school-age children and teenagers to being recognized as something that happens at all age levels, in all demographics, and in many different types of social circles. Popular culture has long served as a barometer for American life, and it continues to serve as a barometer in the case of bullying behaviors. Bullies have been antagonists in television programs, books, and movies for years. Take, for example, *Back to the Future* from 1985. Marty McFly and his father, George McFly, are the very clear cut "good guys" of the film. They are meek, they generally don't talk back, and they act appropriately. There is, however, an established bully, Biff, who is an antagonist throughout. Also consider the more recent *Harry Potter* books and movies, where Harry is the relatable and lovable protagonist, and Draco Malfoy is an antagonist from his first scene.

These black and white distinctions that viewers have grown accustomed to seeing have changed to varying shades of gray in recent years. Scholarly research is indicating that there are unique considerations regarding bullies and victims, and it is necessary to examine the entire situation in order to understand all its perspectives. Bullying is a social issue, typically occurring in a manner to facilitate or deteriorate social groups or individuals. While always social, the varying representations of bullying in popular culture creates interesting dynamics between characters, and, on a macro-level, between media. Therefore, the purpose of this collection is to offer a variety of perspectives regarding bullying in popular culture to show the development and manifestations of such behaviors across media. These essays discuss bullying in education, in texts, movies, and television shows. This collection also addresses the increasingly gray middle area of bullying behaviors, and how behaviors are complicated by popular culture and today's media.

Bullying behaviors are most traditionally thought of, or sometimes referred to, as "schoolyard bullying." Undoubtedly, bullying has a deeply engrained role in the American education system. Stopbullying.gov, the program of the U.S. Department of Health and Human Services to stop bullying, has an entire section of its site devoted to educators and bullying within the education system. This program found, through the National Center for Education Statistics and Bureau of Justice Statistics, that in 2010–2011, "28% of students in grades 6–12 experienced bullying," and, according to the Center for Disease Control and Prevention, that "20% of students in grades 9–12 experienced bullying" in 2013. The Stopbullying program offers a wealth of good resources to teachers and administrators looking to combat specific elements of bullying behaviors in their schools.

Although bullying in the educational setting is not always directly tied to popular culture, the population of bully and victim in these scenarios often are. Middle school- to high school-aged students are one of the most impressionable demographics for a variety of reasons. Behaviors that they witness in their popular media, as well as perceived behaviors that deliver desired results, are not always the most well-informed actions. As previously stated, bullying has a huge impact on social groups and processes. In a time of immense social pressure and personal development, bullying, popular culture, and education have very clear connections.

In recent years, young adult (YA) novels have found increasing popularity across demographics and now have a place among readers of all ages. The *Harry Potter, Twilight, Hunger Games,* and *Divergent* series have not only been immensely popular novels, but have also been blockbuster films. The film adaptations of the *Harry Potter* books is one of, if not the, highest grossing film franchises of all time, making almost $8 billion (Box Office Mojo). The *Twilight* series, the only other one of these series to have all of its books transformed into films (as of publication of this text), grossed more than $3 billion worldwide (Box Office Mojo). For a genre that once had a very limited readership, YA novels (and their subsequent films) have gained a tremendous following.

All of the series listed above have antagonizing characters that often display bullying behaviors toward one or more of the main characters. Draco Malfoy, Crabbe, Goyle, Deatheaters, the members of the Capitol, other Tributes, Jeanine ... these bullies take on different roles but all play integral roles in the development of the protagonists, the creation of the heroes, and the resolution of the storylines. Therefore, discussions of YA novels, and their film adaptations, are a popular point of discussion in this collection. These texts and films are not only geared to the demographic most often associated with bullying behaviors—youths—but are also immensely successful in popular culture.

Bullying in television and movies is discussed at length throughout this collection. Television and movies create many opportunities for critical analysis of bullies and victims because the incorporation of a bully as a stereotypical antagonist is so prominent. Bullying can take on many forms including, but not limited to, name calling, social isolation, physical abuse and rumor spreading, to name just a few. Displaying these behaviors in popular media designates a clearly defined behavioral pattern for the audience—especially one that can be easily resolved in a twenty-some-minute episode of a television show. Some bullies, and behaviors, though, have much more significant, lasting effects with characters and audiences, making them important considerations for scholarly conversations.

The collection starts with an historical account of bullying research and its connection to popular culture in the past. This essay sets the stage for much of the discussion that occurs throughout the work and serves as background for all the essays and the subject of bullying as a whole. Throughout this collection, bullying is discussed in many varieties of social groups and participants. For instance, "The Power of Praise" analyzes the impact of bullying behaviors on students' educational processes by interviewing students who were involved in bullying as primary research and making connections to similar situations found in popular culture. Other essays, such as "Bullying Boundaries" and "It Gets Better (When You Come Back from the Grave and Kill Them All)," discuss bullying in specific genres of media—reality television and horror, respectively. The essays use some of the most popular media of the present to illuminate the representations and metamorphoses of the bullying cycle. Also, these essays address different types of bullying relationships (such as parents that bully) and analyze characteristics of both bullies and victims.

More specifically, the first essay, Kulwinder P. Kaur's "The Changing Faces of Bullying in Popular Culture: An Historical Account of Research in Bullying," provides an historical analysis of the research pertaining to bullying to inform and frame the conversation of this work. By looking at the development of research, we can better understand bullying behaviors in their many contexts and relationships. Though the research being analyzed is not specific to bullying in popular culture, understanding the many forms and faces of bullying in varying contexts does inform one's overall understanding of bullying and how it is depicted and tolerated in popular culture today.

"Bullying Boundaries: How Are Reality Television Programs and School Policies Shaping Youth Perceptions of Acceptable Aggressive Behaviors?" by Tamara Girardi looks at the impact that reality television has on educational culture and school policy. Physical altercations certainly remain an issue in high schools across the country, but bullying has advanced beyond "Kick Me" signs and groups of boys waiting around the corner for a quiet, unsuspecting kid to walk home from school alone. Perhaps it is the influence of zero tolerance policies that have caused bullies to revise their approaches or be removed from the classroom altogether. Bullying, as it is portrayed in contemporary literature and film, focuses on emotional and mental attacks. The current generation is also influenced by reality television shows where verbal altercations are common, emotional and mental attacks are part of the shows' appeal, and the one violation that will ensure a cast member is removed is if he or she ever physically strikes another cast member. This essay investigates current boundary lines drawn to combat bullying. Specifically, its author questions whether zero tolerance policies in schools and similar policies in reality television shows illustrate to students and audiences that verbal, mental, and emotional bullying is acceptable, perhaps since it cannot be easily measured and corrected, but physical bullying is not. Furthermore, how do the outcomes of verbal, mental, emotion, and physical bullying differ, if at all?

Eduardo Barros-Grela's "Bullying Bullies: Narratives of Territoriality in American Popular Culture" examines a movie and a television show that have been paradigmatic in the contemporary perception of perpetuated harassment in the American educational system, as seen from international audiences: first, Jared Hess's film *Napoleon Dynamite* (2004) added a comical turn to the already-alarming popularity of such harassing practices, and second, Chuck Lorre's sitcom *The Big Bang Theory* (2007–) successfully reaffirmed the positive prominence of characters that have been traditionally depicted as susceptible to bullies. Today, bullying is still common in American schools, but different approaches have been taken to critically observe the complexity of this phenomenon.

Based on the discrepancies in the current perceptions of bullying as a practice to gain "popularity" at school, this essay looks at the problematic nature of bullying through then lens of two rather distant narratives. First,

Dan Houser's video game *Bully* (2006) gave the audience the opportunity to *enact* the role of a bullied teenager in a hostile educational center. As a sandbox type of video game, players participate in the development of the game, and have to make decisions about their attitude toward other characters (including bullies and potential victims). In this sense, this essay is interested in seeing how individuals react to bullying (both as victims and perpetrators) when "protected" by a fictional distance. Also, this essay examines the struggle for territoriality that is inherent to the act of bullying is resignified through the heterotopic space of a videogame.

The second case explored in this essay through a comparative approach is Matt Reeves's film *Let Me In* (2010). In the analysis of this film, this essay also looks at the original Swedish film (Tomas Alfredson's *Let the Right One In*, 2008) to analyze how the identification of the audience with bullied children precipitates the inversion—or, rather, the problematization—of traditional roles in situations of teenager victimization.

Even the terrible act of death by dismembering is received in these films with joy by spectators who long for a rather resilient response instead of the option of an educational process. Both cases refer to the extreme complexity of bullying. Addressed from angles that include humor and terror, this concept is explored in this essay from a theoretical approach based on the study of space and violence and is articulated within the sphere of (de/re)territorialization. Although no specific sections are devoted to theory, its presence is implicit in the analysis of the proposed texts.

In "*The Chocolate War* and Anti-Bullying Novels in Popular Culture" Nina Marie Bone examines popular YA literature and its impact on school-related bullying programs. In addition to teen book series focusing on wizards and vampires, there has developed a new sub-genre in young adult literature, a new wave of literature focusing on the problem of bullying in schools. While much research is being conducted on effective anti-bullying programs, young adult novels are the missing piece of the puzzle. When students see their lives in contexts that are meaningful and relevant to them, they are given the confidence to speak out about bullying and identify effective tools for dealing with this ever-increasing issue. The genre of anti-bully literature may seem new to most, but it actually began in the 1970s with the release of Robert Cormier's book *The Chocolate War* and its sequel *Beyond the Chocolate War*. In these books, we follow the main character, Jerry Renault, through high school and his dealing with a gang of bullies known as the Vigils. The two classic novels offer the viewpoints of not only the bullied, Jerry, but also of the bullies and the bystanders; these two books should be used as the gateway and introduction to other anti-bully novels such as *The Misfits* by James Howe, *Scars* by Cheryl Rainfield, and others. This essay will show (1) anti-bullying young adult novels are being used effectively all over the country to reduce bullying; (2) anti-bullying literature fosters a sense of belonging; and (3) what needs to be done for future success in classrooms with this untapped resource of anti-bullying young adult literature.

"The Power of Praise" by Mary-Lynn Chambers addresses the role of a positive, praise-giving adult figure in the life of a student who has been wounded by bullying. The effect of bullying is seen in the classroom where a student who has been bullied becomes the bully or where the bullied student retreats into the safety of his or her own world. In situations like these, the healthy adult has an opportunity to bring healing through words of praise. Media has captured the role of the encouraging mentor in movies like *The Karate Kid*, where the handyman believes in the hidden talents of a young boy, *Precious*, where an illiterate teen is supported by a teacher and social worker, and *17 Again*, where Alex is bullied by Stan but emboldened by Mark, his magically transformed father. These mentors have the opportunity to infuse the life of a bullied student with the power of praise. Hirschstein et al. affirm the role of praise in a bullied student's life; thus, as instructors we need to add to our pedagogy an element of praise. This essay will examine the stories of a 12-year-old white boy from the upper-middle class and a 19-year-old African American male from the lower class. Both students faced bullying, both students encountered a positive, encouraging mentor, and both students went on to experience success. This essay concludes with practical guidance regarding the incorporation of praise into instructional time and the benefits it will provide to bullied students.

In "Not Just for the Kids: Parents Who Cyberbully" Abigail G. Scheg examines an episode of the popular television series *Law and Order: Special Victim's Unit* (*SVU*) in which a parent is bullying a pregnant teenage girl to get back at her for causing strife among her family members. By looking critically at this episode of *SVU*, this essay demonstrates that bullying is not limited to school-related negative behaviors or kids in middle through high school. Rather, bullying occurs across many demographics and in a number of places.

Katherine Lashley's "'Fire is catching!' and So Is Bullying: *The Hunger Games*" focuses on the bullying—extreme bullying—in *The Hunger Games* trilogy by Suzanne Collins. The bullying takes the forms of the tributes taunting one another during practice and in the arena. There is an even more potent kind of bullying which is not addressed often enough: bullying across social strata and ages: the lower classes are bullied by the upper classes and Katniss is bullied by President Snow.

Although the Capitol poses bullying and its awful effects of injury and death as a game (within the Hunger Games specifically), it is anything but a game, especially as the Hunger Games turn into a rebellion. Bullying leads the bullied and oppressed to eventually stand up for themselves. Bullying is not only imagined as the awful physical and verbal actions toward one another, but as a bloody, gory, and battle-like incident that will not resolve itself until the oppressed stand up for themselves. No longer is bullying an individual occurrence, but something that affects an entire community, for instance, District 12. *The Hunger Games* trilogy and movies demonstrate that bullying occurs in more lethal instances, against more groups of people and not only individuals, and that if allowed to continue, will result in war. Suzanne Collins shows what is possible when it comes to bullying not only for a dystopian future, but also for the present.

"Queerness and Bullying in Popular Culture" by Kylo-Patrick R. Hart explores queerness in relation to bullying as it is represented in the Fox television series *Glee* (2009–present) and the 2003 feature film *The Mudge Boy*. Although bullying is a prominent theme throughout many episodes of *Glee*, this analysis of the television series focuses primarily on the powerful storyline which has the openly gay high school student Kurt Hummel (played by Chris Colfer) bullied relentlessly by the football player Dave Karofsky (played by Max Adler), to the extent that he ultimately decides to enroll in a different school. The analysis of the film concentrates on how the queerness of the farm boy Duncan Mudge (played by Emile Hirsch), who has a chicken as his best friend, is misread as homosexuality by a local bully, who enters into a sadomasochistic relationship with the boy as a result.

One of the common themes foregrounded in both of these narratives is that the bullies' own latent homosexual tendencies are what cause them to feel so threatened by the otherness of the young males around them and to lash out at them in such deleterious and disturbing ways. Another is that queerness (in the sexual orientation sense) does not always manifest itself in blatant or stereotypical ways. Relevant insights offered in the psychological literature on bullying are employed to critique the effectiveness of both of these influential media representations.

Kasey Butcher's "Swatch Dogs and Plastics: The Codification of Female Bullying" looks specifically at female bullies in popular culture. "It's one thing to want someone out of your life, but it's another thing to serve them a wake-up cup full of liquid drainer," Veronica Sawyer says, resisting a plan to kill her best friend, in the 1988 movie *Heathers*. Although female bullies had been portrayed before in films such as *Carrie* (1976), *Heathers* emerged as the first popular film to focus primarily on female bullies. Over the course of the 1990s and early 2000s, psychologists and educators increasingly studied bullying behavior between girls, noting the tendency toward passive-aggressive or relational and hierarchy-based bullying. This trend reached its height with Rachel Simmons' *Odd Girl Out* (2002), Rosalind Wiseman's *Queen Bees and Wannabes* (2002), and *Mean Girls* (2004). These works sought not only to shed light on the politics of female aggression, but also to analyze how to cope with the rules of what *Mean Girls'* Cady Heron calls "girl world." By examining film and television representations of microagressions between girls including the above, *My So Called Life* (1994), *Drive Me Crazy* (1999), *Never Been Kissed* (1999), *Gilmore Girls* (2000–02), *Veronica Mars* (2004–07), *Friday Night Lights* (2006–10), and *Gossip Girl* (2007–12), this essay argues that the representation of high school female bullying has become increasingly codified, based on predictable rules, in a way that makes the signs of bullying easy to spot, but also an expected part of young women's experiences. This essay further asserts that, although some works playfully subvert the rules (notably all before *Mean Girls*), the persistent representation of adolescent female hierarchy makes it hard to imagine an alternative, thus portraying this aggression as inevitable rather than a problem worth addressing.

"It Gets Better (When You Come Back from the Grave and Kill Them All): Bullying and the Horror Film and the Indeterminany of the Monster" by Fernando Gabriel Pagnoni Berns, Mariana S. Zárate and Canela Ailen Rodriguez Fontao examines bullying in the popular horror genre. Bullying has been one of the most used topics in horror cinema since the opening of *Carrie* (Brian de Palma) in 1975. It is not that rare if we take into account that many fans of fantastic fiction are introverts (especially teenagers) who suffered bullying on a daily basis. Some audience members may find in cinema a possibility of catharsis.

We may also wonder how the bullied teenagers in a genre constructed around real social anxieties are represented. There are three main groups of films which represent bullies. In films such as the aforementioned *Carrie* (and its sequels and remakes), *Terror Train* (Roger Spottiswoode, 1980) or *The Pit* (Lew Lehman, 1981), the bullied kids are depicted as monsters who kill their peers for revenge. Other films represent them as victims or heroes, as in *Return of the Living Dead Part II* (Ken Wiederhorn, 1988),

The Burning (Tony Maylam, 1981) and *A Nightmare on Elm Street Part II: Freddy's Revenge* (Jack Sholder, 1985). Finally, a third group has bullied kids as hybrids between the above mentioned categories: in *Christine* (John Carpenter, 1983), *Let Me In* (Matt Reeves, 2010) or *Fido* (Andrew Currie, 2006), the bullied ones have a supernatural being that help them against the bullies.

What do these different films have in common? Here, a bridge between bullying and horror film reappears in the notions of the abject and the Other, figures used when trying to analyze bullying since both speak about the anxieties of social exclusion in a stage of life (childhood and adolescence) where the formation of identity is crucial. Historically, these notions are used with great frequency to analyze horror fiction, since the anxieties from a particular society are embodied in an abject monster considered as an Other that must be destroyed to produce the return of the status quo. Now the question would be what status quo is restored at the end of horror films with bullying? Which order is established when, for example, Carrie dies?

Many of these films have endings that avoid a possible restoration of the established. The authors argue that this is because the position of the abject/monster is very fluid in bullying situations. Usually the Other is the victim of the bully, but sometimes the abject Other is the bully. Thus, there is a permanent shift of poles which makes explicit how complicated bullying is and that the horror film portrays through its metaphors created from a deep fear of loss of control. This essay's aim is to analyze a large corpus of horror films to demonstrate that bullying is represented as a mobile social intra-activity rather than a static phenomenon.

Chantelle MacPhee, in "Bullying, Quidditch and the Golden Snitch: *Harry Potter and the Philosopher's Stone*," examines bullying relationships in the first book of the popular Harry Potter series. A bully belittles and berates a victim to feel empowered, in control. The way in which the aggressor controls the victim may vary: manipulation, innuendo, lies, gossip, and so on. This sense of power is intoxicating as the bully becomes ever more enraptured by the actions and reactions of his or her victim(s). If the victim responds, then he or she begins to lose control and the aggressor may become even more domineering. The victim's self-worth is attacked, effaced, regarding his or her own importance or role in the community, with family, friends. In *Harry Potter and the Philosopher's Stone*, J.K. Rowling appears to address this issue quite substantially. Harry Potter is the victim of bullying by Dudley, Aunt Petunia, Uncle Vernon and Draco Malfoy. However, as the novel progresses, Quidditch becomes the metaphor for the bullying and the novel becomes ever more intriguing as our understanding of the game unfolds.

In "'Carrie White burns in hell': Re-Evaluating *Carrie* in the Post-Columbine Era," Don Tresca examines Stephen King's 1974 novel *Carrie* and its cinematic adaptations in 1976 (by Brian DePalma) and 2013 (by Kimberly Peirce) to evaluate the evolution of reader and viewer response to the character of Carrie White and her actions within the story. This essay shows how Carrie's actions have moved from justified based on her victimization status (in King's novel and DePalma's film) to the actions of a vengeance-driven monster whose justification is much less clear-cut (in Peirce's film). This alteration of Carrie's motivations and activities has largely been caused by recent real-life bully retribution dramas (such as Columbine) which paint the bullied shooters as dangerous sociopaths and the targets of their "vengeance" as innocent victims. Like the shooters at Columbine, Carrie's vengeance carries far beyond those who tormented her and causes the untold destruction and trauma to the guilty and innocent alike. This essay also examines some of the minor characters (such as Chris Hargensen, Sue Snell, Tommy Ross, Billy Nolan, Miss Collins/Desjardin, and Carrie's mother Margaret White) to show how their actions (or lack of action) are colored by the reader/viewer's knowledge of recent real-life tragedies involving bullied teens.

In "Dauntless Bullying in Veronica Roth's *Divergent*," Katherine Lashley examines the bullying behaviors occurring in the popular novel *Divergent*. One of the most shocking elements in the popular young-adult novel is the prevalence of bullying. Yet, the role of bullying in *Divergent* challenges the roles of gender, class, and disability as well, making the presentation of bullying worthy of analysis. The female protagonist, Tris, is bullied because of her gender, size, and class, which leads the bullies to assume she is inferior, not as able-bodied as they are. In effect, they view her as disabled. When she demonstrates her speed, strength, and resilience, the bullies attempt to disable her. A similar scenario occurs with Edward, except the bullies do manage to disable him, thereby forcing him out of Dauntless.

The result of the bullying proves that being disabled in some way is undesirable because the characters, particularly Tris, know that being disabled will result in being bullied, which will result in even further disabilities. Yet Tris, being a divergent individual due to her cognitive dis/ability, learns that in order for her to escape bullying and further damage to herself as a disabled individual, she needs to stop the bullying and negative perceptions of disability. Thus, *Divergent* reveals that bullying is caused by disability and it results in disability, which presents a circular trap for those being bullied, as the goal is not only to avoid being bullied but avoid being disabled.

"The Post–9/11 John Wayne vs. Bullying: A Tale of a Schadenfreude Obsessed Culture" by Kelly F. Franklin examines well-known male characters in popular culture to address a shift in gender roles, particularly in young adult (YA) literature. In particular, this essay discusses Sherman Alexie's character Junior in the novel *Absolutely True Diary of a Part-Time Indian,* the post–9/11 American male character, bullying, reality television, and the phenomenon of Schadenfreude.

The target audience for this collection includes individuals teaching or researching bullying or popular culture, as well as those interested in literature or media, particularly media targeted at adolescents, the demographic most likely to be engaged with bullying behavior in some capacity.

Works Cited

BoxOfficeMojo. *Franchises.* BoxOfficeMojo, 9 Dec. 2014. Web.
Stopbullying.gov. *About Bullying.* Stopbullying.gov, 9 Dec. 2014. Web.

The Changing Faces of Bullying in Popular Culture

An Historical Account of Research in Bullying

Kulwinder P. Kaur

Bullying is not a pop culture problem; rather, it has always been there as one of the animal desires like any other evil. The present-day concept of bullying may seem relatively new, but the phenomenon is part of the history of mankind that has changed faces in terms of predominance of its components and recognition by the general public, researchers, and policy makers. The evolution has changed our physical, mental, emotional, social, and psychological tolerance regarding bullying behaviors. We have also evolved intellectually and become more unstable emotionally. Though bullying was not studied systematically by researchers, it had been referred to in the literature. Hyojin Koo, a Korean researcher, has reviewed the status of bullying in his journal article "A Time Line of the Evolution of School Bullying in Differing Social Contexts." Koo mentioned that the first significant journal article by Burk appeared in 1897 and addressed bullying among young people. It was followed by a Scandinavian researcher, Olweus, in 1978. Since then the issue of bullying has become important news, giving way to many research approaches in various social contexts as well as new laws. Also, bullying has taken different forms from traditional to cyberbullying. Cyberbullying is more closely associated with pop culture. In this essay I will review Koo's article and other studies to traverse the path bullying has taken from past to present. The purpose is to study how the behavior has developed and the consequences associated with it.

Perceptions of bullying are subjective based on one's character, family background, community, and the context in which the bullying, or bullying situation, occurs. At some places and specifically more so in earlier times, it was considered a normal part of personal relationships, whereas more presently it may be treated as a crime, depending on the social context and time period.

Definitions of Bullying

Koo states that aggression can be considered an inclusive term for unacceptable behavior, and researchers have agreed that bullying or school violence are usually considered subsets of aggression (Roland and Idsoe; Smith, Cowie, Olafsson and Leifooghe). Koo selected three definitions of violence that cover the spectrum of bullying behaviors. Olweus defines violence as "aggressive behavior where the actor or perpetrator uses his or her own body, or an object, to inflict injury or discomfort upon other individuals" (in Smith et al. 12). The World Health Organization defines "violence as intentional use of physical and psychological force or power, threatened or actual, against oneself, another person or against a group or community, that either results in or has a high likelihood or resulting in injury, death, psychological harm, maldevelopment, or deprivation." Third, the Encarta Dictionary defines violence in two statements: "the use of physical force to injure somebody or damage something; the illegal use of unjustified force, or the effect created by the threat of this." These definitions share two features: first, violence is harmful and damaging, or at least threatens harm or damage; and second, violence is intended and therefore accidental damage or hurt done by someone is not usually thought of as violent behavior. However, there are differences as well; for instance, two of the definitions suggest that violence should be physical, but solely identifying physical violence as violent behavior is not agreed upon by all. There are other types of violence besides physical that can be equally, or more, harmful. Violence can be non-physical and still cause lasting impacts on the victim and perpetrator.

Further, bullying is a subset of aggression and, like violence, it involves intentional harm to others. Over time, the definition of bullying has been modified. Olweus (*Bullying at School*) explains that a person is being bullied when he or she is exposed, repeatedly, over time, to negative actions on the part of one or more other students (9). According to Farrington, bullying is repeated oppression of a less powerful person by a more powerful one. Smith and Sharp define it as "systematic abuse of power," like

Farrington. Rigby states that bullying involves a desire to hurt another, a harmful action, a power imbalance, repetition, an unjust use of power, evident enjoyment by the aggressor, and generally a sense of being oppressed on the part of the victim. Most of the definitions have common elements that bullying is a type of aggression, and it involves repetition and imbalance of power. Also, it is not limited to physical actions alone. Further, Pikas clarifies that the meaning of bullying may cover multiple types of relationships: a single bully attacking an individual or groups of individuals. Even though for victims of bullying external characteristics could be a part of the reasons for being bullied, there could be many other reasons as well (including, but not limited to, personality).

According to the Centers for Disease Control (CDC), the initial release of *Bullying Surveillance Among Youths: Uniform Definitions for Public Health and Data Elements, Version 1.0* is a starting point that will need to be revised periodically as more becomes understood about bullying behaviors. The CDC's latest (2014) uniform definition of bullying explains bullying among youths as

> any unwanted aggressive behavior(s) by another youth or group of youths who are not siblings or current dating partners that involves an observed or perceived power imbalance and is repeated multiple times or is highly likely to be repeated. Bullying may inflict harm or distress on the targeted youth including physical, psychological, social, or educational harm [17].

This definition clarifies that a single act of aggression is not classified as bullying, but in order to be considered bullying, the behavior either is repeated, or has the likelihood to be repeated.

Modes and Types of Bullying

As per the latest CDC compilation of information on bullying, there are two modes of bullying: direct and indirect. Direct modes of bullying include aggressive behavior(s) that occur in the presence of the targeted youth. Examples of direct aggression include, but are not limited to, face-to-face interaction, such as pushing the targeted individual, or directing harmful written or verbal communication at an individual. Indirect behavioral modes include aggressive behavior(s) that are not directly communicated to a targeted individual. Examples of indirect aggression include, but are not limited to, spreading false and/or harmful rumors or communicating harmful rumors electronically.

In agreement with other researchers, the CDC identifies three types of bullying: physical, verbal, and relational. Physical bullying refers to the use of physical force by the perpetrator against a targeted individual. Examples include, but are not limited to, hitting, kicking, punching, spitting, tripping, and pushing. Verbal bullying involves oral or written communication by the perpetrator against the targeted individual that causes him or her harm. Examples include, but are not limited to, mean taunting, name calling, threatening or offensive written notes or hand gestures, inappropriate sexual comments, or verbal threats. In relational bullying, the behaviors by a perpetrator are designed to harm the reputation and relationships of the targeted individual. Direct relational bullying includes, but is not limited to, efforts to isolate the targeted individual by keeping him or her from interacting with their peers or ignoring them. Indirect relational bullying includes, but is not limited to, spreading false and/or harmful rumors, publicly writing derogatory comments, or posting embarrassing images in a physical or electronic space without the individual's permission or knowledge.

History of Bullying

Koo explains that "in the 19th century, although the term bullying was not mentioned, the pattern of it has been described as interpersonal violence in everyday life (e.g. D'cruze, 2000)" (109). Swift pointed out that in the UK, the Irish were victims of racist violence in urban and rural areas. In the same vein, Heinmann pointed out victims' external characteristics (such as being an immigrant, and using a dialect) as reasons for being bullied. Koo states that

> defining these situations as everyday violence or interpersonal violence does not imply that this violence was insignificant. Rather than looking down on these experiences, the everyday or interpersonal relationship is a useful way of understanding the dysfunctional interaction between people known to each other, but who are operating at a different power level [109].

Koo shares a good example of introducing bullying and discussing the term in early Victorian times. Koo reports that *Tom Brown's Schooldays*, first published in 1857, contains a famous example of bullying in school: "'Very well, then, let's roast him,' cried Flashman, and catches hold of Tome by the collar; one or two boys hesitate, but the rest join in" (Hughes 188). This excerpt from the popular book indicates that school bullying was a well-recognized circumstance in Victorian England, even if it was not officially reported. The review of literature suggests that there are "not many other examples of bullying in popular books of that time" (109) and thus is difficult to determine the development of the phenomenon of bullying in schools until systematic research on bullying began in the 1970s when Olweus took the lead to study this growing issue.

A daily newspaper, *The Times*, introduced the first bullying incident on August 6, 1862, after the death of a soldier named Flood, according to Koo. He states that "the serious problem of bullying and its consequences warranted official mention and this was the first published announcement on bullying in *The Times* for the period covered since 1790" (109). Koo also reports how the news writer defined bullying:

> The bullying propensities of human nature have, generally speaking, these remarkable characteristics that they are not wandering, volatile fluttering, oscillating, unsteady appetites, hopping about and changing from one object to another, but that they settle upon some one object and stick close and faithfully and perseveringly to it. They are about the most unchangeable thing that this fickle world possesses [*The Times* p. 8, col. f].

It is obvious that according to the writer, even at that time, bullying was considered a part of human nature manifested; this includes systematic bullying in the army, and according to the author, the soldier died as a result of bullying: "It is clear from the evidence that this unfortunate man, dreadfully as he retaliated upon his tormentors, was the victim of long, malignant, and systematic bullying" (*The Times* p. 8, col. f).

Koo is correct in stating that these examples clearly indicate the elements of bullying—that is, the victim had retaliated against the bully, who was one of the officers, and was singled out for a long time by the rest as an object of constant exasperation and attack. According to Koo, around this time, bullying was construed as a misadventure of young schoolboys, particularly those in boarding schools, which was carried out by senior pupils and teachers. The death of a boy in the King's School in Cambridge serves as a prime example of bullying in schools. Significant attention in the UK was given to an incident where a twelve-year-old boy in the King's School died from bullying behavior by an older group of students in 1885. After the death of the boy, a former student of King's School wrote a letter to the editor of *The Times* on April 27, 1885, reporting on the tragic incident and the ignorance of the teachers about the phenomenon, as well as how a few physically stronger boys bullied peer group members and senior groups as a replacement of harsh punishment by teachers as follows:

> Bullying of the kind mentioned constantly occurred during the seven years I was at the school, and in no case can I remember a porter interfering—indeed, I doubt whether old Tomas knew that was considered part of his duty ... as for the masters, they naturally spent the short break in the middle of the day in getting their own luncheon. In my time a favourite habit of some of the elder boys was to link arms and rush down the long corridor at the top of their speed, and woe betide any unfortunate youngster [*The Times* p. 7, col. e].

It is disturbing to realize what Koo has narrated about the accident, that caused the death of a twelve-year-old boy, prompted people to write letters to the council in order to investigate the death. Inspectors of the council examined the death and saw bullying as a "misadventure." There was no punishment given to the boys involved. People from the council also believed that this behavior could be a normal part of a boy's school life. It can be assumed that at that time the meaning of bullying was presented as an acceptable behavior among young male students.

Recently, we have become more concerned about the repercussions of bullying after Olweus' study. Rabinowicz and King state that "we are much more sensitive to violence than were our less civilized ancestors" (10). Koo questions the change in our attitude towards bullying. He considers World War II as a factor that significantly altered and affected our awareness of human rights and dignity of life. This includes the notion that citizens have a right to be safe from the threat of violence as "everyone has the right to life, liberty and security of person" (UN, article 3) as reported by Koo.

In the past, simple behaviors associated with bullying were more clearly specified than we experience in our world today. Bullying behaviors were generally described, and understood, as physical or verbal harassment that related to death, strong isolation, or extortion in school children. Bullying was largely seen as misbehavior in direct physical aggression and verbal taunting until around 1950, according to Koo. Koo quoted Morgan, stating that in the early 1950s, studies of children's behavior found that aggressive behavior among children involved mainly robbery and stealing as the two most serious misdemeanors for children. In the 1960s, the perceptions of children's misdemeanor became more complicated as Greenberg's 1969 list of student misbehaviors include persistent inattention, carelessness, underhandedness, and smoking. Since the 1970s, children's behavior has increasingly included bullying behavior, and the first systematic study on bullying was conducted by Olweus in 1978, using a "self-report questionnaire." Since then, a number of researchers in varied disciplines, ranging from education and psychology, to criminology and policy, have been working to determine the solution to the bullying epidemic. Olweus studied overt behavior among school children and described bullying as physical harm, but facial expressions and other forms of indirect bullying were not mentioned in the descriptions of bullying behavior, and only more direct and harmful behavior used to be considered as bullying. However, in contrast to the forms of bullying in earlier times, and the first descriptions of bullying as one or a few physically strong boys directly and harshly treating weaker ones, bullying in modern contexts includes more psychological and verbal threats as well.

Until the 1980s, bullying behavior referred to direct, physical forms, and later it was expanded to include indirect forms of bullying, as well such as rumor spreading (Bjorkqvist, Lagerspetz, and Kaukiainen, 992). Olweus also indicated that more indirect ways of bullying such as unkind gestures and facial expressions were still considered bullying behaviors. Other researchers have included other forms of indirect behaviors such as gossiping, unkind gestures, and spreading rumors (Rigby and Smith). The nature of bullying has become more physical and psychological in nature in the popular culture of today.

Recently, a new type of bullying, known as "cyberbullying," has developed and grown rapidly. Cyberbullying refers to "an aggressive, intentional act carried out by a group or individual, using electronic forms of contact, repeatedly and over time against a victim who cannot easily defend him or herself" (Smith et al., 376). As with traditional bullying, estimates of cyberbullying vary across studies depending on the age and gender of the participants sampled, the time, parameters assessed, and the venue where the cyberbullying occurs (Monks, Robinson, and Worlidge; Raskauskas and Stoltz; Sakellariou, Carroll, and Houghton; Williams and Guerra). According to Nansel et al., traditional bullying occurs predominantly at school during the school day whereas cyberbullying can occur anywhere and any time of the day or night since it occurs via technology (Koalski, Morgan, and Limber).

Growing awareness of cyberbullying has led people to believe that the actual instances of cyberbullying are also increasing. There is no reason to doubt that cyberbullying has increased, as relevant technology has become more and more sophisticated and accessible anonymously. Also, as the proportion of students in most communities having access to mobile phones and the Internet has approached saturation, cyberbullying is continuing to rise instead of leveling off. It may be explained by other technological advances. Rigby and Smith have found that cyberbullying involving abusive text messages and/or emails rose for young teenage students in the north of England between 2002 and 2004, but reduced slightly thereafter. With respect to frequency of cyberbullying ("once a week or more often"), the prevalence rose from 1.1 percent in 2002 to about 1.8 percent in 2004 and went down to about 1.1 percent in 2006. Further analysis by Rivers and Noret indicated that increases in occasional cyberbullying were greater for girls, but for more frequent cyberbullying, trends were similar for boys and girls. This study did not include other aspects of cyberbullying involving social media websites that have also grown exponentially in popularity.

Several differences between cyberbullying and more traditional forms of bullying have been identified. Specifically, cyberbullying is "perceived as different from other types of bullying by victims" (Slonje and Smith) and "more likely to occur outside of school" (Smith et al.). Victims of cyberbullying are more likely to report depressive symptoms than cyberbullies, or traditionally-bullied victims (Wang et al.). Current research suggests that cyberbullying occurs with less prevalence than the other types of bullying, but still affects around 10 to 20 percent of adolescents who report being bullied, or bullying others electronically (Ybarra, Boyd, et al.; Ybarra, Mitchell, et al.). Litwiller emphasizes the importance of studying the experience of bullying in childhood and adolescence, as research has shown that childhood bullying predicts adult suicide attempts (Meltzer et al.) as well as suicide deaths by the age of 25 (Klomek et al.).

Popular culture cyberbullying is a recent variant of the traditional bullying process, in which individuals use electronic communication as a medium to harass, degrade, embarrass, and deliberately hurt others (Kowalski et al.). Cyberbullying using mobile phones and the Internet may involve sharing unpleasant or confidential emails, instant messages, pictures, videos, or text messages about a victim to others or sending such messages to a victim. Numerous venues exist on the Internet where cyberbullying can take place; the most popular of these include chat rooms, personal blogs (online journals), polling sites, and social networking sites such as Facebook, MySpace, and Bebo (Kowalski et al.). Although the concepts of bullying and victimhood have been the focus of research since the 1970s, several areas relating to these constructs require further delineation. Stability over time of bullying and victimization and the nature of the relationships between bullying and victimization over time require further specification, and their extension to the world of cyberbullying and cyber victimization is needed as well (Jose et al.).

Bullying Among Special Populations

Most research on childhood bullying focuses on peer bullying, mainly in schools. Researchers have indicated that children who are consistently bullied by peers have an increased risk of developing new mental health-related symptoms, and children who have high levels of mental health problems are more likely to be bullied (Fekkes et al.; Salmon et al.). Students who have disabilities are subjected to bullying more than their peers. Factors associated with victimization were identified in children with autism spectrum disorders (ASD) including age, internalizing and externalizing mental health problems, communication difficulties, number of friends at school, and a parent's mental health problems (Cappadocia, Weiss, and Pepler). It has been reported that variables such as age and having a diagnosis of Asperger's syndrome are found to be predictive of victimization, with children having special needs bullied at greater frequencies than other youth (Carter; Little).

Although a nationally representative U.S. sample shows that about one third of adolescents have experienced some form of bullying in school (Nansel et al.), research shows that bullying is even more prevalent among lesbian, gay, and bisexual (LGBT or sexual minority) youth (Berlan, Corliss, Field, Goodman, and Bryn Austin; Hunt and Jensen; Kosciw, Greytak, Bartkiewicz, Boesen, and Palmer). For instance, in analyses of pooled youth risk behavior survey data from states that gathered information on sexual orientation, Kann et al. noted that significantly more LGB than heterosexual high school students reported being in a physical fight and missing school because they felt unsafe there. Recent evidence suggests that aspects of victimization such as frequency, duration, and severity increase the risk of negative health outcomes (Wilsnack, Kristjanson, Hughes, and Benson, 2012). Obviously, the reported prevalence of bullying among the LGB population is significantly higher than the non–LGB population (Berlan et al.; Kann et al.); this group may be at increased risk for health problems across their lifespans.

The evolution of the study of bullying can be identified in the analyses of gender (Carrera-Fernandez et al.). At first, studies focused almost exclusively on analyzing bullying among young males, who were considered more involved as perpetrators and victims than young females (Byrne; Olweus; Ortega and Mora-Merchan). The analysis of the phenomenon was ignored in girls, neglecting their bullying associations (Gruber and Fineran; Keddie; Osler & Vincent) from what could be considered a "gender-blind position" (Carrera et al.). This analysis covered research from the 1970s to the 1990s, when "relational aggression" was identified and started to receive attention. From this perspective, there are not only quantitative differences, but more importantly, qualitative differences between both the genders related to bullying. Boys are more often involved in direct physical and verbal incidents of abuse than girls, who are significantly more likely to be involved in relational or social kinds of aggression than boys (Bjorkqvist and Osterman; Losel and Bliesener; Smith).

Contrary to the traditional approaches, where the study of bullying was limited to school children only, modern diverse approaches to studying bullying behaviors have included adult populations as well. Workplace bullying refers to a prolonged and repeated negative behavior at work directed against one or more employees who are unable to defend themselves (Einarsen et al.; Leymann), leading to numerous negative outcomes for the affected workers (Einarsen and Mikkelsen) as well as organizations (Hoel et al.). Researchers have identified workplace bullying as one of the most harmful social stressors in organizations (Hauge, Skogstad, and Einarsen; Zapf, Knorz, and Kulla). Workplace bullying has been reported to be a relevant issue in almost every type of organization (see, e.g., Einarsen and Skogstad; Hoel and Cooper), with social, health, public administration and education being reported to have the highest rate of occurrence (Zapf et al.). Zabrodska and Kventon state that given the prominence of education on the list of risk sectors, it is interesting that, until the beginning of the new millennium, bullying in higher education was on the margins of research interest (Keashly and Neuman; for exceptions see Björkqvist et al.; Lewis; Spratlen). The research interest in bullying has seen some shift in focus since the last decade. The reportedly growing number of researchers in this area have begun to explore the ways in which the academic environment provides opportunities for workplace bullying (Keashly and Neuman) that may be attributed to the diversification of bullying research and the restructuring of higher education in western Europe and the U.S. (Zabrodska and Kventon).

Anti-Bullying Laws

There has been significant pressure from parents who have lost their children because of bullying behaviors for government officials to enact anti-bullying laws. States around the nation are responding to the tragedies resulting from bullying in schools. Seth's Law was enacted as a bill named after a thirteen-year-old who hanged himself after being bullied for being gay (Mayer). It was enacted after a school district in California failed to "adequately investigate or respond appropriately" to the bullying. Just prior to this tragedy, schools in New York were mandated to "thoroughly train a staff member to handle sensitive issues of harassment and discrimination" (Hadam 17) under the Dignity for All Schools Act (DASA). DASA prohibits harassment and discrimination of individuals on school property, or at school functions, based on a person's actual or perceived race, color, weight, national origin, ethnic group, religion, religious practice, disability, sexual orientation, gender, or sex. In response to the suicide of Rutgers University student, Tyler Clementi, New Jersey has also enacted new anti-bullying legislation where schools must coordinate efforts with state law enforcement officials "to address potential crimes and serious acts of bullying in schools" (State of New Jersey). Under the law, educators must receive training, designate an anti-bullying coordinator, report incidences of bullying within several days, and provide counseling and intervention for children who are victims and bullies. The New Jersey law requires educators to report acts of bullying on or off school grounds to the principal within two days. Forty-nine out of 50 states have bullying intervention laws as of now (Carter). There are 11 key components suggested by the Department of Health and Human Services through the anti-bullying education website for states to consider while creating anti-bullying laws. The components are helpful in creating or improving the anti-bullying laws. These components include statements of purpose and scope, specification of prohibited conduct, enumeration of specific characteristics, development and implementation of LEA (local education agencies) policies, components of LEA policies, review of local policies, communication plan, training and preventive education, transparency and monitoring, and a statement of rights to other legal resources (Key Components in State Anti-Bullying Laws).

Conclusion

Bullying in American popular culture has become an epidemic with stories in the news on a regular basis. There have been many reported bullying-related deaths among people of all ages and demographics that garner attention and attract more conversation to this topic. Obviously, researchers are doing their best to bring the facts to this emotionally-charged conversation, and the government is also investigating sufficient and appropriate bullying control. We, as parents, caretakers, teachers, and friends need to observe behavior, especially changes in behavior, in order to identify the bullies and victims and intervene early on before this behavior continues and perpetuates. Victim identification is equally as important as the victims of bullying often don't express their problem to others and keep suffering, which may lead to suicide or mental health problems. Support is needed for the efforts to control bullying and help the bullies, as well as the victims, to save precious lives.

Notes

1. Montana is the only state with only anti-bullying policy without any law. Arizona, Illinois, Indiana, Kansas, Minnesota, North Dakota, Tennessee, and Texas have anti-bullying state laws but no policies. The rest of the states and U.S. territories have both anti-bullying policies and state laws. At present, no federal law directly addresses bullying.

2. At stopbullying.gov, there are examples of all the 11 key components in state bullying laws.

Works Cited

Berlan, Elise D., Heather L. Corliss, Alison E. Field, Elizabeth Goodman, and S. Bryn Austin. "Sexual Orientation and Bullying Among Adolescents in the Growing Up Today Study." *Journal of Adolescent Health* 46.4 (2010): 366–71. Print.

Björkqvist, Kaj, Kirsti M. J. Lagerspetz, and Ari Kaukiainen. "Do Girls Manipulate and Boys Fight? Developmental Trends in Regard to Direct and Indirect Aggression." *Aggressive Behavior* 18 (1992): 117–27. Print.

Björkqvist, Kaj, and Karin Österman. "Finland." *The Nature of School Bullying: A Cross-national Perspective*. London: Routledge, 1999. 56–67. Print.

Björkqvist, Kaj, Karin Österman, and Kirsti M. J. Lagerspetz. "Sex Differences in Covert Aggression Among Adults." *Aggressive Behavior* 20 (1994): 27–33. Print.

Burk, Frederic L. "Teasing and Bullying." *The Pedagogical Seminary* 4 (1897): 336–71. Print.

Byrne, B. "IRELAND." *The Nature of School Bullying: A Cross-national Perspective*. London: Routledge, 1999. 112–128. Print.

Cappadocia, M. Catherine, Jonathan A. Weiss, and Debra Pepler. "Bullying Experiences Among Children and Youth with Autism Spectrum Disorders." *Journal of Autism and Developmental Disorders* 42 (2012): 266–77. Print.

Carrera-Fernandez, M.-V., M. Lameiras-Fernandez, Y. Rodriguez-Castro, and P. Vallejo-Medina. "Bullying Among Spanish Secondary Education Students: The Role of Gender Traits, Sexism, and Homophobia." *Journal of Interpersonal Violence* 28.14 (2014): 2915–940. *Academic Search Complete*. Web. 15 Oct. 2014. [doi:10.1177/0886260513 488695]

Carter, Susan. "The Bully at School: An Interdisciplinary Approach." *Issues in Comprehensive Pediatric Nursing* 35.3–4 (2012): 153–62. Print.

Cooper, Leigh A., and Amanda B. Nickerson. "Parent Retrospective Recollections of Bullying and Current Views, Concerns, and Strategies to Cope with Children's Bullying." *Journal of Child and Family Studies* 22.4 (2013): 526–540. Web. 15 Oct. 2014. [doi: 10.1007/s10826-012-9606-0].

Cruze, Shani. *Everyday Violence in Britain, 1850–1950: Gender and Class*. Harlow, England: Longman, 2000. Print.

Einarsen, Ståle. "The Concept of Bullying at Work." *Bullying and Emotional Abuse in the*

Workplace: International Perspectives in Research and Practice. London: Taylor & Francis, 2003. 3–30. Print.

Einarsen, Ståle, and Anders Skogstad. "Bullying at Work: Epidemiological Findings in Public and Private Organizations." *European Journal of Work and Organizational Psychology* 5.2 (1996): 185–201. Print.

Farrington, David P. "Understanding and Preventing Bullying." *Crime and Justice*, Vol. 17. Chicago: University of Chicago Press, 1993. 381–458. Print.

Farrington, David P., and Brandon C. Welsh. "Family-based Prevention of Offending: A Meta-analysis." *Australian and New Zealand Journal of Criminology* 36 (2003): 127–51. Print.

Fekkes, M. "Do Bullied Children Get Ill, or Do Ill Children Get Bullied? A Prospective Cohort Study on the Relationship Between Bullying and Health-Related Symptoms." *Pediatrics* 117 (2006): 1568–574. Print.

Gladden, R.M., A.M. Vivolo-Kantor, M.E., Hamburger, and C.D. Lumpkin. "Bullying Surveillance Among Youths Uniform Definitions for Public Health and Recommended Data Elements Version 1.0." National Center for Injury Prevention and Control, Centers for Disease Control and Prevention and the United States Department of Education, 1 Jan. 2014. Web. 5 Nov. 2014. http://www.cdc.gov/violenceprevention/pdf/bullying-definitions-final-a.pdf.

Greenberg, Bernard. *School Vandalism: A National Dilemma: Final Report, Prepared for the Stanford Research Institute, Research and Development Program*. Menlo Park, CA: Stanford Research Institute, 1969. Print.

Gruber, James E., and Susan Fineran. "Comparing the Impact of Bullying and Sexual Harassment Victimization on the Mental and Physical Health of Adolescents." *Sex Roles* 58 (2008): 13–14. Print.

Hauge, Lars Johan, Anders Skogstad, and Ståle Einarsen. "The Relative Impact of Workplace Bullying as a Social Stressor at Work." *Scandinavian Journal of Psychology* 51 (2010): 426–33. Print.

Heinemann, P.P. *Mobbing Ruppvald Bland Barn Ochunxna*. Stockholm: Naur Och Kultur, 1972. Print.

Henry, Kimberly L., Peter J. Lovegrove, Michael F. Steger, Peter Y. Chen, Konstantin P. Cigularov, and Rocco G. Tomazic. "The Potential Role of Meaning in Life in the Relationship Between Bullying Victimization and Suicidal Ideation." *Journal of Youth and Adolescence* 43.2 (2014): 221–32. Web. 28 Nov. 2014. [doi:10.1007/s10964–013–9960–2]

Hoel, Helge, and Cary L. Cooper. *Destructive Conflict and Bullying at Work*. Manchester: Manchester School of Management, UMIST, 2000. Print.

Hoel, Helge, Stale Einarsen, Dieter Zapf, and Maarit Varita. "Empirical Findings on Bullying in the Workplace." *Bullying and Emotional Abuse in the Workplace: International Perspectives in Research and Practice*. London: Taylor & Francis, 2003. 103–126. Print.

Hoel, Helge, and Denise Salin. "Organisational Antecedents of Workplace Bullying." *Bullying and Emotional Abuse in the Workplace: International Perspectives in Research and Practice*. London: Taylor & Francis, 2003. 203–218. Print.

Hughes, Thomas. *Tom Brown's Schooldays*. London: Charles H. Kelly, 1913. Print.

Hunt, Ruth, and Johan Jensen. *The School Report: The Experiences of Young Gay People in Britain's School*. London: Stonewall, 2007. Print.

Idsoe, Thormod, Atle Dyregrov, and Ella Cosmovici Idsoe. "Bullying and PTSD Symptoms." *Journal of Abnormal Child Psychology* 40.6 (2012): 901–11. Web. 28 Oct. 2014. [doi:10.1007/s10802–012–9620–0]

Jose, Paul E., Moja Kljakovic, Emma Scheib, and Olivia Notter. "The Joint Development of Traditional Bullying and Victimization with Cyber Bullying and Victimization in Adolescence." *Journal of Research on Adolescence* 22.2 (2012): 301–09. Web. 28 Oct. 2014. [doi:10.1111/j.1532–7795.2011.00764.x]

Kann, Laura, et al. "Sexual Identity, Sex of Sexual Contacts, and Health-Risk Behaviors Among Students in Grades 9–12: Youth Risk Behavior Surveillance, Selected Sites, United States, 2001–2009 Surveillance Summaries." *Morbidity and Mortality Weekly Report.* Centers for Disease Control and Prevention, 60.SS07 (10 June 2011): 1–133. Print.

Keashley, Loraleigh, and Joel Neuman. "Faculty Experiences with Bullying in Higher Education: Causes, Consequences and Management." *Administrative Theory and Praxis* 32.1 (2010): 48–70. Print.

"Key Components in State Anti-Bullying Laws." *Stopbullying.gov.* U.S. Department of Health and Human Services. Web. 28 Oct. 2014. http://www.stopbullying.gov/laws/key-components/index.html.

Klomek, Anat Brunstein, Andre Sourander, Solja Niemelä, Kirsti Kumpulainen, Jorma Piha, Tuula Tamminen, Fredrik Almqvist, and Madelyn S. Gould. "Childhood Bullying Behaviors as a Risk for Suicide Attempts and Completed Suicides." *Journal of the American Academy of Child & Adolescent Psychiatry* 48: 254–61. Print.

Koo, Hyojin. "A Time Line of Evolution of School Bullying in Differing Social Concepts." *Asian Pacific Education Review* 8.1 (2007): 107–16. Print.

Kosciw, Joseph G., Emily A. Greytak, Mark J. Bartkiewicz, Madelyn J. Boesen, and Neal A. Palmer. *The 2011 National School Climate Survey: The Experiences of Lesbian, Gay, Bisexual and Transgender Youth in Our Nation's Schools.* New York: GLSEN, 2012. Print.

Kowalski, Robin M., and Susan P. Limber. "Electronic Bullying Among Middle School Students." *Journal of Adolescent Health* 41 (2007): S22–30. Web. 28 Nov. 2014. [doi:10.1016/j.jadohealth.2007.08.017]

Kowalski, R. M., C. A. Morgan, and S. P. Limber. "Traditional Bullying as a Potential Warning Sign of Cyberbullying." *School Psychology International* 33.5 (2012): 505–19. Web. 28 Oct. 2014. [doi:10.1177/0143034312445244]

Levine, Emily, and Tamburrino, Melissa. "Bullying Among Young Children: Strategies for Prevention." *Early Childhood Education Journal* 42.4 (2014): 271–78. Web. 15 Oct. 2014. [doi:10.1007/s10643–013–0600-y]

Lewis, Duncan. "Workplace Bullying—Interim Findings of a Study in Further and Higher Education in Wales." *International Journal of Manpower* 20 (1999): 106–19. Print.

Leymann, Heinz. "The Content and Development of Mobbing at Work." *European Journal of Work and Organizational Psychology* 5.2 (1996): 165–84. Print.

Little, Liza. "Middle-class Mother's Perceptions of Peer and Sibling Victimization Among Children with Asperger's Syndrome and Nonverbal Learning Disorders." *Issues in Comprehensive Pediatric Nursing* 25.1 (2002): 43–57. Print.

Litwiller, Brett J., and Amy M. Brausch. "Cyber Bullying and Physical Bullying in Adolescent Suicide: The Role of Violent Behavior and Substance Use." *Journal of Youth and Adolescence* 42.5 (2013): 675–84. Web. 28 Oct. 2014. [doi:10.1007/s10964–013–9925–5]

Meltzer, Howard, Tamsin Ford, Robert Goodman, and Panos Vostanis. "The Burden of Caring for Children with Emotional or Conduct Disorders." *International Journal of Family Medicine*, 2011 (2011), Article ID 801203, 8 pages, 2011. Web. 28 Oct. 2014. [doi:10.1155/2011/801203]

Menesini, Ersilia, Marina Camodeca, and Annalaura Nocentini. "Bullying Among Siblings: The Role of Personality and Relational Variables." *British Journal of Developmental Psychology* 28.4 (2010): 921–39. Web. 28 Oct. 2014. [doi:10.1348/026151009X479402]

Monks, C. P., S. Robinson, and P. Worlidge. "The Emergence of Cyberbullying: A Survey of Primary School Pupils' Perceptions and Experiences." *School Psychology International* 33.5 (2012): 477–91. Print.

Morgan, John Jacob Brooke. *The Psychology of the Unadjusted School Child.* New York: Macmillan, 1952. Print.
Nansel, Tonja R., Mary Overpeck, Ramani S. Pilla, W. June Ruan, Bruce Simmons-Morton, and Peter Schmidt. "Bullying Behaviors Among US Youth: Prevalence and Association with Psychosocial Adjustment." *JAMA: The Journal of the American Medical Association* 285.16 (2001): 2094–100. Print.
Olweus, Dan. *Aggression in the Schools: Bullies and Whipping Boys.* Washington, D.C.: Hemisphere Press, 1978. Print.
Olweus, Dan. *Bullying at School: What We Know and What We Can Do.* Oxford: Blackwell, 1993. Print.
Ortega, R., and A. Mora-Merchan. "Spain." In P. K. Smith, Y. Morita, J. Junger-Tas, D. Olweus, R. Catalano, and P. Slee (eds.), *The Nature of School Bullying: A Cross-National Perspective.* London: Routledge, 1999: 157–173. Print.
Osler, Audrey, and Kerry Vincent. *Girls and Exclusion: Rethinking the Agenda.* London: Routledge/Falmer, 2003. Print.
Pikas, A. "A Pure Concept of Mobbing Gives the Best Results for Treatment." *School Psychology International* 10 (1989): 95–104. Print.
Radzinowicz, Leon, and Joan F. S. King. *The Growth of Crime: The International Experience.* New York: Basic, 1977. Print.
Raskauskas, Juliana, and Ann D. Stoltz. "Involvement in Traditional and Electronic Bullying Among Adolescents." *Developmental Psychology* 43: 564–75. Print.
Rigby, Ken. *A Meta-Evaluation of Methods and Approaches to Reducing Bullying in Preschools and Early Primary School in Australia.* Canberra: Attorney General's Department, Crime Prevention Branch, 2002. Print.
Rigby, Ken. *New Perspectives on Bullying.* London: J. Kingsley, 2002. Print.
Rigby, Ken, and Peter K. Smith. "Is School Bullying Really on the Rise?" *Social Psychology of Education* 14.4 (2011): 441–55. Web. 28 Oct. 2014. [doi:10.1007/s11218-011-9158-y]
Rivers, Ian, and Nathalie Noret. "'I H8 U': Findings from a Five-year Study of Text and Email Bullying." *British Educational Research Journal* 36.4 (2010b): 643–71. Print.
Rivers, Ian, and Nathalie Noret. "Participant Roles in Bullying Behavior and Their Association with Thoughts of Ending One's Life." *Crisis: The Journal of Crisis Intervention and Suicide Prevention* 31.3 (2010a): 143–48. Print.
Sakellariou, T., A. Carroll, and S. Houghton. "Rates of Cyber Victimization and Bullying Among Male Australian Primary and High School Students." *School Psychology International* 33.5 (2012): 533–49. Web. 28 Oct. 2014. [doi: 10.1177/0143034311430374]
Schroeder, J. H., M. C. Cappadocia, J. M. Bebko, D. J. Pepler, and J. A. Weiss. "Shedding Light on a Pervasive Problem: A Review of Research on Bullying Experiences Among Children with Autism Spectrum Disorders." *Journal of Autism and Developmental Disorders* 44.7 (2014):1520–1534. Web. 28 Oct. 2014. [doi:10.1007/s10803-013-2011-8]
Skinner, J. A., and R. M. Kowalski. "Profiles of Sibling Bullying." *Journal of Interpersonal Violence* 28.8 (2013): 1726–736. Web. 28 Oct. 2014. [doi:10.1177/0886260512468327]
Slonje, Robert, and Peter K. Smith. "Cyberbullying: Another Main Type of Bullying?" *Scandinavian Journal of Psychology* 49 (2008): 147–54. Print.
Smith, Peter K. *School Bullying: Insights and Perspectives.* London: Routledge, 1994. Print.
Smith, Peter K., Helen Cowie, Ragnar F. Olafsson, and Andy P. D. Liefooghe. "Definitions of Bullying: A Comparison of Terms Used, and Age and Gender Differences, in a Fourteen-Country International Comparison." *Child Development* 73 (2002): 1119–133. Print.
Smith, Peter K., Jess Mahdavi, Manuel Carvalho, Sonja Fisher, Shanette Russell, and Neil Tippett. "Cyberbullying: Its Nature and Impact in Secondary School Pupils." *Journal of Child Psychology and Psychiatry* 49 (2008): 376–85. Print.
State of New Jersey. "An Overview of Amendments to Laws on Harassment, Intimidation

and Bullying." *Keeping Kids Safe, Student Behavior—Harassment, Intimidation & Bullying.* State of New Jersey, Department of Education, 1 Jan. 2011. Web. 5 Nov. 2014. http://www.state.nj.us/education/students/safety/behavior/hib/overview.pdf.
Stellwagen, Kurt K., and Patricia K. Kerig. "Ringleader Bullying: Association with Psychopathic Narcissism and Theory of Mind Among Child Psychiatric Inpatients." *Child Psychiatry & Human Development* 44.5 (2013): 612–20. Web. 28 Oct. 2014. [doi:10.1007/s10578–012–0355–5]
Swift, Rogers. "Heroes or Villains? The Irish, Crime, and Disorder in Victorian England." *Albion: A Quarterly Journal Concerned with British Studies* 29.3 (1997): 399–421. Print.
Thornberg, Robert, Robert Rosenqvist, and Per Johansson. "Older Teenagers' Explanations of Bullying." *Child & Youth Care Forum* 41.4 (2012): 327–42. Web. 28 Oct. 2014. [doi: 10.1007/s10566–012–9171–0]
Trépanier, Sarah-Geneviève, Claude Fernet, and Stéphanie Austin. "Workplace Bullying and Psychological Health at Work: The Mediating Role of Satisfaction of Needs for Autonomy, Competence and Relatedness." *Work & Stress* 27.2 (2013): 123–40. Web. 28 Oct. 2014. [doi:10.1080/02678373.2013.782158]
Ttofi, Maria M., and David P. Farrington. "Bullying Prevention Programs: The Importance of Peer Intervention, Disciplinary Methods and Age Variations." *Journal of Experimental Criminology* 8.4 (2012): 443–62. Web. 28 Oct. 2014. [doi:10.1007/s11292–012–9161–0]
Twemlow, Stuart W., and Frank C. Sacco. "Bullying Is Everywhere: Ten Universal Truths About Bullying as a Social Process in Schools & Communities." *Psychoanalytic Inquiry* 33.2 (2013): 73–89. Web. 28 Oct. 2014. [doi:10.1080/07351690.2013.759484]
United Nations. "Event for Human Rights: Adoption by the General Assembly of the Convention on the Prevention and Punishment of the Crime of Genocide." New York: United Nations. 1948. Print.
Williams, K., and N. Guerra. "Prevalence and Predictors of Internet Bullying." *Journal of Adolescent Health* 41.6 (2007): S14–21. Web. 28 Oct. 2014. [doi: 10.1016/j.jadohealth.2007.08.018]
Wilsnack, Sharon C., Arlinda F. Kristjanson, Tonda L. Hughes, and Perry W. Benson. "Characteristics of Childhood Sexual Abuse in Lesbians and Heterosexual Women." *Child Abuse & Neglect* 36.3 (2012): 260–65. Print.
Ybarra, Michele L., Danah Boyd, Josephine D. Korchmaros, and Jay (Koby) Oppenheim. "Defining and Measuring Cyberbullying Within the Larger Context of Bullying Victimization." *Journal of Adolescent Health* 51.1 (2012): 53–58. Print.
Ybarra, Michele L., Kimberly Mitchell, and Dorothy Espelage. "Comparisons of Bully and Unwanted Sexual Experiences Online and Offline Among a National Sample of Youth." *Complementary Pediatrics.* Rejeka: InTech, 2012. 203–216. Print.
Zabrodska, Katerina, and Petr Kveton. "Prevalence and Forms of Workplace Bullying Among University Employees." *Employee Responsibilities and Rights Journal* 25.2 (2013): 89–108. Web. 28 Oct. 2014. [doi:10.1007/s10672–012–9210-x]
Zapf, Dieter, Carmen Knorz, and Matthias Kulla. "On the Relationship Between Mobbing Factors, and Job Content, Social Work Environment, and Health Outcomes." *European Journal of Work and Organizational Psychology* 5.2 (1996): 215–37. Print.
Zou, C., J. P. Andersen, and J. R. Blosnich. "The Association Between Bullying and Physical Health Among Gay, Lesbian, and Bisexual Individuals." *Journal of the American Psychiatric Nurses Association* 19.6 (2013): 356–65. Web. 28 Oct. 2014. [doi:10.1177/1078390313510739]

Bullying Boundaries

How Are Reality Television Programs and School Policies Shaping Youth Perceptions of Acceptable Aggressive Behaviors?

Tamara Girardi

Although not a new issue in academic environments, the act of bullying has become the focus of research and legislation in recent years as a national public health issue. In 2001, the surgeon general published a report arguing the need to focus on bullying, and researchers complied. According to one study, 72 percent of teens who responded reported experiencing bullying online while 85 percent experienced bullying in school (Juvonen and Gross 496). The numbers are significant because, as the researchers report, "even a single incident of bullying encountered at school is associated with elevated daily levels of anxiety. Similarly, single episode of cyberbullying has been shown to be related to emotional distress" (497). Furthermore, "victims of bullying exhibit high levels of suicidal ideation and [are] more likely to have attempted suicide compared with non victims" (Klomek, Sourander and Gould 282). And victims of bullying are not alone when it comes to the detrimental effects of the acts. Research also shows that teens involved in bullying behavior are more likely to experience suicide ideation or attempts (Klomek, Sourander and Gould). Whether there has been a significant increase in instances of bullying in recent years or researchers and concerned parties are simply paying more attention to the issue, the fact is bullying is a cause for concern; as such, further discussion on the problem is necessary.

Before moving forward with that discussion, it is relevant to note exactly what constitutes bullying. Although cyberbullying is a frequently used term in the bully discussion, Klomek, Sourander and Gould identify bullying behavior in four categories: "direct-physical (for example, assaults or theft), direct-verbal (threats, insults, or nicknames), indirect-relational (for example, social exclusion and spreading nasty rumors), and the newest form, cyber" (283). Although the researchers categorize the types of bullying, some experts argue that there is no clear, universal definition of bullying. Yahn argues that researchers tend to compartmentalize bullying and referring to specific behaviors as illustrated above. "Rather than developing a holistic understanding of this phenomenon as a dynamic continuum of aggression behaviors that interact with social influences, what has developed is a methodology that favors rigid, static definitions which are primarily dependent on each researcher's own conceptualization of what constitutes bullying and what can most easily be measured" (Yahn 20). Since this chapter represents a theoretical debate rather than quantitative research on acts of bullying, Yahn's broader definition can more easily apply. Additionally, considering the references to reality television and zero tolerance policies in schools, it is appropriate to define bullying as "a dynamic continuum of aggression behaviors that interact with social influences." The argument is not the age old claim that violence in the media sparks violence in culture. On the contrary, the argument is that violence in reality television is actually changing the way our society defines what violence is; all the while, teens are perpetuating violence among each other to potentially fatal consequences.

Reality television evolved from *An American Family*, a show airing on PBS in 1973 that featured the Loud family. "The televised decision of the parents to divorce and the on-screen coming out of their gay son shocked audiences" and prompted sociologist Margaret Mead to argue that a new name was necessary for this kind of television. According to the Writers Guild of America, reality TV includes such shows as *Unsolved Mysteries, America's Funniest Home Videos,* and *Dateline NBC*. However, MTV's *The Real World* "moved the format ahead by staging an environment in which 'reality' could occur in 1992" and "the wide range of reality television series that we recognize today followed" (Slocum). The popular reality television shows such as *Survivor, American Idol,* and *The Amazing Race* were part everyday life, part game show competition. The shows are a clear win for networks because, as Slocum notes, "in virtually every line of the production budget, reality-based programming is cheaper than traditional programming." Slocum argues that the questions of whether reality television can contribute or tear down are for sociologists and historians as the implications for economists is clear. Researchers indeed have several options for exploration with reality television. As a teen viewer of *The Real World*, I recall the "no fighting" policy. As a result of this rule, stars of the show might argue intensely, but they would often show some self-control in stopping themselves before the disagreements escalated to physical violence. "Whether on *Real World* or its spinoffs including *Road Rules* and *The Challenge*, housemates have avoided coming to blows due to the belief that, in doing so, they'd lose their coveted spot on the season, and have managed to talk out their disputes in more level-headed ways" (Marechal). In other words, the participants realized there would be consequences for their actions, and they acted appropriately to avoid such consequences. However, Marechal reports "there is no contractual policy against fighting on *Real World*, contrary to what many viewers and cast members may have thought" although what the producers refer to as "physical aggression" *could* result in a cast member leaving.

Consequences of cases of violence are determined individually by producers and cast members, but no clear cut rules are outlined. Therefore, the suggestion to audiences is that there are no clear cut rules regarding what kinds of behaviors are acceptable or unacceptable in everyday life, the environment these shows aim to mimic.

> All too often, these shows portray violence—and I don't mean gang violence or Bruce Willis movie violence. I am talking about the violence that we don't think of as violence anymore: roommates screaming at each other, items being thrown, walls being punched and head butted, name calling and bullying, and physical violence against women and men (perpetrated by both sexes) [Espitia].

Espitia argues that what audiences are watching on reality television is actually domestic violence. "The pervasiveness of this violence and the fact that it is widely accepted as having a high entertainment value has served to confuse people, especially youth, about what constitutes domestic violence" (Espitia). For many psychologists the prevalence of reality television shows is a cause for concern in terms of bullying, which occurs both inside and outside of domestic environments. Psychologist Sarah Coyne argues that "our own concepts of aggression are activated in the brain when we watch these shows, and we are primed to behave aggressively" (Christensen).

> Nightmarish behavior is the stuff reality TV shows are made of. [Gordon] Ramsay is certainly not alone. Tami Roman on VH1's *Basketball Wives* calls her friends "bitches" and physically attacks one of them in front of a fancy Miami

restaurant. A study of the U.K.'s version of *The Apprentice* found it depicted 85 aggressive acts an hour. *American Idol* showed 57 aggressive acts an hour [Christensen].

The argument of how television shows, media, video games, and so on, influence behavior has been debated for decades, often basing itself in social cognitive theory and script theory. These theories "propose that children can learn aggressive behavior by observing media models and the consequences of their actions. However, the acquisition of aggressive scripts depends on the attention paid to the actions depicted on the screen" (Matos, Ferreira, Haase 76). While Coyne doesn't argue that modeling the behavior of reality television stars is instant, she does contend that "it can creep slowly into the ways the viewers react in real life" (Christensen).

One study by the Girl Scouts of America found that the current generation of girls is in fact watching reality television and, as a result of paying the attention Matos, Ferreira, and Haase reference, are being influenced by it. Of the 1,100 girls surveyed between the ages of 11 and 17 across the United States, 86 percent agreed that the shows "often pit girls against each other to make the shows more exciting." Seventy-three percent believe the shows "make people think that fighting is a normal part of a romantic relationship," and 70 percent said reality TV makes "people think it is okay to treat others badly" (Real to Me). Respondents who watch reality TV regularly are more accepting of gossip as "a normal part of a relationship between girls" and girls' tendencies to be catty and competitive with each other. From a bullying perspective, the results were also telling. Girls who watch reality TV report that lying and being mean more often result in getting what you want (Real to Me). Earlier in the chapter, the four categories of bullying were discussed, and they included assault, threats, insults, and spreading nasty rumors. The research from the Girl Scouts of America shows that young girls identify such actions as normal and are accepting of them. In other words, bullying might be a negative term they don't quite believe they're engaged in; in fact, the girls could be subconsciously condoning the behavior due to the potential for positive outcomes.

The definition of bullying itself is inconsistent and based on changing perceptions. Yahn argues that bullying should be more clearly defined, and she does so with what she classifies as "definitions" and "criteria." Here is her definition:

> Bullying is a form of aggression manifested through a range of behaviors that include, but are not limited to, physical, non-physical, sexual, verbal, visual,

and relational antisocial reactions. Bullying consists of the *motivation* (underlying reason or catalyst) of the perpetrator to overpower, control, subjugate, force into submission or otherwise dominate the victim coupled with the *intent* (purposeful action) to harm, intimidate, humiliate, terrorize or otherwise hurt the victim [21].

While Yahn's intention of clearly defining bullying as a starting point for more appropriate discussion on the issue is admirable, the definition itself is problematic. Among her criteria, she argues "*both* the motivation for dominance and the intent to hurt *must* be present to constitute bullying" (21). Yahn addresses the aspect of implicit power in her article, but the potential flaw with the definition is that some teens might not believe that a friend or classmate possesses the intention to harm them. The Girl Scouts of America study shows that girls are becoming more and more accepting of some behaviors other generations might view as bullying. If that is the case, then the criteria that intent to harm must be in place creates an inconsistency that Yahn's definition aims to combat. In other words, girls might dismiss bullying behavior based on such a definition due to the influence that reality television has had on their perceptions of which behaviors are acceptable and which are not.

Aggressive behaviors, by nature, possess the motivation to overpower, control, subjugate, force into submission or otherwise dominate the victim. Yet some researchers distinguish bullying from aggressive behavior. Cuadrado-Gordillo supports Yahn's claim and writes that in the 30 years of bullying research, scholars haven't agreed upon an exact definition of the term but seem to agree on three criteria "that distinguish bullying from aggressive behavior" (1890). The criteria are "power imbalance in favor of the aggressor, with the victim of bullying finding him- or herself in an inferior status that makes it very difficult to put up any defense, intent to cause another person physical, social or psychological harm, and repetition of aggressive behavior" (1890). However, students don't necessarily agree on the three criteria perpetuated by researchers. Regarding the criterion of repetition, results from several studies vary with the lowest percentage of participants citing repetition as an aspect of bullying at 3 percent (Madsen) and the highest at 30 percent (Frisen et al.).

However, the majority of the studies noted less than 10 percent of participants including repetition as a criterion of bullying. Results for the criterion "intent to hurt" ranged from only 1.7 percent (Vaillancourt et al.) to 17 percent (Everett and Price). Finally, results for the criterion of power imbalance range from 16 percent (Madsen) to 40 percent (Guerin and Hennessey). So, if students are not identifying the same criteria researchers utilize to define bullying, how do they define the act? Although this chapter contends from a purely theoretical perspective that young people's exposure to reality television could negatively influence their perceptions of acceptable behavior in friendships and romantic relationships, there are likely other factors at play as well. Nevertheless, the earlier arguments in this chapter supported by the Girl Scouts of America study are also supported by Cuadrado-Gordillo's work. Researchers define bullying more broadly than students, according to the research. "Some studies indicate that teenagers' perception of the various modes of bullying is very limited, generally being restricted to physical and verbal abuse" (1891). For instance, a study by Boulton et al. of 600 teenagers aged 11–16 years old:

> found that about 4 out of every 5 mention bullying situations that involve fighting and pushing (82.9%), threats (82.9%), and forcing someone to do things against their will (78.2%), and somewhat smaller proportions mention giving offensive nicknames (65.9%), stealing someone's personal belongings (59.4%), spreading false rumors (54.1%), and making fun of others (41.8%). Only 20.6%, however, identified social exclusion as a manifestation of bullying [1891].

Although there is quite a bit of discrepancy among the results from the studies, the results are still interesting to consider since they address students' perceptions of bullying, which are likely to vary widely in any case. Most notably, the teens' perceptions of bullying differ from researchers. Cuadrado-Gordillo surveyed 2,295 teenagers between the ages of 12 and 16 and found that "very few of the respondents consider repetition, intent to hurt, and abuse of power simultaneously as criteria to classify aggressive behavior as bullying ... 45 percent of teens still think that bullying is any behavior that hurts somebody else even though the aggressor did not mean to do so" (1901). The results are promising in that teens believe that bullying could be identified in situations where researchers might not. Nevertheless, the results of the study feature general questions about bullying rather than specific incidents. In other words, although teens have a clear view of bullying when asked, that does not account for the many circumstances they encounter daily and how they choose to react to them.

On the one hand, they might rationalize such behavior as appropriate in certain contexts. For instance, as Coyne notes, reality television perpetuates the belief that behaving aggressively will result in success as many of the people who exhibit bullying-type behavior on reality TV programs are "very rich and very successful" (Christensen). Therefore, teens might believe that their intent is not to harm someone else but to get what they want, a claim that contradicts Cuadrado-Gordillo's results. When it comes to the influence of reality television or television in general, Huesmann et al. argue that "aggressive scenes will be more salient if children perceive the violence as realistic and identify with the perpetrator of the aggressive behavior" (Matos, Ferreiera and Haase 76). In other words, although teens might appropriately define bullying as any action that causes harm even if the aggressor did not intend to cause harm, they have also been sensitized to the idea of circumstance. They are influenced by reality television programs in which choosing sides is often part of the expectation. Therefore, in their everyday lives, when their friends cause harm to classmates, they might not identify such acts as bullying. In fact, it would be interesting to study how teens define behaviors they and their friends engage, especially when those behaviors are traditionally viewed as bullying. To be fair, I should note that several studies ask participants if they are aggressors, and many teens do respond that they are. Nevertheless, viewing situations objectively is a difficult, if not impossible, task for most humans, and influences of what kinds of behavior are acceptable in reality television programming further clouds teens' judgment of what constitutes bullying in their everyday lives.

School policies further confuse the issue. Students look to their parents and their school authorities to define what behaviors are appropriate in the educational environment, but not all policies define such behaviors as well as they could. The policies tend to address the consequences of certain behaviors rather than a clear explanation of the behaviors that can lead to those consequences. Curious about my local community, I searched online until I found a guide for high school students in the school district where I reside. The guide does in fact address bullying with a section entitled "Bully Prevention Program." Below the brief explanation is an italicized, underlined statement "No from of bullying will be tolerated at Highlands Middle School." Yet, the definition of bullying itself is so vague that it could perhaps benefit the school officials aiming to enforce it and the students and parents trying to protect their children from possible consequences. It reads, "A person is being bullied or victimized when he or she is exposed, repeatedly and over time, to negative actions on the part of one or more persons" (Student Agenda 15). The explanation goes on to detail the consequences for the five offenses. Interestingly, the consequences are clear. The behaviors that lead to them are not. Additionally, as noted in the introduction, becoming a victim of bullying only once is likely to negatively influence a student's ability to feel safe and perform well in school. Additionally, teens believe that bullying need not be repetitive, yet this program identifies bullying as something persistent, that occurs over time. I don't mean to criticize my local middle school's policy on bullying. Quite frankly, it is refreshing to know that the district is attentive to the issue and has put a program in place to address it. Whether or not that program works for the school cannot be argued here due to lack of evidence. Nevertheless, the issue of how we define bullying in order to prevent it is illuminated in this discussion. If we too closely define bullying as Yahn does, we could create a situation in which teens experience bullying but don't define it as such. On the contrary, if the definition is too broad, students engaging in bullying behavior could argue that what they have done is not, in fact, bullying.

To further explore how schools are addressing bullying in school policy documents, I found the Pittsburgh Public Schools online handbook from the 2013-2014 academic year. The district has more broadly defined bullying; the statement in the handbook states:

> The Board prohibits all forms of bullying, including cyberbullying by students. Bullying means an intentional electronic, written, verbal or physical act or series of acts directed at another student or students, which occurs in a school setting, that is severe, persistent or pervasive and has the intent or effect of:
> 1. Creating an intimidating or hostile environment that substantially interferes with a student's education; or
> 2. Physically, emotionally or mentally harming a student; or
> 3. Placing a student in reasonable fear of physical or emotional harm; or
> 4. Placing a student in reasonable fear of damage to or loss of personal property
>
> Bullying includes cyberbullying and/or bullying on social networking websites and may include acts that occur outside of school if certain criteria are met. The complete policy, complaint and investigation procedures are posted on the district website, in every building and classroom [The Code of Student Conduct 9].

The Pittsburgh Public Schools policy is more specific in that it includes cyberbullying, a growing form of bullying. It identifies bullying as acts that occur in a school setting with an addendum that bullying might occur outside of school in some cases. While some of the language might contradict other areas of the policy, generally it is both broad enough to include nearly anything an administrator might want to punish as bullying while also being specific enough that students and parents can't argue that they haven't violated the policy. The definition also aligns with Cuadrado-Gordillo's research results illustrating how teens define bullying in that it does not require repetitive action, nor does it require the intent to harm.

Although the Pittsburgh Public Schools policy clearly represents many students' definition of bullying, it seems that the best way to engage students in a discussion on bullying lies in seeking their voices when developing policies and consequences. In addition to moving away from what the Education Law Center refers to as "harmful zero-tolerance policies that disproportionally impact students of color and students with disabilities" (ELC Applauds Pittsburgh), Pittsburgh Public Schools also welcomed student voices by way of a "student-proposed bill of rights" (Chute). Just as was the case with the Highlands Middle School's clarity among potential consequences, the proposal approved by the Pittsburgh school board focuses on language regarding disciplinary action. Rather than a uniform approach to all behavioral issues, the district has made a commitment to considering cases individually. However, part of the proposal addresses students' perspectives and their rights, which s promising. The statement reads that "students have the right to a positive and inclusive learning environment that feels safe, respectful and welcoming for all students" (Chute). In the new Code of Conduct for 2014-2015, the language regarding student behaviors has not changed. However, the policy is now available online, and the district offers the caveat that copies are available in languages other than English. Therefore, accommodations and considerations are being made to include student populations that might have previously met with difficulty when it comes to understanding and honoring school policies. Nevertheless, the changes prompted by the Education Law Center, while admirable, might not address the heart of the bullying issue, not that they are intended to.

As research cited in this chapter shows, experts and students will not always agree on what bullying is, when it occurs or what to do about it. However, it's not necessary for experts and students to agree. Perhaps what is necessary is a dialogue between the relevant parties, which include school officials. Research shows that girls, in particular, are being influenced by television programming such as reality television. They believe that the situations in the programs are real, and therefore, by paying attention to the aggressive behaviors on the screen, they are acquiring an understanding of what behaviors are acceptable and what behaviors are unacceptable. In turn, those behaviors become part of their lives, or they are overlooked as potentially harmful, or both. While scholars argue that some of the behaviors girls noted in the Girl Scouts of America study are, in fact, unacceptable acts of bullying, the girls don't necessarily view the acts as representative of bullying. Yet, teens surveyed more widely did view such acts and others as bullying. What is the cause of the disconnect?

Could the cause lie in perception in given situations? Do teens not view their own actions or actions of their friends as hurtful to others? Do they feel justified, for whatever reason, to engage behavior they might otherwise define as bullying? Or do they simply accept that bullying is a part of life, as some of the research on the influence of reality television suggests? These are all questions worth pursuing in formal research or perhaps in informal conversations among academic environments. If school districts are addressing bullying with policies in their codes of conduct, why not create a bullying task force that addresses issues of bullying in their school communities. Perceptions of acceptable behaviors vary, as research shows, among age groups; therefore, the policies that work for elementary students might not apply appropriately to high school students. And while experts and school officials are certainly welcome to offer suggestions and ideas when it comes to acceptable behavior in schools, the students live the environments every day. They see behaviors that occur when teachers heads are turned. They are the best populations to voice what is truly occurring, and more importantly, without their commitment to identify bullying behaviors, even those engaged by themselves and their friends, and their commitment to ending such behaviors, all of the policies and research possible is likely to be less transformative. Researchers survey students as the central foci of their studies for a reason: they are the ones experiencing the phenomenon. The time has come to stop telling students what bullying is and to combat the images they see of aggressive behavior on television by engaging them in real-world conversations about the issue and expecting them to create "the positive and inclusive learning environment that feels safe, respectful and welcoming for all students" as the Pittsburgh Public Schools student bill of rights requests.

Works Cited

Christensen, Jen. "Our Unhealthy Love of Reality TV Bullying." *CNN*. 28 Feb. 2013. Web. 27 Aug. 2014.

Chute, Eleanor. "Proposed Changes in Pittsburgh Schools' Student Conduct Code Emphasize Progressive and Positive Discipline." *Pittsburgh Post-Gazette*. 20 July 2014. Web. 29 Aug. 2014.

"The Code of Student Conduct: Updated for 2013-2014." *Pittsburgh Public Schools*. Web. 29 Aug. 2014.

Cuadrado-Gordillo, Isabel. "Repetition, Power Imbalance, and Intentionality: Do These Criteria Conform to Teenagers' Perception of Bullying? A Role-Based Analysis." *Journal of Interpersonal Violence* 27.10 (2011): 1889–1910. Web. 28 Aug. 2014.

"ELC Applauds Pittsburgh Public Schools' New Code of Student Conduct." *The Education Law Center*. 5 Aug. 2014. Web. 29 Aug. 2014.

Espitia, Amanda. "The Reality of Reality TV." *Huffington Post*. 13 Feb. 2012. Web. 6 Aug. 2014.

Everett, Sherry A., and James H. Price. "Students' Perceptions of Violence in the Public Schools: The metLife Survey." *Journal of Adolescent Health* 17.6 (1995): 345–352. Web. 27 Aug. 2014.

Guerin, Suzanne, and Eilis Hennessy. "Pupils' Definitions of Bullying." *European Journal of Psychology of Education* XVII (2002): 249–261. Web. 27 Aug. 2014.

Juvonen, Jaana, and Elisheva F. Gross. "Extending the School Grounds? Bullying Experiences in Cyberspace." *Journal of School Health* 78.9 (2008): 496–505. Web. 6 Aug. 2014.

Klomek, Anat Brunstein, Andre Sourander, and Madelyn Gould. "The Association of Suicide and Bullying in Childhood to Young Adulthood: A Review of Cross-Sectional and Longitudinal Research Findings." *La Revue Canadienne de Psychiatrie* 55.5 (2010): 282–288. Web. 6 Aug. 2014.

Madsen, Kirsten C. "Differing Perceptions of Bullying and Their Practical Implications." *Educational and Child Psychology* 13 (1996): 14–22. Web. 27 Aug. 2014.

Marechal, AJ. "Violence on MTV: Why Did Producers Stop Intervening on 'Real World'?" *Variety.* 7 Aug. 2013. Web. 28 Aug. 2014.

Matos, Armanda Pinto Da Mota, Joaquim Armando G. Alves Ferreira, and Richard F. Haase. "Television and Aggression: A Test of a Mediated Model with a Sample of Portuguese Students." *The Journal of Social Psychology* 152.1 (2012): 75–91. Web. 28 Aug. 2014.

"Real to Me: Girls and Reality TV." *Girl Scout Research Institute.* Web. 27 Aug. 2014.

Slocum, Charles B. "The Real History of Reality TV or, How Allen Funt Won the Cold War." *Writers Guild of America, West.* 2014. Web. 27 Aug. 2014.

"Student Agenda." *Highlands Middle School.* Web. 30 Aug. 2014.

Vaillancourt, Tracy, Patricia McDougall, Shelley Hymel, Amanda Krygsman, Jessie Miller, Kelley Stiver, and Clinton David. "Bullying: Are Researchers and Children/Youth Talking about the Same Thing?" *International Journal of Behavioral Development* 32 (2008): 486–495. Web. 27 Aug. 2014.

Yahn, Mimi. "The Social Context of Bullying." *Encounter: Education for Meaning and Social Justice* 25.4 (2012): 20–28. Web. 8 Aug. 2014.

Bullying Bullies

Narratives of Territoriality in American Popular Culture

Eduardo Barros-Grela

Two narrative events have been paradigmatic in the contemporary perception of perpetuated harassment in the American educational system, as seen from international audiences: First, Jared Hess's film, *Napoleon Dynamite* (2004), which added a comical turn to the already alarming popularity of such harassing practices. Second, Chuck Lorre's sitcom *The Big Bang Theory* (2007–2014; in progress), which successfully reaffirmed the positive prominence of characters that had been traditionally depicted as susceptible to be bullied. Today, bullying is still a common practice in American schools, but different approaches have been opened to critically observe the complexity of this phenomenon.

Based on these discrepancies in the current connotations of bullying as a practice to gain "popularity" in schools, this essay looks at the problematic nature of bullying through the lens of two rather distant narratives: first, Dan Houser's video game *Bully* (2006) gave the audience the opportunity to *enact* the role of a bullied teenager in a hostile educational center. As a sandbox type of video game, players participate in the development of the game, and have to make decisions about their attitude toward other characters (including bullies and potential victims). In this sense, this essay is interested in seeing how individuals react to bullying (both as victims and perpetrators) when "protected" by a fictional distance. Also, this essay will look at how the struggle for territoriality that is inherent to the act of bullying is resignified through the heterotopic space of a videogame.

The second case, explored in this essay through a comparative approach, is Matt Reeves's film *Let Me In* (2010). In this analysis of this film, this author will also look at the Swedish original film (Tomas Alfredson's *Let the Right One In*, 2008) to analyze how the identification of the audience with bullied children precipitates the inversion—or, rather, the problematization—of traditional roles in situations of teenager victimization. Even the terrible act of death by dismembering is received in these films with joy by spectators who long for a rather resilient response instead of the option of an educational process. Both cases refer to the extreme complexity of bullying. Addressed from angles that include humor and terror, bullying is explored in this essay from a theoretical approach based on the study of space and violence, and is articulated within the sphere of (de/re)territorialization. Although no specific sections are devoted to theory, its presence is implicit in the analysis of the proposed texts.

The concept of "territory" has already been mentioned in this introduction, and the reason of its particular relevance springs from the way this discussion looks at the intimate relationship between the spaces of violence that derive from a struggle for territory and the process of becoming a bully. According to Gilles Deleuze and Felix Guattari in *A Thousand Plateaus* (*ATP*), the concept of territory evades its generally accepted meaning as a fixed and permanent space with clear boundaries and with connotations of sedentary nature, and becomes a space of transit whose functionality depends on the recognition of its own malleability (326). This evolution from a concept of territory as a certain place that is susceptible to be owned by specific individuals into the notion of territory as an assemblage of different—and constantly changing—subjectifications of space directly reverberates on how bullies interpret their functions and on how they are conceptualized by/in society.

Napoleon Dynamite builds upon this reconceptualization of spatial discursivity. In one of the final—and best-known—scenes in the film, the protagonist, a stereotypical victim of social harassment in centers of education, delivers a surprising dancing performance in front of the entire school body. Bullies in the audience witness with astonishment what might be interpreted as a territorial threat against their spatial hegemony and social dominance. Napoleon (Jon Heder) gradually transitions from a space of humiliation and social annihilation to an adult domain in which the values that characterized him as a nerd renew their connotations as physiognomies of the successful entrepreneur. This transition is opposed to the social and professional decrepitude of the bully, whose most valued virtues as a successful teenager are now deprived of their positiveness and acquire diminishing social connotations.

That typical development of events in films that contemplate in their plots the circumstances of bullies and nerds is, nonetheless, further explored in *Napoleon* from different perspectives. First, the film provides a sardonic look at what Penny Crofts referred to as the "bullying's gray zone." Characters who have internalized their social function at school as recipients of pranks and harassment turn the table and internally transform their spaces of aggravation into spaces of self-confidence. Their reterritorialization[1] of the connotations that are normally associated with their actions is naturally produced through the film and inherently subjectivized by viewers. As we are about to see in the analysis of the two audiovisual narratives proposed, the dynamics that are prominent in situations of social abusive behavior are contested through processes of place reappropriation and, again, the influence of parody appears as fundamental to bring up the question of how bullying is being socialized today and how effective the measures to counteract its consequences actually are.

Another facet that is discussed in *Napoleon* and that can be applied to the examination of *Bully: The Videogame* and *Let the Right One In/Let Me In*[2] is the contrast between open and closed spaces. Repeatedly throughout *Napoleon* we can see cases of bullying against victims that are depicted in a typically stereotyped nerd fashion. These abuses occur, almost without exception, in interior places, in which it is, apparently, much easier for bystanders to react against those forms of harassment. However, bullies and victims seem to have interiorized these dynamics of abuse as a cause, a consequence, or both of the passivity expressed by fellow students before those acts. This "semi-private sphere" (the high school, the karate classes, etc.) allows bullies to act freely against their victims, and at the same time it motivates the fact that victims naturalize and internalize their assigned role as social misfits. Even in the private sphere, represented mainly by Napoleon's grandmother's residence or other houses from the neighborhood, the same dynamics prevail, and abusive power relations are established between bullies and victims, although in some cases those roles can be adopted by individuals who would not be traditionally considered as belonging to that side of the conflict. For instance, Napoleon's uncle, Uncle Rico (Jon Gries), is clearly portrayed as an unsuccessful adult who continuously tries to revert his appearance and feign happiness and power as a successful entrepreneurial man. Within the parcel he inhabits—he is portrayed as a homeless man who lives in his van and who spends most of his time outside his vehicle in a deserted space—he is a winner in front of his illusionary spectators, as he is—or tries to be—in situations with Napoleon's brother Kip (Aaron Ruell). However, as soon as he enters any given interior space, he automatically becomes a nonentity and is bullied by a jealous husband or ridiculed by an anonymous online seller who pitilessly swindles him.

However, not only Uncle Rico is presented following these spatial premises. Napoleon himself, as many other bullied boys do, shares the same identity confusion epitomized by the protagonist's uncle. He is normally attacked by bullies when he finds himself in interior spaces (at school or in his grandmother's house). However, in those moments when he is in places of transition (school bus) or in exteriors (his grandmother's yard or the road back to the school festival), Napoleon assumes features that are typical of bullies, such as talking back to schoolmates, mistreating animals, and driving around in low-rider cars with apparent gang members.

There are two other examples of the grey zone of bullying and the transformations it implies. First, a student is bullied by another obviously taller and stronger student in the hallways of the school. However, when they leave the school premises and the bully tries to attack the victim again, he is instantly repelled by the presence of two gangsters, who come in support of the victimized student. In that moment, the bully loses all his connotations as a strong and threatening person in power to become a ridiculed specter of himself, while the bullied student becomes empowered and assumes what has the appearance to be a role of domination. The second case would be defined by the concretization of the online relationship Kip has repeatedly claimed to have. When he finally manages to meet his date in person, she happens to be LaFawnduh, portrayed as a powerful and secure woman who transforms Kip's appearance to have the looks of a tough person.

Both examples join Uncle Rico's instances of how space has a determining influence in the configuration of one's identity, specifically when it comes to deal with relations of power and also in interactions between subjects within a situation of abuse of power. Lorraine Ryan, in her analyses of Spanish film *La lengua de las mariposas* (José Luis Cuerda 1999), discusses the influence of space in the formation of children with adaptation difficulties, and claims that

> this typology consists of the ecological center, composed of the family and home, a zone characterized by warm emotional relationships with a high degree of dependency; ecological proximity, the neighborhood in which the child grows up, and establishes his first relation with the external world; ecological sectors, such as the school, where the child is expected to conform to predetermined roles; and the ecological periphery, a space that the child encounters infrequently [453].

According to Ryan's view, space has a defining role in the production of social identifications, but as we have seen with our brief analysis of *Napoleon Dynamite* the parody of those elements can also be interpreted as fundamental for the dynamics of identity production.

Along the same lines, Sonia Sharp argues that the possession of space in the school area tends to be a determining factor in the use of violence among teenagers (148). In this sense, both the videogame *Bully*—as well as its 2008 re-edition for PC, *Bully: Scholarship Edition*—and the two versions of the film *Let Me In* (and *Let the Right One In*) display a profound preoccupation for the articulation of space in atmospheres of power-based relationships. The complete first part of the videogame, for instance, takes place within the walls of Bullworth Academy, an independent boarding school especially designed for troublesome teenagers. In it, the main character struggles to survive the school system by completing missions directed to harass other students or to abuse other bullies. As part of the Rockstar Games open world series, this game also radiates violence in its treatment of human relationships, both in interior and exterior places. In this sense, it slightly moves away from the other two narratives discussed in this chapter, but it compensates this shortage with players' territorialization of becoming a bully, just another expression of the gray zone of bullying. We will discuss this aspect with thoroughness in the following pages, but let us first briefly refer to how *Let Me In*—and *Let the Right One In*—deal with the use of interior spaces to show legitimation of violence.

There are three fundamental sequences in these two films that directly refer to the problem of space: first, the scene in which the bullied protagonist is intimidated and physically abused by a group of fellow students in the high school swimming pool. Main character Oskar (Kåre Hedebrant)/Owen (Kodi Smit-McPhee) carries out his normal school duties when he is suddenly surrounded by a group of classmates who first harass and then attack him. He subsequently enters in a state of panic and is dragged around the swimming pool locker room, while the aggressors laugh and mock the victim. Unable to confront them, the abused student will have to wait until the moment he finds an opportunity to oppose the bullies, non-coincidentally in an open-space environment.

A second situation arises when Oskar/Owen finds himself again in a compromised position when he is pestered by the same group of fellow students while in a school trip to a frozen lake. In this case, however, he finds the courage to respond to his assaulters, but fails to avoid violence in the actions he perpetrates. Using the snow pole he holds in his hands, he attacks the leader of the bullying gang, and severely wounds him to cause the bully a permanent hearing impairment.

The third and last instance from *Let the Right One In* occurs in one of its most notable scenes, when the abused individual happens to be innocently practicing water sports in the school swimming pool, only to be interrupted by the raging gang of bullies that, in this occasion, brings along the older brother of the former leader of the group. Angered by his relative's injury, the bully threatens Oskar and makes him go underwater for an inconceivable amount of time. Again, the film creates a claustrophobic atmosphere in which space appears as a constrictive affection to the protagonist's emotions—as well as to his physical integrity. In this case, the claustrophobic effect is epitomized by the momentary feeling of asphyxiation experienced by the young protagonist, whose violent lack of air is transferred to the viewer.

The transmission of a constrictive sensation to the spectators' environment emphasizes the choking spatial construction that the bullied individual undergoes when exposed to a violent situation. The resolution of this swimming pool scene—the vampire girl who the bullied boy has befriended enters the scene and decapitates/mutilates the aggressors— is a representation of the genealogy of violence within Oskar's—and Owen's—production of identity. His interior demons are stimulated by the extreme situation of violence he is forced to confront, and therefore both internalizes and legitimizes another act of extreme violence against the perpetrators. This way, both Oskar and the spectators of the film feel relieved and satisfied when the group of children is brutalized by a form of monstrosity, squaring thus the circle of violence.

From these three scenes from *Let the Right One In*, we can infer a certain parallelism with the aforementioned discussion about interior and exterior spaces that we used to examine *Napoleon Dynamite*. There is an obvious isolation that directly affects Oskar in his relationships with the environment he inhabits. According to Espelage and Mrinalini, the creation of "safe spaces" will be critical to fight the stigmatization of children in disadvantaged positions at school (151). However, the very notion of "safe space" is problematic and must be questioned from a perspective of conflicting territories.

Speaking literally, "safe space" may refer to a particular location where abused children find a spot where they feel comfortable and do not perceive a threat against their physical or emotional integrity. On the other hand, the production of a safe space possibly perpetuates and legitimizes the hegemony of those spaces that have been collaterally defined as unsafe.

Let the Right One In addresses this issue brutally, and looks at how the reterritorialization of spaces might be a more plausible move for bullied children, as long as they grow a conscience of belonging on those spaces. Following Ann Friedberg, Jørgen Bruhn refers to the conflictive interaction of spaces in *Let the Right One In* arguing that

> the window is an opening, an aperture for light and ventilation. It opens, it closes; it separates the spaces of here and there, inside and outside, in front of and behind. The window opens onto a three-dimensional world beyond: it is a membrane where surface meets depth, where transparency meets its barriers [13].

From a more general approach, these two films (*Let Me In* and *Let the Right One In*) provide an initial scenery of fear that gradually becomes a territory of confidence for the bullied children. The spectator, though, is driven along a path of violence that blurs the deep aims of the film. Instead of participating in the educational process that Oskar pursues to overcome his lack of social abilities, viewers are deceived into a thirst for vengeance that brings to the discussion the position of violence in human nature. Although it is not the purpose of this study to analyze the problematic character of violence,[3] it is important to remind its influence on space, as *Evy Varsamopoulou* argues to analyze *Let the Right One In*.[4] Space can be understood as a phenomenon of violence as long as spatialities are involved. The construction of spaces as part of human identities has been widely discussed within the theoretical patterns of postmodernism,[5] and inevitably, the production of identities goes hand in hand with the proliferation of different types of violence. Rather, the purpose of this essay is to consider how the spectators of these two films support the production of violence[6] through their participation in the resignification of space, a position that will find its prime performance in *Bully: Scholarship Edition*, as will be explained in the next pages.

Michel Foucault, Henri Lefebvre, and Edward Soja, among others, have been prolific in their references to heterotopic spaces and to spatiality to refer to epistemological instances that have a direct repercussion in the formation and shaping of *actual* space. Their discussions have been particularly relevant in the analyses of photographical and film narratives, since these discourses provide an ample range of sceneries to establish dialogues with the viewers, making them participant in the construction of their uniqueness. Viewers' involvement in the production of space in film is, subsequently, metaphorical of human participation in the construction of space, and the best model of these discursive practices of space would be represented by heterotopias. Captured in between traditional modes of spatial representation, heterotopic spaces exist in separate planes of perception, but contribute to the questioning of physicality and standard geography to explain space. Defined as spaces that do exist and do not exist at the same time—or, rather, as *places* that exist elsewhere from any other known place in a society[7]—these heterotopias accomplish the mission of rendering the dialogue between text and reader—in this case viewer—to produce different relations in the heterotopic space. A frequently referred example of this sort of space in cinema[8] is the scene from David Lynch's *Inland Empire* in which a crying woman watches the white noise coming from a television screen, right before her stare blurs with an allegedly existing dramatic scene within the television set.

The sequence from Lynch's film contributes to establish the parameters of a renewed space that does not obey to laws of physical nor traditional conceptions of location. Rather, it portrays a sequence of the production of spatiality, one that is defined by the intervention of human subjectivity not only in the perception of space, but also in its very production. Furthermore, the resulting category should be paralleled to that of heterotopia, since the dramatic scene the extradiegetic spectator watches comes only from the interaction of the crying woman and the white noise screen, and can only have viability within that context, but it is a complete space nonetheless: it does not exist as a physical entity, but it does have an existence as spatiality and should not be categorized below traditional space in a hierarchical organization of locations. Given the syllogism, therefore, that if space is formed after the relationship between subjectivities and the environment, and space goes hand in hand with violence in its relation with identity production, then violence ought to present other forms besides the traditional conceptions we have, and violence should probably be investigated in terms of its function in that heterotopic space.

In this sense, *Let Me In*—as well as *Let the Right One In*—manifests the relevance of violence in Owen and Abby's—or Oskar and Eli's—production of their heterotopic space. Bullying comes and goes in different directions, but is never absent in any of the human relationships that are developed throughout the film(s). The only connection that is free from that sort of violence is, paradoxically, the one that is endorsed by the nonhuman, by the monster. The fact that Abby/Eli is condemned by her nature to be confined in either concealed or dark places makes of her an individual prone to create transitions between real and imagined spaces. Violence is her nature, but she fights her own instincts in order to protect the integrity of Owen/Oskar, the person who has been able to penetrate her space to see her as an equal, rather than as a marginal menace. Abby is, in fact, an abused child who has been permanently bullied by society, and perfectly understands the critical situation Owen is undergoing at school during their relationship.

Violence, therefore, is inherently constructed along the production of spaces. If these two characters seem to be able to inhabit a heterotopic space, created by themselves, in which violence is apparently suspended, viewers require from them some type of retaliation against all those factors that prevent them from continuing their lives. The viewer, thus, participates in the transformation of their heterotopic space into a place of heterotopic violence. As Rasmussen argues, "there is a sense that everyone can enter into a safe space, but these heterotopic spaces may only offer the illusion of inclusivity" (162). Viewers are tempted to be a part of that inclusivity, and in order to do so they must question the safe space that is supposed to be crucial in the well-being of Owen and Abby. In that sense, the viewer requires that a gang of bullies attack Owen (and Oskar) at a swimming pool, and that Abby/Eli responds vehemently with a demonstration of the violence that seemed to be suspended. Consequently, we look at the presentation of violence in this film not as the punctual attitude of a certain group against one specific individual. What *Let Me In/Let the Right One In* do is to refer to the different forms of bullying that subjects endure in their performed spatialities, integrated as they are in the collective appraisal and acceptance of violence as a terminal act of justice.

From that point of view, these two films represent an invitation to reflect upon the consequences of the legitimization of bullying in western epistemologies, and they follow the parodical criticism around bullying epitomized by the other narrative that is discussed in this study: the video game *Bully: Scholarship Edition*, developed and published by Rockstar in 2006.

Played from a third-person perspective, the player controls James Hopkins, also known as Jimmy, in an open-world scenery located in a school at Bullworth. The town academy where he becomes a boarding student is ruled by numerous gangs that bully on a regular basis the student body in the school. The mission of the player who is controlling Jimmy will be to impersonate this character in order to end the hierarchical dominance of those bullies. To that end, he will have to go through a series of missions and violent encounters.

The game clearly looks at how society works in environments of cohabitation. Based on the successful style of the *Grand Theft Auto* franchise, Rockstar Games brings to an educational space the impersonation of characters that are able to, under the controller's commands, become criminals by being abusive against other people, stealing, assaulting, kidnapping, or even murdering. Although the spatial component in the *GTA* games is undoubtedly recognizable—Los Angeles, New York or Miami—the living situations performed by the characters are far from being realistic for the average player to identify with them: the leader of a dangerous gang, an unscrupulous killer from the underworld, or a crooked businessman, to name just a few. Although the degree of violence in these games is extremely high, the spatial distance that is established between the fictional characters and the possible identifications performed by the players is fairly prominent (DeVane 270).[9]

That is not the case in *Bully: Scholarship Edition*. As Peter Rauch explains, "staffed by sadists, incompetents and perverts, Bullworth [Academy] represents both a parody of the stated aims of modern education and a microcosm for the whole world" (114). The metaphorical significance of this game's environment provides a diaphanous space of identification for its implied gamers. The person who controls Jimmy becomes a secondary school student who has to deal with the problems that arise from the interaction with groups of other teenagers in the same educational institution. Prone to be involved in fights and misdemeanors, Jimmy has access to a very limited range of minor weapons, including a slingshot, a baseball bat, or a paintball rifle, and his only traffic offenses come from jay walking, skating or riding his or stolen bicycles. However, the main actions of the game take place within the school walls, and involve hiding from bullies and school staff and administrators, flirting with fellow students, or attempting to succeed with class assignments. Peter Rauch describes the game as

> a story in and of itself, a story that is fundamentally about the relationships between children and power, and like most examinations of power, it is nuanced and unsettling. Although the controversy over *Bully* had mostly dissipated by the time the game was released, the content of the game itself would very likely have raised its own share of media attention even if it had been released by an unknown company with a less provocative title [113].

It seems evident that players involved in this game can identify with this character's experiences to a much higher extent than *GTA* players. The events Jimmy goes through are probably closer to the player's own— past or present—episodes at school, and therefore they incorporate to the gameplay a relevant factor of genuineness that the *GTA* series lacks.

From a point of view of the analysis of violence, bullying and space, the identification of the players with the characters in the game becomes critical. Comparable to the way *Let Me In* gives its audience a possibility to participate in the inherent violence that the film brings up, *Bully* goes a step further. Not only does it emphasize the role of its audience—in this case, the video game players—as *accomplices* in, or at least, contributors to the production of violence, but it also makes the players responsible for the violence the game proffers. Enshrined by both the relatively low level of criminality and the allegedly legitimate violence under cases of social survival, players spare no expenses in accepting the role they have been assigned with by the game developers, and they plunge into the sometimes subtle and sometimes explicit violence available in the game.

As far as the translation of violence into bullying is concerned, the case of *Bully: Scholar Edition* is clearly paradigmatic. Most of the missions the protagonist has to complete are based on the idea of spatial appropriation. The very first mission in the game presents the young character as a newcomer in the school, where he is received first by the administrators, who let the boy know very clearly which his place is, and which environments he should not even dare to get close, and then by a group of school mates who pester and force him to start a fight in order to establish their position in the social hierarchy of the school.

The character at this point, and as a ventriloquized extension of the player, has no option other than accepting the proposed violence and justify it as a mode of survival—and therefore as a legitimate dynamics in their relationship with the other members of the academy. From that moment on, the player will show no mercy at bullying vulnerable students and at defending others from gangs of bullies. In short, the practice of bullying becomes natural in this particular space, even if the game belongs to the category of "open world" adventures and therefore the players have the option to explore the game in a different approach; in fact, they are explicitly directed into performing violence, but at the same time they have many alternative missions of a different nature. About the violence in this video game, Clare Bradford argues in "Playing at Bullying: The Postmodern Ethic of *Bully (Canis Canem Edit)*" that

> despite widespread moral panics about video game violence, *Bully* exercises tight controls over the kinds of violence permitted in the game, and the characters against whom violence is tolerated; for instance, Jimmy can fight bullies or trip up prefects, but he cannot behave violently toward girls or young characters or nerds without consequences such as detention [71].

Detention, however, occurs only after a pursuit and potential fight with guards that becomes in itself just another mission in the game. The game invites players, actually, to amuse themselves in different fashions within the game, and one of those entertaining activities—as it happens in the *GTA* series and many of the open-world games—is to escape from and fighting forces of order, including police officers, army soldiers and school guards. In this sense, attacking "girls or young characters or nerds" in the game should not be read as a source for punishment, but rather as just another door to amusement through violence. I do not discuss Bradford's accurate critique of the moral tendency to judge violent video games for their supposed connections to reality and the—according to those points of view—actual consequences in the daily lives of young players (73), but I would suggest a more detailed analysis about the archeology of violence and the ways it is performed within the sets of representations that make up subjectivity.

Particularly, the reconceptualization of violence according to spatial reformulated values would add another crucial component to Bradford's discussion of *Bully* as a postmodern narrative (75). Other authors, such as Jasmina Kallay in "Rethinking Genre in Computer Games: How Narrative Psychology Connects Game and Story" or Sue Saltmarsh in *Rethinking School Violence: Theory, Gender, Context*, explain that there is a direct connection through psychological narratives between the actual game and the story it tells. In this sense, as discussed above, the player participates in the production of the game narrative, and therefore becomes part of the resulting discursive subjectivity, and participates in the abusive practices against other characters in the game.

There is a particular scene in the game that evidences this position. One of the many missions in the game related to the act of bullying includes some extra points gained by the player after completing a terrorizing action against other students with an ample set of violent activities, including dunking those students' heads in toilets. The territorial hostility represented by those acts is to be played by gamers as parodical forms of spatiality.[10] They create a heterotopic space in which the fictional pact with the game narrative is constantly transgressed, and the actions performed by Jimmy under the commands of the players are coherent with the narrative objectives of the game.

The production of this heterotopic space in the game, in other words, implies the production of an inherent violence to those spaces. The player, in a way, is inside the space of the game, but they are also distant from their own physicality. Such a present-absent spatiality of the player goes hand in hand with their experience of the violence in the game, which becomes distant but also part of their identities. It reinforces the subjective alienation of players through spatial identifications, and the territorialization of the spaces within the game, something that has a direct repercussion on the spatial perception that derives from the game.

Bully: Scholarship Edition can be perceived as the epitome of the connections between space and the violent act of bullying. The processes of legitimization of violence that have been described here work within the same pattern in regular situations of harassment at schools. Spaces are territorialized by the abusive executors of violence and, as it happened in *Let Me In*, the resignification of spaces is put up within the dichotomy of interior and exterior places. The Bullworth Academy becomes a repressive place of discipline and punishment, whereas the open urban environment around the school performs violence following a much more complex pattern.

Besides their polarized view of space, both *Bully* and *Let Me In* offer a heterotopic representation of violence that requires, respectively, the participation of the player and the viewer. In this view, such a dislocation of these extradiegetic elements pursue an honest problematization of the act of bullying, not from a deontologized distance, but from the experimentation of violence as an inherently subjective discourse and as a problematic structure of both identification with and alienation from bullied individuals and bullies.

As indicated in the introduction, the complexity of bullying resides in its secrecy. The non-verbalization of harassment, from both sides, has been interpreted as a symptom of plausible irresolution, and the texts that have been analyzed in this chapter advocate for a straight up conviction that the heterotopic implication of observers in the acts of violence in educational institutions will manifest a deeper, and possibly clearer understanding of bullying.

Notes

1. "De/Re-territorialization" are concepts directly related to Deleuze's discussion on space and territory. They refer to the process of resignification of a given spatiality through a process of detaching its denotation from an ideologically-inherited meaning (deterritorialization) and reconstructing its connections to new sets of meanings (reterritorialization).

2. As aforementioned, Reeves' version is based on Alfredson's. They are both interpretations of John Ajvide Lindqvist's novel *Låt den rätte komma in* (2004).

3. There is a whole corpus of rigorous studies on the concept of violence, particularly reinvigorated in the last few years. See, for instance, Slavoj Žižek, *Sobre la violencia: seis reflexiones marginales* (2009); *Violence: Six Sideways Reflections* (2008); Randall Collins,

Violence: A Micro-Sociological Theory (2008); Peter Gelderloos, *The Failure of Nonviolence: From the Arab Spring to Occupy* (2013); Bruce Lawrence and Aisha Karim, *On Violence: A Reader* (2007); Charles Tilly, *The Politics of Collective Violence* (2003); or James Tyner, *Space, Place, and Violence: Violence and the Embodied Geographies of Race, Sex and Gender* (2012).

4. Evy Varsamopoulou, "Violence and the Poetics of (un)heimlich Space in *Let the Right One In*,'" *Film-Philosophy Conference 2012* (N.p., 2012), www.film-philosophy.com.

5. See, for instance, Fredric Jameson, Jean Baudrillard, or David Harvey.

6. It would be fair to say that they do participate as well in the production of nonviolence, as defined by Gelderloos, and therefore they could be systematically placed within the concept of non-violent violence (Žižek and Critchley).

7. Foucault, "Of Other Spaces."

8. I talked about this scene elsewhere in order to explain the semiotic hierarchies established by Lynch among the different acting components in his films. See Barros-Grela 78.

9. This does not mean that the game is exempt of controversy due to the negative stereotypes it provides of society and populations. Along these lines, DeVane argues that "critics charged that this portrayal of African-American and Latino communities as hubs for violence and criminality both reifies discriminatory stereotypes and provides young adolescents with negative role models" (269).

10. In my argument I do not discriminate between ages. I have found the reaction of teenagers to these scenes very similar to those of players in their thirties. In both cases, they saw these actions as mere acts of parody.

Works Cited

Barros Grela, Eduardo. "Tópicos rizomáticos y espacialidad posmoderna en Estados Unidos." In *La pantalla ficcional. Literatura y tecnologías de la comunicación.* Eds. José María Paz and Pilar Couto. Madrid: Pigmalion, 2014.
Baudrillard, Jean. *Simulacra and Simulation.* Trans. Sheila Faria Glaser. Ann Arbor: University of Michigan Press, 1995.
Bradford, Clare. "Playing at Bullying: The Postmodern Ethic of *Bully (Canis Canem Edit)*." *Digital Culture & Education (DCE)* 1.1 (2009): 67–82.
Bruhn, Jørgen, Anne Gjelsvik, and Henriette Thune. "Parallel Worlds of Possible Meetings in *Let the Right One In*." *Word & Image* 27.1 (2011): 2–14.
Critchley, Simon. *How to Stop Living and Start Worrying: Conversations with Carl Cederstrm.* Malden, MA: Polity, 2010.
Crofts, Penny, and Honni van Rijswijk. "'What Kept You So Long?' Bullying's Gray Zone and The Vampire's Transgressive Justice in *Let the Right One In*." *Law, Culture and the Humanities* (2012): 1–22.
Deleuze, Gilles and Félix Guattari. *Anti-Œdipus.* Trans. Robert Hurley, Mark Seem and Helen R. Lane. London and New York: Continuum, 2004.
____, and ____. *A Thousand Plateaus.* Trans. Brian Massumi. London: Continuum, 2004.
DeVane, Ben, and Kurt D. Squire. "The Meaning of Race and Violence in Grand Theft Auto San Andreas." *Games and Culture* 3.3–4 (2008): 264–285.
Espelage, Dorothy L., and Mrinalini A. Rao. "Bullying and Harassment." *Creating Safe and Supportive Learning Environments: A Guide for Working with Lesbian, Gay, Bisexual, Transgender, and Questioning Youth and Families.* Eds. Emily S. Fisher and Karen Komosa-Hawkins. New York: Routledge, 2013: 140–160.
Foucault, Michel. "Of Other Spaces." Trans. from French Jay Miskowiec. *Architecture/Mouvement/Continuité* (October 1984).

Friedberg, Ann. *The Virtual Window: From Alberti to Microsoft*. Cambridge: MIT Press, 2009.
Harvey, David. *Spaces of Global Capitalism*. New York: Verso, 2006.
Inland Empire. Dir. David Lynch. Perf. Laura Dern and Jeremy Irons. Absurda, 2006. DVD.
Jameson, Fredric. *Postmodernism, or, the Cultural Logic of Late Capitalism*. Durham: Duke University Press, 1990.
Kallay, Jasmina. "Rethinking Genre in Computer Games: How Narrative Psychology Connects Game and Story." *Interdisciplinary Models and Tools for Serious Games: Emerging Concepts and Future Directions*. Ed. Richard Van Eck. Hershey, PA: IGI Global, 2010: 30–49.
Lefebvre, Henri. *The Production of Space*. Hoboken, NJ: Wiley, 1992.
Let Me In. Dir. Matt Reeves. Perf. Kodi Smit-McPhee and Chloe Moretz. Hammer, 2010. DVD.
Let the Right One In. Dir. Tomas Alfredson. Perf. Kåre Hedebrant and Lina Leandersson. EFTI, 2008. DVD.
Lindqvist, John Ajvide. *Låt den Rätte Komma In*. Stockholm: Ordfront Förlag, 2004.
Napoleon Dynamite. Dir. Jared Hess. Perf. Jon Heder and Efron Ramirez. 20th Century–Fox, 2004. DVD.
Rasmussen, Mary Louise. *Becoming Subjects: Sexualities and Secondary Schooling*. New York: Routledge, 2006.
Rauch, Peter. "Coming of Age at Bullworth Academy." *Journal of Social Science Education* 7/8.2/1 (2008/09): 112–118.
Rockstar Games. *Bully: Scholarship Edition*. N.p.: BMG Interactive, 2004. Computer software.
Rockstar North. *Grand Theft Auto Series*. N.p.: BMG Interactive, 1997–2014. Computer software.
Ryan, Lorraine. "The Development of Child Subjectivity in *La lengua de las mariposas*." *Hispania* 95.3 (September 2012): 448–460.
Saltmarsh, Sue, Kerry Robinson, and Cristyn Davies. *Rethinking School Violence: Theory, Gender, Context*. New York: Palgrave Macmillan, 2012.
Soja, Edward W. *Postmodern Geographies: The Reassertion of Space in Critical Social Theory*. London: Verso, 1989.
Varsamopoulou, Evy. "Violence and the Poetics of (un)Heimlich Space in *Let the Right One In*." *Film-Philosophy Conference*. N.p., 2012 www.film-philosophy.com.
Žižek, Slavoj. *Violence: Six Sideways Reflections*. London: Profile Books, 2009.

The Chocolate War and Anti-Bullying Novels in Popular Culture

Nina Marie Bone

Parents have always been dragged to the theaters by their children for the latest blockbuster, but they may have never dreamed that one day their children's influence would not only have them shelling out eight bucks for a movie ticket, but also dictating what movies are in demand. As the rise in popularity of the teen book series *Twilight* by Stephenie Meyer (2005) grew, so did Hollywood's interest in adapting it for the big screen. The final *Twilight* movie, in what later became a saga, grossed over $676 million in the U.S. alone (Whitehouse 240). Following suit was *The Hunger Games* and the *Divergent* series, causing others to take a second glance at the treasures held in young adult (YA) novels. Jeff Kinney's *Diary of a Wimpy Kid* pulled the focus of the young adult media to the bullying problem many schools across America are facing. Thus, a new sub-genre of anti-bullying literature has emerged and is continuing to grow in influence. Tracking this trend back to its roots, all signs would lead to one unlikely author: Robert Cormier.

Cormier spent his entire life in and around Leominster, Massachusetts, where his grandfather immigrated as this area recruited laborers for its new comb factories. His grandfather married then bought a three-story tenement house, where he raised his family. When his sons grew, they too moved their families into the tenement house and in 1925 Cormier became the second of eight children. Throughout his life, Cormier remained surrounded by a loving and close family, both close in love and close in proximity, as his grandparents remained on the ground floor and Cormier's parents, aunts, uncles, and cousins occupied the remaining floors and rooms. Cormier was able to lean on his close-knit family for the love and support he needed which remains ironic because all of Cormier's characters come from broken homes and some even suffer horrendous abuse. As for Cormier, he remained a quiet and shy young man, socializing mostly with his family, using his pen as his voice (Campbell).

Cormier's first job was working the night shift of the Leominster bureau of the *Worcester Telegram*; later he moved to the *Fitchburg Sentinel* as a reporter, wire editor, and worked his way up to an associate editor. He had been with the *Fitchburg Sentinel* for twenty-three years when he left in 1978 to pursue fiction writing full-time (Campbell). His first novel, *A Little Raw on Monday Mornings* (1963), details the story of a middle-aged widow with two children who finds herself pregnant after a one-night stand with a co-worker. She now must decide to bring into her life another mouth to feed or to hide and expel her shame without anyone knowing. This novel's content is hardly suitable for young adults, as Cormier intended.

However, it was *The Chocolate War* (*TCW*), published in 1974, that sent this shy and reserved author into the spotlight. Cormier put the spotlight on bullying, showing its potentially fatal consequences, and making it a topic of dialogue. From those roots, the new sub-genre of YA anti-bullying novels has grown. Cormier paved the way for YA authors today to break away from the "happily ever after" ending, and to paint the grim reality that bullying is. Sometimes, the bad guys win. Finally, Cormier pushed the limits regarding the content discussed in YA novels, allowing YA authors today to write in the sometimes crude manner that most young adults hear in their school hallways, thus making the YA novels more relatable and realistic. The portrayal of bullying in popular culture permeates movies, books, advertising, and even jewelry, but Robert Cormier is the grandfather of this trend.

The Chocolate War was Cormier's first YA novel and the breakthrough book for anti-bullying literature. This novel depicts Jerry, who is new to Trinity High School, a private Catholic school for males. Brother Leon is the current headmaster, and in order to impress those above him, and earn extra money from Trinity High's annual chocolate sale, he has ordered 20,000 boxes of chocolates, double the normal amount, to be sold at double the normal cost. While the brothers think they run the school, behind the scenes lurks a gang of students known as "The Vigils," run by the cold, manipulative, and sly Archie Costello. The Vigils coerce or blackmail students into performing assignments that prey upon their weaknesses in order to keep the students under their control.

Archie singles Jerry out to refuse to sell the chocolates to show Brother Leon who rules the school and the assignment turns deadly. When we analyze *TWC* for literary quality or semantics, scholars agree that Cormier was undisputedly a master. Cormier uses vibrant words and metaphors to paint the spaces of his novels, drawing in readers. One fine example of this is when Jerry (*TCW* main protagonist) is being pummeled on the football field. We read, "On the third play, he was hit simultaneously by three of them: one, his knees; another, his stomach; a third, his head—the helmet no protection at all. His body seemed to telescope into itself but all the parts didn't fit" (Cormier 2). It was this ability to be short, blunt, and to the point that made Cormier an easy author to read and it was his ability to capture his readers that made him an author to be loved. *TCW* received rave book reviews upon its release and remained unchallenged until the 1980s. Even now, the debate continues as to what audience, adult or teen, is best suited for this work.

The Chocolate War was inspired when Cormier's son Peter came home from school one day with bags of chocolate he was supposed to sell to help the school raise money. Peter did not want to go door-to-door bothering his neighbors and family members, so Cormier wrote him a note to excuse him from the chocolate sale. Peter was excused, and that was the end of it. But Cormier let his mind ruminate over other possible outcomes of his son's lack of participation in this private school's long-held tradition of a fall chocolate sale fund raiser (Campbell 27). *TCW* was then born out of Cormier's rumination over different endings to his son's real life chocolate sale dilemma. When Cormier presented his work to his literary agent, Marilyn Marlow, she changed the course of Cormier's career forever. After reading the first few chapters, she told Cormier that he had written a young adult novel. This shocked Cormier and made him wonder if he would need to clean up the language, but Marlow told him to write what he felt was true and she would worry about how to market it (Campbell 28). The task that Marlow undertook was not easy as many publishers thought that Cormier's writing was not suitable for young people. Publishers felt that *TCW* was too downbeat and the ending must be changed. The idea of an innocent protagonist ending in failure was unheard of in the YA world and after several rejections; it was Pantheon publishing that realized the quality of Cormier's writing style and put *TCW* into print (Campbell).

The first review of *TCW* was published on March 12, 1974, in *Kirkus Reviews*. Expecting nothing less than something wonderfully dark and morbid from Cormier, the initial review praised the action and fast pace of the author's fourth novel. The overall theme of the review was positive, but it noted, "Mature young readers will respect the uncompromising ending that dares disturb the upbeat universe of juvenile books" (Kirkus Reviews). While the first review raved over this work by Cormier, this subtle remark about the novel's dark content set the stage for the subsequent debate that would surround *TCW*. The *New York Times* published the second review on May 5, 1974; Theodore Weesner believed that this novel was a great book for young adults because it had a message for them. Weesner believed that, when used as a high school read, it could start discussions about identity, power, and the function of power in society (Weesner). Weesner opened his article by stating that the novel was written for teenagers, "but a strong read for adults" (Weesner), and he closed his article by saying, "an easy out does not occur" (Weesner). The reviews indicate that the serious content was not customary of YA literature in the mid–1970s, and this shock to the YA genre had lasting impact.

On November 3, 1974, the *New York Times* ran a feature entitled "Outstanding Books," selected by the children's editor. What is interesting about this particular issue is that not only does *TWC* make the outstanding books list for teenage fiction, but on the same page, it also makes the 9–12 age list. The teen-age section remarks that *TCW* is a "masterfully structured novel about the misuse of power" ("Outstanding Books"). When we go across to the column to the 9–12 age groups, the critic says that *TCW* shows "how the dormant, indiscriminate cruelty of a mob can be easily mobilized by the absolute evil of any cruel leader" ("Outstanding Books"). While both reviews are positive, it is clear that the critic was not sure into what category Cormier's novel fell. For older teens, the editor enjoys the book for its message about the "misuse of power." This editor believes that this novel would work well in a classroom setting for the same reasons that Weesner thought it would work. While the editor may have been torn as to how to categorize *TCW* he was not torn as to whether or not the message of *TCW* should be heard. While admittedly *TCW* is tells the blunt dark side of bullying its message is true and honest and one that this editor felt should be read by all age groups.

When the editor looks at it as a pick for the 9–12 age range, it is praised for an anti-bullying theme comparable with Judy Blume's *Blubber*. Yet, while Blume's book is a good read for the 9–12 age group, *Blubber* does not contain any of the language, violence, or sexual reference that Cormier's does. Up to this point in time, YA literature remained focused on plot, setting, and protagonist formatted in basic beginning, rise in climatic action, climax, and ending. Traditionally, the protagonist is presented with a problem, typical to young adult problems, and by the books ending the problem is neatly wrapped up and the protagonist has come out on top with lessons learned. Parents mislead by reviews may have thought *TCW* was as child friendly as Blume's would have been outraged upon reading *TCW*, and thus began a parental pushback. Parents demanded that *TCW* be taken off their children's reading list, in other states, parents had *TCW* banned from their schools library, and some went as far as to write letters to Cormier and his editors appalled by the garbage they felt he created. Cormier, both with language and content, was far beyond the normal standards for YA fiction, let alone for children's fiction. Young adults responded well to the relatable characters and were enthralled by the book's sudden and shocking ending. In later criticism, some scholars believe that Cormier should not have been marketed as a YA author to begin with. His first book, *Now and at the Hour*, was said to be for the morbid reader, and each novel after deals with life from its darker side and often, as in life, there is no happy ending.

In March 1975, *The School Library Journal* released its notable children's books of 1974. Along with Maya Angelou's *My Name*, and *Watership Down*, by Richard Adams, *The Chocolate War* also stands alongside them ("Notable Children's Books—1974"). On May 11, 1975, the *New York Times* published its Paperbacks: New and Noteworthy section where the book *Alive*, that recounts the real-life story of the Uruguayan rugby players, also made the list along with *The Chocolate War*. The fact that *TCW* can stand along such a harrowing tale of human will and heroism speaks volumes about the quality of Cormier's writing style, not to mention that this 1974 review also marks it as a book about the cruelty of bullying ("Paperbacks: New and Noteworthy").

Again, these two reviews feed into the increasing confusion about where Cormier's novel fits, but the message is clear. Cormier brought the topic of bullying into the spotlight, he made teachers, and students engage in dialogue about the real and serious consequences of bullying for all of those involved. The first review, noted above, places *TCW* alongside Maya Angelou, framing it in the same manner as the earlier review did with Blume. This gives the buyer the impression that Cormier's writing is as safe and poetic as Maya Angelou listing them both in their children's book section. The second review lists Cormier as a general paperback and while they do give a brief synopsis about its anti-bullying theme that would make it a good sell for children; they list it alongside *Alive*, a noteworthy paperback, yet not for young children.

Sylvia Iskander picked up the conversation about *TWC* in her 1987 article by stating what she sees as a problem. "The young-adult novels of Robert Cormier—*The Chocolate War*—have been criticized for the bleak, hopeless world they describe" (Iskander 7). She then quotes some of the things that have been said about his works: "there are no adults worth emulating" and "*The Chocolate War* presents a frightening universe" (Iskander 7). Iskander argues that *TCW* accurately describes the problems that exist in the real world. But school boards in New York, Massachusetts, South Carolina, and Arizona worked to ban Cormier's novels from the classroom (Campbell 71).

Iskander asks her readers to consider: what are the characteristics of YA literature audiences. She asserted that since students are, in essence, in limbo between being children and being adults. They cling to idealism. Therefore, since *TCW* leaves Jerry beaten and Archie in the winner's seat, what does Cormier want from his readers (Iskander 8)? This brings us back to the words of Cormier's editor who told him to "write what you feel is true" and that is what Cormier sought to do. He chose to write about a teenager's problem with bullies from the viewpoint of the teen and to tell the story the way real life sometimes turns out to be. Cormier dose not solve the problem for his readers and by leaving the story without a conclusion it is up to the readers to solve the problem in their own lives.

Iskander relates that if readers find Cormier's books as hopeless they have missed the "positive elements because these are presented ironically and indirectly" (Iskander 8). A successful reader, the author writes, must realize there are various levels at work in Cormier's novels, and moral development extends past the end of the novel. Iskander argues that because Cormier's novels are so complex, they challenge the notion of relationships. She then goes on to give examples of young adults who, after reading one of Cormier's novels, were moved to action in some way or another.

Parents of young readers have the hardest time with Cormier's novels because of a preconceived idea of young adult novels containing a moral protagonist that triumphs over evil. For *The Chocolate War*, Iskander defends, we do have the moral character Jerry who, by all accounts, does everything right. However, while readers expect a happy ending, "the hero is crushed and brutally beaten, his very survival in question, many readers feel betrayed and disoriented" (Iskander 12). Iskander says the reason readers complain about Cormier is because he has "defie[d] their expectations" (Iskander 12). In conclusion, Iskander asserts that Cormier's books "argue for justice" (Cormier 18) and are an effective tool to demonstrate moral responsibility.

Maia Mertz, noting that young adult novels have received much attention for their usefulness in the classroom, points out that the books "can be used to enhance students' literary understandings" (1). Mertz's first subheading is entitled "Transition Literature," which is one of the many categories young adult literature (YAL) falls into. YAL is the middle ground between children's books and adult fiction. Mertz goes on to highlight two books that she feels meets a high quality of YAL: Paul Zindel, author of *The Pigman*, and Robert Cormier. She notes that both books have a complexity that draws in and engages the readers. Mertz says, "Cormier's novel is particularly appropriate for dealing with two concepts that inexperienced readers seem to find particularly elusive: style and structure" (Mertz 30). Mertz goes on to explain that both adults and adolescents are challenged by its structure, style, and theme (Mertz 32). Mertz admits that some YA work is best for casual reading by young people, but she firmly states that YAL will continue to grow and mature, and the two authors she looked at (Zindel and Cormier) can help young readers grow in their understanding of literature. Mertz emphasizes that helping adolescent readers "understand how writers achieve their effects" is also helping them to grasp "the power of language to evoke thought and feelings" (Mertz 32).

A dissenting view is expressed by Anita Tarr, who does not share the previous authors' belief about the value of *TWC*. Tarr does not agree that Jerry is a hero fighting against a corrupt system. Tarr claims instead, "Cormier presents only the *illusion* of moral agency, and his refusal to sell chocolates is *not* the result of a moral dilemma" (Tarr 96).

Not only does Tarr feel that Cormier's work is anti-female, she also argues that Cormier's work lacks narrative structure, with the entire novel going back and forth between "loose and tight." Tarr believes that Jerry is not a hero, and that his rebellion is merely an illusion. This critical perspective demonstrates the power of Cormier's writing to evoke strong responses of all types. The topic of bullying strikes a chord with everyone, at some level or another, and *TCW* is so well crafted that it can be debated and argued among scholars, teens, parents, school boards, antifeminists, feminists, and LGBTQ groups. *TCW* is able to transcend barriers and what remains is the cold hard truths about bullying.

Ciara Bhroin takes the opposite stance of Anita Tarr. Bhroin argues that Cormier's novel is exactly what young adults need. Bhroin argues, "Jerry's strength is that he had the courage to make a stand at all. It is clear to the reader that he would not have failed if others showed similar individual courage and persistence" (Bhroin 25). Bhroin notes that "the fact that his books are marketed and sold under the 'Young Adult' label means that criticism of them will invariably involve questions of appropriateness" (Bhroin 29). Bhroin rebuts that argument by explaining that books have the role of expanding children's minds, not to shelter them and protect their innocence. He explains that many YA books today that are problem focused are as "didactic" as any children's literature book (Bhroin 29). Bhroin reasserts that Cormier asks his readers tough questions that teach them not to be complacent.

Lourdes Lopez-Ropero writes that *TCW* was a precursor to a new sub-genre of anti-bullying literature. Lopez-Ropero establishes that "anti-bullying novels transcend the confines of the single-issue problem novel, addressing matters of difference and bias in society. So, Jerry Renault, Stargirl, and Leonard Grey are victimized for the value they attach to their personal convictions, and, in other novels, teenagers are mistreated on specific grounds such as their class, sexual orientation or race" (Ropero 49). The issue of bullying has permeated our popular culture as authors follow in Cormier's steps and have chosen to take on bullying and present it in a true and relatable light for both parents and young adults.

Contemporary books that show such mistreatment include *The Misfits* by James Howe, *Stargirl* by Jerry Spinelli, and *Wonder* by R.J. Palacio. James Howe's *The Misfits* (2001) focuses on four middle school students who use the very insults used against them to become empowered. This group of students bans together, creating a third party in the student council elections. Howe addresses the issue of name calling, put-downs, and gossip so well that his book inspired a national movement. In 2004, No Name-Calling Week was implemented and has been adopted by schools across the nation, becoming one of the largest bullying-prevention initiatives in the country (Bott 5).

Jerry Spinelli's book takes place in high school, where new student Stargirl celebrates her uniqueness. She does not have a cohort to lean on as in *The Misfits*, nor does she allow her oppressors to take away her spirit. With Spinelli, readers receive the story from a bystander and one-time boyfriend. Like Jerry in *TCW*, Stargirl appears to have no other choice but to conform to Mica High's environment; and even though Mica High is void of a corrupt headmaster and gang like the Vigils, the pressure to conform is just as intense, but she refuses.

Endgame, by Nancy Garden, shows how systematic long term bullying can escalate into a live shooter in the hall. Main character Gray Wilson has no cohort to draw strength from, he has no determined spirit that allows him to rise above his abuse, and in many ways he resembles

Cormier's Jerry, who is slowly beaten down. Gray, like some teens have decided to do, takes matters into his own hands and forces the world around them to take notice by bring a gun to school. Many schools have safety protocols in place for "live shooters," and *Endgame* allows teachers to start a discussion, in a safe and controlled environment.

Wonder by R.J Palacio has recently been named a *New York Times* best seller. While this is a story of bullying, a young reader may often forget with the books quick wit and lighthearted nature. What draws younger audiences to this story of a boy with a facial deformity is its typical fifth-grader banter. When describing Auggie's feelings about attending school for the first time he says, "So here's why I changed my mind.... It wasn't so I wouldn't have to hear Mom give me a whole lecture.... Ahhh, I suddenly felt really bad" (Palacio 141). The book is an easy and quick read that alternates among multiple narrators keeping young readers engaged. In the novels by Cormier and Garden, the authors keep a somber and serious tone throughout their books. Howe, Spinelli, and Palacio's writing is far more upbeat causing their books to be a popular choice for a pre-teen middle school age group.

Authors today have free range to discuss this difficult topic in a language and with situations that are real and relatable to the students and teachers that read them. From names being called to live shooters on campus, these stories are allowed to flourish in the hands of young readers because of *The Chocolate War* and Robert Cormier. Cormier spearheaded the way through school boards and parental lash outs so that the bullying can be discussed honestly, instead of a tidy ending where everyone wins. It was his use of langue and dark tones that gave other writers permission to write in the same fashion and, in turn, this has allowed film makers adaptations to be as real as the words they were crafted after. This has brought much needed discussion to the topic of bullying. Bullying is more of a problem than it ever was and if words are the weapon, then we can thank Cormier for giving us the courage to fight back.

Works Cited

Bhroin, Ni. "Cynical or Compassionate? The Young Adult Novels of Robert Cormier." *Journal of Children's Literature Studies* (2004): 23–33.
Bott, C.J. *More Bullies In More Books*. Lanham, MD: Scarecrow Press, 2009.
Campbell, Patty. *Robert Cormier: Daring to Disturb the Universe*. New York: Random House, 2006.
Cormier, Robert. *The Chocolate War*. New York: Dell Laurel-Leaf, 1974.
Iskander, Sylvia Patterson. "Readers, Realism, and Robert Cormier." *Children's Literature* (1987): 7–18.

Kirkus Reviews. "Rev. of *The Chocolate War.*" *Kirkus Reviews* (12 March 1974).
Lopez-Ropero, Lourdes. "You Are a Flaw in the Pattern: Difference, Autonomy, and Bullying in YA Fiction." *Children's Literature in Education* 43.2 (June 2012): 145–157.
Mertz, Maia. "Enhancing Literary Understandings Through Young Adult Fiction." *Publishing Research Quarterly* (1992): 23–33.
Moss, Barbara. "The Common Core Text Exemplars: A Worthy New Canon or Not?" *Voices from the Middle* (2013): 48–52.
"Notable Children's Books—1974." *School Library Journal* (1975): 64.
"Outstanding Books." *New York Times* 3 November 1974: F52.
"Paperbacks: New and Noteworthy." *New York Times* 11 May 1975: BR13.
Tarr, Anitia. "The Absence of Moral Agency in Robert Cormier's *The Chocolate War.*" *Children's Literature* (2002): 96–123.
Weesner, Theodore. "Rev. of *The Chocolate War.*" *New York Times* 5 May 1974: 15.
Whitehouse, Ginny. "Case and Commentaries." *Journal of Mass Media Ethics* (2011): 240–253.

The Power of Praise

Mary-Lynn Chambers

Bullying is a phenomenon that directly impacts almost one-third of students and is recognized as a school-based violence that impacts the greater part of the student body (Cooper and Nickerson). Thus, it is a societal issue that needs to be addressed. Within the United States, there has been a growing concern regarding bullying and the implications it is having on our children and adolescents. In response to school shootings, the United States adopted the "zero-tolerance" policy, and as we entered the new millennium, there was growing evidence that this policy included bullying. Yet, education mandates a "free and appropriate education" (Espelage and Swearer 366) for all students, so suspension or expulsion for aggressive bullying behavior is often avoided. However, in 2003 the U.S. government responded with the DARE (Drug Abuse Resistance Education) campaign that launched a national bullying public awareness and prevention program with the hope of becoming more strategic in dealing with bullying in the school setting (Espelage and Swearer). In 2014, the problem of bullying continues to brew in the academic setting. Georgiou and Stavrinides define bullying as "a physical, verbal or psychological attack or intimidation that is intended to cause fear, distress or harm to the victim" (165). These authors continue to explain that the act must be intentional and systematic in order to be considered bullying. In order for society to respond appropriately to bullying within our schools, we need a stronger focus on the causes of bullying, the impact bullying has on the victim, and the power of praise rooted in an appropriate plan of action that will censure bullying activity.

Bullying is not a socio-economic, racial, or even gender specific challenge; bullying affects the young and the more mature students, the students in the suburbs and in the urban school settings, those with money and those without money, it even affects those inside and outside (Milsom and Gallo) of the United States. Studies show that sixty percent of elementary school-aged children have been a victim of bullying (Davis, Galford, and Lovell). However, there are also students who see bullying take place and are affected by that experience. Cooper and Nickerson surveyed two hundred and sixty adults, ninety percent of whom indicated a memory of seeing or being involved in bullying as a child, which demonstrates the long lasting imprint bullying has on the psyche. Although bullying can begin as early as kindergarten, the pattern of bullying increases as the students move toward middle school, peaks during middle school and early high school, then declines towards the end of high school (Davis, Galford, and Lovell; Milsom and Gallo).

This chapter will consider the data regarding the causes and impact of bullying, while relating it to three interviewed individuals who will be addressed as Student A, Student B, and Teacher A. Student A is an African American 20-year-old male who is presently a sophomore at a North Carolina university. This student grew up in a low-income, gang-infested city in North Carolina where he experienced bullying at home and at school. Student B is a white 14-year-old who is a freshman in a Canadian high school, but his seventh grade year will be forever branded as a bullied year. He lives in a quaint Canadian town with his parents, sister, and brother. They are a higher income family, and they enjoy the benefits that come with that status. Finally, Teacher A teaches in a low-income area with multi-racial representation at her school. Although she addresses bullying amongst her students, she also experienced bullying when she was a high school student. She grew up in a small rural community where she was considered middle class. Her status as a student-athlete did not keep her from experiencing bullying her sophomore year. All three of the individuals interviewed experienced bullying during the middle school or early high school years. All three individuals also encountered a role model who became a positive, praise-giving mentor for them. Presently, all three individuals are now experiencing greater confidence and success because of the power of praise.

Student A was born into a gang-connected family setting where violence was a common denominator. His birth father was a member of one gang, and his mother was part of another gang. The two never married, and Student A knew who his father was, but he never interacted with his father. His stepfather assumed the role of man of the house, but this man's aggressive and angry actions resulted in physical abuse for Student A. The violence Student A experienced at home had a direct impact on his self-esteem, and he quickly discovered that he was marked as a target for bullying in the school setting. In response to the bullying he was experiencing, he decided to learn how to box. He joined a club and learned the art of self-defense. He used the newly acquired skill to fight off his stepfather's violent advances, but Student A also used the same skills to begin bullying others. Patton, Williams and Allen-Meares explain that "exposure to violence is particularly relevant antecedent to bullying ... among African American youth in low-resourced communities" (256). Georgiou and Stavrinides, researchers from the University of Cyprus, explain that authoritarian parents who use severe punitive discipline on their children are more likely to rear children who bully others. They explain that parental practices at home are related to a child's aggressive activity at school. Student A confessed during the interview that what he had learned at home from his stepfather had a significant impact on his reaction to others. He acknowledged that he became a bully at school, participated in gang-related activities in his community, and fought his stepfather at home, all on a regular basis. Research reveals that bullying behavior results from interrelated influences including family, peers, and the social environment (Espelage and De La Rue). Student A is evidence of the impact of this interrelated system and the resulting aggressive behavior that is identified as bullying. This real life experience represents depictions of bullying in popular culture where the bully is depicted as a villain, but he or she may also be a victim.

The filmmaking industry has acknowledged this interrelated system that leads to bullying and illustrated it for us on the big screen. The movie *Precious* in many ways replicates the family and school setting that Student A shared during his interview. Precious is a 16-year-old African American girl from a welfare home where she is physically, sexually, and emotionally abused. What she experiences at home directly affects her actions at school. Precious lashes out and hits classmates and a younger neighborhood girl. However, these acts of violence mirror the treatment she is receiving at home. Georgiou and Stavrinides explain that being bullied as a child can result in aggressive behavior or antisocial behavior that is filled with anxiety and results in a low self-esteem. In the movie *Precious*, we see the main actress display both of these reactions. Her lashing out is obvious at the beginning of the movie. However, as the movie progresses, we see Precious struggling with her own identity, while longing to be famous and glamorous. Eventually, this troubled girl morphs her own reflection in the mirror into a white, beautiful young woman. At one point in the movie, Precious says, "Sometimes I wish I was dead," and at another point she expresses, "I'm lookin' up, lookin' up for a piano to fall." What is happening in the film is reflective of reality. During the interview, Student A shared that for him aggressive behavior was a defense mechanism, but inside he struggled with anxiety and low self-esteem and wanting a different reality.

This dynamic of violence in the home, community, and school is present within all ethnicities; however, there is a stronger representation in the African American community (Patton et al.). The pattern that surfaced in Goldweber, Waasdorp, and Bradshaw's research was that African American youth are more likely to perceive peer support for aggressive behavior when bullying, they are more likely to experience depression when bullied, and less likely to seek help from adults when bullied. These researchers demonstrated that almost twenty percent of African American students who are bullying fall into the category of bully-victim; they are depressed, looking for peer approval, and fearful to trust adults. These researchers explain that bully-victims experience more aggressive and depressive symptoms than just those who are victims or just bullies because they are more susceptible to "emotion regulation difficulties" (206). For many of these students, the middle school years see a peak in bullying because hierarchies are unstable during these transitional years. This instability provides an opportunity for victimization to occur, thus allowing the bully to claim a higher-ranking position in the school setting. Patton, Hong, Williams, and Allen-Meares support this data by explaining that the hypermasculine male role encompasses bullying behavior, which allows the male to regain self-respect within the hegemonic paradigm that is developing during the middle school years and is often prevalent in the high school years. In other words, when an African American male is unsuccessful academically in school, one way the male gains credibility is by bullying. However, it is not just about lack of academic success, Goldweber, Waasdorp, and Bradshaw also made it clear that African American youth exposed to violence and disproportionate disciplinary actions in the home do have an increased involvement in bullying. Student A recognized that as a victim of bullying, he was looking for peer support, and his gang affiliation provided that support. Yet, his involvement in the gang also perpetuated his own violent acts towards others. In this situation bullying begets bullying; on the other hand, being bullied does not have to result in bullying others, and this was seen during Student B's interview.

Student B was raised in a healthy family setting where the parents loved each other and the family dynamics was supportive. As a child, Student B was fun-loving and full of silly antics. When he started school, he discovered that academics did not come as easily to him as they did to other students. It took him a while to be able to conquer the art of reading, and this created some insecurities in him while he was in the classroom. At the beginning of middle school, Student B moved to a new city and settled into a country home with a privacy gate. He loved his home life, but he was nervous about attending school because he knew he looked younger than many of his peers and he also was aware that he was not strong academically. With these concerns there was some anxiety in place when he began attending his new school. It did not take long for an older boy who had been held back a year to spot Student B and begin picking on him. What began as covert verbal taunts moved to hidden physical assaults that were meant to intimidate Student B but not be seen by the teachers or administration. Student B, wanting to make his new school experience successful, tried to avoid any confrontations and for a while did not share with anyone what was happening. During the interview, Student B explained that when he finally did go to his teachers to report the inappropriate behavior, their first response was to ask some questions. This, at first, gave hope to Student B that the teachers would do something about the bullying. The teachers watched for evidence of the bullying, but the bully was devious and he was able to keep it out of the teacher's vision. Because the two boys had lockers side by side, a teacher decided to take action and moved Student B's locker some distance away. However, the bullying continued, so Student B's mother asked for a parent-teacher meeting. During that meeting, the parent explained what was happening, and the teacher's response was "Well, boys will be boys." This kind of dismissive comment was very frustrating for all involved because the mother wanted action not patronizing comments. Student B became more reclusive as the semester continued. He did not answer questions in class, nor did he interact with the other students. He did not even make eye contact with other people in the school, and he ate lunch on his own. This reclusive, anxiety-filled reaction is not unusual with students who are being bullied (Cooper and Nickerson). What Student B was experiencing is called covert bullying.

Student A both experienced and demonstrated visible forms of bullying, which are easily identified; however, there are also covert forms of bullying. The authors of the article "The Invisibility of Covert Bullying Among Students: Challenges for School Intervention" offer a definition of covert bullying when they write, "Covert forms of bullying are behaviors that are non-physical, subtle, disguised or hidden, but which nevertheless cause emotional distress and damage self-esteem, relationships and social status" (Barnes et al. 207). Covert forms of bullying remain unnoticed or unacknowledged by adults in the school setting, and this lack of awareness is credited to the schools' inattention to covert bullying policy, as well as the limited staff understanding and staff skills to address covert bullying (Barnes et al.). There are many reasons why students are hesitant to report a covert bully, and these reasons include a fear of retaliation from the bully and non-responsiveness from the adult. They also fear being perceived as weak and being rejected by the "in" crowd (Davis, Galford, and Lovell). Student B experienced covert bullying, and during the interview he demonstrated why many students who are bullied hesitate to report the event. A report on bullying presented by the University of Colorado Boulder recommends that the victim needs to be taken seriously, given a school's plan of action, and encouraged to report any new bullying episodes to the teacher or administration. This report also suggests that the teacher or administrator move the aggressor away from the victim and contact the aggressor's parents to let them know the course of action taken ("Bullying Prevention: Recommendations for Schools"). According to this report, the teacher's response to the situation was not the wisest because the teacher moved Student B away from the bully, and the teacher did not provide a plan of action, which left Student B feeling more hopeless. The bully was allowed to keep his locker, and Student B was forced to move his locker location. Student B was not given any plan of action, nor was he encouraged to report further bullying.

This lack of response is not uncommon according to research regarding bullying. Research shows that less than twenty percent of teachers respond appropriately to reports of bullying. Both teachers and students acknowledge that a vast majority of teachers try to ignore bullying with the hopes that it will go away (Frey et al.; Kennedy, Russom, and Kevorkian). Fortunately, for Student B, he had supportive parents who pursued the issue with the administration. During the meeting with the principal, Student B's mother was present. She explained, during the interview conducted with Student B for this essay, that the principal's comment in response to the situation was "Boys will be boys," and the principal's advice to Student B was to be more confident and not let the bully's taunts bother him. This response was very frustrating for Student B's parents, and understandably so because the "Steps to Respect Program" clearly advises teachers to never fall for "the misconception [of] bullying [just being] 'boys will be boys'" ("Steps to..." 28). Also, instructors and school administrators are advised by Davis, Gilford, and Lovell not to ignore bullying or blame the child who is being bullied, yet Student B's principal encouraged the victim to ignore what was happening, and, furthermore, he put the responsibility of managing future bullying on the victim's shoulders rather than addressing the aggressor. This inappropriate response from the school identifies the need for educators to become more aware of the indicators of bullying and how to address bullying (Barnes et al.; Gleason; Frey et al.). The film industry appears to be aware of the general belief amongst students (Frey et al.) that the adults in the school setting are unaware and unprepared to appropriately address bullying.

Daniel Larusso in *Karate Kid* and Alex O'Donnell in *17 Again* are two white characters who illustrate that bullying happens to white students and in middle class suburbia. Both Daniel and Alex are in high school. Daniel is from a single-parent home with a working mother, and Alex is from an upper middle class neighborhood raised by both parents. Both students are being bullied, and when the bullying is first apparent, the adults are missing from the scene. Although the bullying is not as covert as what Student B experienced, both movies project the reality that bullying occurs when adults are not there to witness the actions. Both movies also provide visual insight regarding targeting that can happen in a bullying situation (Georgiou and Stavrinides). Johnny, in *Karate Kid*, targets Daniel because he is smaller; although Daniel tries to fight back, Johnny looks tough when beating up Daniel because Daniel is not able to defend himself. Stan, in *17 Again*, targets Alex because of his size and lack of resistance. Both bullies are out to dominate their victims while trying to impress their peers who are witnessing and/or participating in the assault. Although the characters in this movie do not appear to be worrying about keeping the bullying secret, the directors of the movie have provided a setting where the adults are missing, signaling that bullying occurs in settings where adults are not there to intervene. Therefore, research is demonstrating, adult testimony is confirming, and filmmakers are recognizing that bullying is taking place and the adults are not available to witness the offenses.

The concept of targeting is not just found in the movies, it is seen in research, and it was experienced by Student B. Georgiou and Stavrinides explain that "bullies do not harass random victims. Rather, they deliberately choose to act aggressively towards pre-selected individuals because they value aggression as a useful interpersonal strategy" (176). Student B, who was new to the school, looked younger, had a mild temperament, and little confidence in the classroom, was an easy target for the bully. Kimmel and Mahler cite many examples of victims who eventually become shooters in a school setting, and these shooters were originally targets for bullies. The stories cited by the authors establish how bullies look for students who are weak and different from the established norm, and through visible and covert means, these bullies systematically attack their victims both verbally and physically. The unfortunate perpetuation occurs when these victims become attackers. Luke Woodham is a white 16-year-old who was bullied and eventually opened fire on his fellow students, killing two and wounding seven others. During an interview, Luke explained, "I am angry ... I killed because people like me are mistreated every day. I am malicious because I am miserable" (Kimmel and Mahler 1447). This powerful testimony speaks to the fact that "violence is one of the most urgent issues facing our nation's schools" (1439), and these drastic examples of violence began with the shooters being bullied. There are many adults who give testimony to seeing or experiencing bullying when they were growing up (Cooper and Nickerson). The teacher interviewed for this essay not only experienced bullying, but is witness to bullying in the school where she teaches.

Teacher A was a beautiful, white, athletic, smart student who came from a middle class home where her parents supported her and her sisters were her best friends. She was captain of the volleyball team, an honor roll student, and well known in her smaller rural high school. In her sophomore year, Teacher A became the victim of bullying. The cheerleading squad determined to collectively attack this girl and they chose to do it relationally. Milsom and Gallo explain that boys engage in physical and verbal bullying, but girls tend to revert to relational bullying. The varsity cheerleaders discussed each week what new rumor they would spread about this girl. They reported the girl to the teachers for offenses she had not committed. They challenged people who were friendly to her, and they made it clear that they were out to destroy her. This girl, known now as Teacher A, had a strong personality and didn't want to let the bullying get to her, but it was starting to affect her view of school and the battle seemed endless, so she shared the situation with her parents. They immediately wanted to go to the principal, but the girl was reluctant because she was afraid nothing positive would be done and that the report would only make the situation get worse. She didn't want to look weak, and she was afraid that by reporting the offenses she might be ostracized from the "in" crowd. The fears that Teacher A experienced when she was a sophomore are the same four fears identified by Davis, Galford and Lovell: retaliation from the bully, non-responsive administrator, being perceived as weak, and being rejected from the "in" crowd. Fortunately, the parents did not listen to the girl's fears, and they went to the principal. In this situation, the principal took immediate action, the coach of the cheerleading squad was called into the meeting and supported the established consequences for the bullying. An announcement that included the consequences was made to the squad, and the bullying ended. The next year, Teacher A's younger sister made the varsity cheerleading squad, and through the younger sister's connection to the team, Teacher A soon became friends with the girls who were once her bullies. The cheerleaders shared with Teacher A their strategy of starting rumors and reporting false offenses, and they also shared their reasoning for targeting Teacher A. They were jealous of the attention she was receiving from a few of the males on the football team, and they were hoping to alienate her so that the boys wouldn't notice her. Yes, in some ways this is typical adolescent behavior, but it became bullying when it became an intentional and systematic psychological attack with the intention to intimidate and cause distress (Georgiou and Stavrinides). This type of bullying is common amongst teenage females, and Hollywood picked up on this bullying scenario in the movie *Mean Girls*.

The movie *Mean Girls* captures the nuances of relational bullying that can occur at the middle school and high school levels between females. Cady, a new girl in town, finds herself in the middle of a bullying battle between the powerful leader of the "in" group, Regina, and a social outcast, Janis, who has been bullied by this "in" group. In this movie about bullying and being bullied, there is a systematic "relational" attacking that is meant to destroy. Relational bullying is a covert form of bullying, but is also a very destructive activity. This essay has highlighted racial, physical, sexual, relational, and emotional bullying in the movie *Precious*, physical, verbal, and emotional bullying in *Karate Kid* and *17 Again*, and relational bullying in *Mean Girls*. However, there are many more movie examples that portray relational, verbal, sexual, physical, racial, and emotional bullying like *Remember the Titans, Easy A,* and *The Sand Lot*. The movie industry is recognizing bullying as an adolescent theme, and they are incorporating it into teen movies. Teens know bullying is happening, there are government initiatives regarding it, even the movie industry is recognizing it, so why are the teachers turning a blind eye to bullying?

Teacher A personally experienced relational bullying, but on the high school campus where she presently teaches, she witnesses all types of bullying. Because Teacher A was bullied as an adolescent, she is much more aware of the signs of bullying and the need for an immediate and stringent response to bullying behavior. During the interview, this teacher shared that her co-workers often ignore bullying, and the administration's "arm of discipline" is very limited. Although bullying is a serious offense in the eyes of Teacher A, she believes the majority of adults in her academic setting seem unable or unwilling to address the indicators that bullying is happening because there are so many bigger issues to address. Research regarding bullying has identified a number of reasons why teachers and administrators are unable or unwilling to address bullying on the school campuses.

It is vital that teachers and administrators consider their role in discouraging bullying behavior (Patton et al.) and the importance of presenting a united front while combatting bullying and the effects of bullying (Kennedy, Russom, and Kevorkian). First, there must be a basic understanding of why bullying happens, and what are the pro-violence attitudes and bullying markers (Espelage and Swearer). There are two types of bullies: there is the bully who is acting out his anger (Kimmel and Mahler) or trying to establish status and there is the victim-bully who is doing what was done to her (Goldweber, Waasdorp, and Bradshaw). The markers that help to identify a victim of bullying include anger, anxiety, depression, withdraw, low self-esteem, and excessive dependence on adults (Espelage and Swearer; Georgiou and Stavrinides; Davis, Galford, and Lovell). Once we understand bullying and the indicators that bullying might be happening, then educators have to consider their adult responsibility. Gleason, who wrote an article on how teachers deal with bullying, was a victim of bullying in her youth. Gleason explained that she often asked, "Where are the teachers and why aren't they doing anything to help me?" (Gleason 4). In Gleason's research, she discovered that there is a lack of communication between teachers as well as a lack of communication between the teachers and administration regarding bullying activity. One reason for a lack of communication is that teachers and administrators need more education regarding bullying and how to appropriately address the issue (Gleason; Espelage and Swearer; O'Moore). Improved training of school staff is a crucial part of responding to bullying (O'Moore; Astor et al.).

Once teachers and administrators accept responsibility for being more pro-active in addressing bullying in school, then a systematic approach needs to be established (*Bullying Prevention*). Clear rules, procedures, and training for adults along with improving adult supervision and parental awareness are measures that can be put in place (The Committee for Children). Clear and consistent communication between the adults and students needs to occur so that the students know that bullying is an unacceptable behavior and that there are consequences. A bullying prevention committee might help guide this process of clarification and communication, along with an anonymous survey that is designed to indicate where there are specific issues (*Bullying Prevention*). When bullying incidents arise, the teacher should meet with the bully and victim separately to discuss what happened and to brainstorm how bullying can be avoided in the future. If teachers are ill-equipped to conduct that sort of discussion, then simulation training amongst the staff is a good idea (Gleason). When incorporating these aspects into school policy and practice, it is important to also consider covert bullying.

Physical and verbal bullying are often more obvious to the bystanders, but there are covert types of bullying that are more difficult to recognize. Barnes et al. conducted a survey of 400 teachers who all agreed that there is a need for more staff training, especially regarding covert bullying. An ethos that will actively address covert bullying on campus with a commitment to bullying prevention will help to lessen covert bullying activity. However, in recent years, there has been a shift to cyberbullying, which is a new form of covert bullying that does not occur on the school campus, and teachers are ill-equipped to deal with the shifting settings and the changing behavior connected with those settings (Gleason). One suggestion Gleason makes is to create a campus support group for students who are feeling bullied. This needs to be a place where victims can come together and feel supported by others who are experiencing the same thing. Gleason does warn her readers that respect and confidentiality must be two elements valued within this group setting for a support group to work. Not only do schools need to educate their teachers and create a bully-free atmosphere for the students, but they also need to inform the parents.

If schools are going to take a holistic approach to the issue of bullying, then the subject needs to be addressed in the schools and at home (Patton et al.). Since bullying "may be ... a result of the interrelations among multiple contexts" (Patton et al. 249), then developing parental support that works in conjunction with pro-active school policies and programs will collectively provide a salient protective factor for the students (Patton et al.). Parents need a growing awareness regarding indicators of bullying and tools to address these indicators. Literature and lectures, provided by the school, can help educate parents concerning bullying markers; also, providing steps to guide parental monitoring would be helpful. Parental monitoring "reflects the parents' effort to find out directly through observation how their child behaves" (Georgiou and Stavrinides 167). However, the parent is not at school to see overt bullying, and they are often removed from monitoring covert bullying; thus, to reduce these limitations, disclosure must be controlled by the student. Child disclosure is "the children's free and willing information offering to their parents about where they are during their free time, how they do in school ... who they socialize with" (Georgiou and Stavrinides 169), and these "offerings" help to provide clues regarding potential bullying situations. Many schools recognize that "parent involvement is essential to reducing children's bullying behavior ... [however], increasing the efficacy of parent involvement [is] an area in need of improvement" (Cooper and Nickerson 527). So, how can schools help to improve the efficacy of parental involvement as they partner together to reduce bullying?

Kennedy, Russom, and Kevorkian revealed in their study of bullying that administrators are more comfortable dealing with the bully and family than teachers are, and this is also true in dealing with the victim and the parents of the victim. To help clarify parental misconceptions and equip parents to partner, these authors recommend that administrators become better informed regarding a pro-active approach so they can share it with the parents. In order to equip parents to better partner with the schools, Davis, Galford, and Lovell provide some suggestions that administrators can share with the parents. Here are some of their suggestions: allow your child to talk about their experiences while supporting him emotionally, document everything, and be persistent in addressing the situation at school, work with the school to problem solve while building resilience in your child, role-play bullying scenarios giving him constructive ways to address the bully, teach him to speak assertively and look confident without the need to respond with physical violence, and ask specific questions regarding his day like what is lunch time like or what is it like to ride the school bus. Admistrators have their responsibility and parents have an important role, but Olweus, Limber, and Mihalic also suggest that training should extend to pre-service teachers, lunchroom supervisors, and school bus drivers. These authors suggest a "train the trainers" model that will facilitate the training of all school staff so that all adults are able to actively engage in identifying, managing, and resolving bullying situation. Frey et al. surveyed over 1000 students, and after sharing their findings, these authors explained that the "changing ... dynamics of bullying involves increased adult awareness and interventions, developing clear school policies, and coordinating procedures to track and respond to bullying reports" (479). When there is a systematic plan in place, and a commitment to work the plan by all involved, the results are much stronger. Teachers who "walk the talk" of bullying prevention weave support for positive behavior into daily interactions with students as well as confidently providing coaching for those involved in bullying. According to a study published in the *School Psychology Review*, the benefits of putting a good plan in place and consistently working that plan is less aggression, victimization, and encouragement of bullying within schools (Hirschstein et al.).

Research provides many helpful suggestions for educators as they address the issue of bullying; however, the interviews that were conducted for this essay provided further insight regarding the power of praise in the healing process after bullying has taken place. Student A, during his interview, identified a few aspects that helped to move him beyond the negative impact of being bullied and into a better mental place. This student shared how learning to box gave him more confidence to defend himself from physical bullying. He also shared that he joined the band and discovered a non-violent group that built positively into his identity. However, what was most significant in his healing process was the role the band director played in his life. This teacher praised Student A daily regarding his musical talent, his ability to positively impact the class dynamic, and he provided this student with a vision of a different future where he could become a music teacher and have a positive impact on other students. The praise Student A received from his music teacher has had a powerful impact on his present status and future dreams. Student A is now a sophomore in college, he is proud of the saxophone that hangs around his neck, he is removing the tattoo that identifies him as a gang member, and he is planning on returning to his neighborhood as a music teacher who can change the course of other high school students who are trapped in gang related violence. Student B discovered the power of praise, and he wants to give the same gift to others.

In the movie *Precious*, this same gift of praise has a powerful impact on this 16-year-old African American girl who feels trapped in her violent circumstances. When Precious transfers to a new school, her teacher, Ms. Rain, encourages Precious in the classroom, celebrates this girl's accomplishments, and casts a vision for a different future for Precious. The producers of this movie saw the power of praise and incorporated it into the storyline that detailed the beginning of the emotional healing process for Precious. The movie ends with Precious and her two children confidently walking towards a better future.

Student B also shared what helped him in his healing process. During the interview, Student B reflected on the value of the self-defense class that was offered to him when he was moved to an alternative school for grade eight. This student's parents eventually withdrew him from the school he had been attending, where he was bullied, and they put him in an alternative school where the teacher was trained to help abused students heal emotionally and then re-integrate back into the public school system. Student B spent his eighth grade year with this teacher, where he experienced praise daily. Initially, when Student B began his eighth grade classes with this teacher and the new group of students, he was hesitant to speak to anyone. Slowly, Student B began to trust Mr. K, his new teacher, and Mr. K was quick to celebrate this student's accomplishments. At the end of the school year, there was a graduating ceremony, and when each of the students were called up to receive their middle school diploma, the teacher shared with the audience what was so amazing about that student. This school understood the power of praise, and they incorporated it regularly into the students' educational experience. When Student B re-integrated back into public high school the next year, he knew the importance of finding a group where he felt safe and could implement some of his strengths, so he joined the Robotics Club. Now, as a freshman in high school, Student B does encounter unkind words or rudeness from time to time, but his confidence has grown and he is able to acknowledge that "the other person is having a bad day. It is not about me. So, I just ignore it." Student B is evidence of the power an educator will have when he learns enough about a student to be able to accurately praise the student, while encouraging his or her strengths.

The movie industry has also picked up on the positive role of a mentor who discovers the student's strengths and then encourages him to find his identity and self-esteem outside of the bully's opinion and actions. In *Karate Kid*, Daniel, the bullied character, has Mr. Myagi come to his rescue. Mr. Myagi becomes Daniel's mentor, teaches him how to protect and defend himself with the art of karate, while giving him hope for the future. At one point in the movie, Mr. Myagi says to Daniel, "You trust quality of what you know." This mentor not only gave Daniel the ability to defend himself, but he also praised him in his new found ability, and helped him to see his new identity is filled with hope. A similar pattern happens in *17 Again* when Alex, who is being bullied by Stan, finds a new friend in Mark. Mark, through an odd twist in time, has physically reverted from a 37-year-old father back to a 17-year-old teenager. Mark, aware of the age change believes the fates have allowed this so that he can help his bullied son. In this movie, the odd twist of time is a bit far-fetched, but the lessons regarding bullying are not. In the cafeteria, Mark challenges the bully, Stan, by saying, "Stan is a bully ... he preys on the weak." The producers seize a comical moment and have Mark share the reasons why a bully does what he does, and two of those reasons are insecurities and lack of self-control. Mark, although he appears to be the same age as Alex, takes Alex under his "parental" tutelage and helps build Alex's confidence on the basketball court. Eventually, Alex makes the team, finds a place where he belongs where he is able to succeed. Throughout the movie, Mark assures Alex that he has talent, that he can get the girl, and that he can win the game. In both these movies, a mentor comes into the lives of the victims, helps them discover what they are good at, praises them when they succeed, and gives them a vision of a better future. If the film industry has figured out the importance of praise while helping a bullied student find their strengths and security in a better future, then educators should take their lead and consider doing the same.

Research has confirmed the need for teachers and administrators to rise to the bullying challenge. Bullying is a reality. Charach, Pepler, and Ziegler, authors of "Bullying at School: A Canadian Perspective," help their readers recognize that bullying is an international issue that face all educators. These authors explain the misconception that teachers believe they are aware of at least seventy percent of bullying activity within the school, but students in the same study indicate that teachers are only aware of about twenty-five percent of the bullying. It is time that educators drop the misconceptions that bullying is not a crisis. Instead, they need to recognize that bullying occurs more frequently than they are able to witness. In response, educators need to put effective bullying policy into place, collectively work toward improving the overall climate in the schools, and develop an accountability system that will work. For those students who still experience bullying, teachers are the key to their healing process. Take the situation seriously and act quickly to discover the best action plan. Once the bullied student is removed from the situation, help that student find his or her strengths through healthy dialogue. Praise the student whenever you have an opportunity (Hirschstein et al.). Direct him or her to a group on campus that will help him or her feel connected. A student's ability to join a group increases his success with peers and reduces potential for bullying ("Steps to Respect..."). Finally, do your best to include parents in the process. A program with positive disciplinary actions and strong parental involvement has less bullying incidents (Espelage and Swearer).

We live in a broken world where bullying fights for a prominent position. Bullying happens to the rich and poor, to the colored and white students, to males and females, and it is not just an American phenomenon; it is worldwide crisis (Milsom and Gallo; Barnes et al.; Kennedy, Russom, and Kevorkian; Espelage and De La Rue; Charach, Pepler, and Ziegler; and

O'Moore). Bullied students are being wounded emotionally and physically. Therefore, it is time for educators to rise to this challenge and consider their role as a mentor for bullied students. Put praise at the top of the priority list because a kind and encouraging word will go a long way to help heal and restore.

Works Cited

Astor, Ron, Heather Meyer, Rami Benbenishty, Roxana Marachi, and Michelle Rosemond. "School Safety Interventions: Best Practices and Programs." *Children & Schools* 27.1 (2005): 17–32.

Barnes, Amy, Donna Cross, Leanne Lester, Lydia Hearn, Melanie Epstein, and Helen Monks. "The Invisibility of Covert Bullying among Students: Challenges for School Intervention." *Australian Journal of Guidance and Counselling* 22.2 (2012): 206–226.

"Bullying Prevention: Recommendations for Schools." *Center for the Study and Prevention of Violence*, 2014. Web. 20 March 2014.

Charach, Alice, Debra Pepler, and Susan Ziegler. "Bullying at School: A Canadian Perspective." *Education Canada* 35 (1995): 12–18.

Cooper, Leigh, and Amanda Nickerson. "Parent Retrospective Recollections of Bullying and Current Views, Concerns, and Strategies to Cope with Children's Bullying." *Child Family Studies* 22.4 (2012): 526–540.

Davis, Elsa-Iris, Kyler Galford, and Rachel Lovell. "Bullying." *PISD Bullying Presentation—Center for Couples & Families*, 2014. Web. 20 March 2014.

Espelage, Dorothy L., and Lisa De La Rue. "School Bullying: Its Nature and Ecology." *International Journal of Adolescent Medicine and Health* 24.1 (March 2012): 3–10.

_____, and Susan Swearer. "Research on School Bullying and Victimization: What Have We Learned and Where Do We Go from Here?" *School Psychology Review* 32.3 (2003): 365–383.

Frey, Karin, Miriam Hirschstein, Jennie Snell, Leihua Van Schoiack Edstrom, Elizabeth MacKenzie, and Carole Broaderick. "Reducing Playground Bullying and Supporting Beliefs: An Experimental Trial of the *Steps to Respect* Program." *Developmental Psychology* 41.3 (2005): 479–491.

Georgiou, Stelios, and Panayiotis Stavrinides. "Parenting at Home and Bullying at School." *Social Psychology of Education* 16 (2013): 165–179.

Gleason, Katherine. "How Teachers Deal with Bullying: Best Practices for Identifying and Dealing with Bullying Behaviors Among High School Students." Oswego State University of New York. ERIC, 2012: 1–34.

Goldweber, Asha, Thomas Waasdorp, and Catherine Bradshaw. "Examining Associations between Race, Urbanicity, and Patterns of Bullying Involvement." *Journal of Youth and Adolescence* 42.2 (2013): 206–219.

Hirschstein, Miriam, Leihua Van Schoiack Edstrom, Karin Frey, Jennie Snell, and Elizabeth MacKenzie. "Walking the Talk in Bullying Prevention: Teacher Implementation Variables Related to Initial Impact of the *Steps to Respect* Program." *School Psychology Review* 36.1 (2007): 3–21.

Kennedy, Tom, Ashley Russom, and Meline Kevorkian. (2012). "Teacher and Administrator Perceptions of Bullying in Schools." *International Journal of Education Policy & Leadership* 7.5 (2012): 1–12.

Kimmel, Michael, and Matthew Mahler. "Adolescent Masculinity, Homophobia, and Violence: Random School Shootings, 1982–2001." *American Behavioral Scientist* 46 (2003): 1439–1458.

Milsom, Amy, and Laura L. Gallo. "Bullying in Middle Schools: Prevention and Intervention." *Middle School Journal,* January 2006: 12–19.
Olweus, Dan, Susan Limber, and Sharon Mihalic. "Blueprints for Violence Prevention: Bullying Prevention Program." *Institute of Behavioral Science,* 1999. Regents of the University of Colorado.
O'Moore, Mona. "Critical Issues for Teacher Training to Counter Bullying and Victimisation in Ireland." *Aggressive Behavior* 26 (2000): 99–111.
"Steps to Respect Program Guide: Review of Research." *Committee for Children,* 2014. Web. 22 March 2014.

Not Just for the Kids
Parents Who Cyberbully

Abigail G. Scheg

Bullying is often associated with vicious behaviors of elementary, middle, and high school students, both virtually and face-to-face. However, bullying can take place in any groups of one's life, including professional and recreational activities. Although research about bullying has been conducted for several decades, many of those studies have been limited to students and in-school, or playground, bullying experiences. Recently, though, scholars have been exploring bullying in many different facets including adults who are, or are victims of, bullying at their workplaces, and cyberbullying among various age groups. In fact, cyber bullying has grown so much that there are government-developed organizations to help educate and combat this epidemic. According to the website for Stop Bullying (a part of the U.S. Department of Health & Human Services), cyberbullying encompasses any bullying, or threatening behavior, that occurs via technology including cellular phones, tablets, personal computers, or via electronic communications ("What Is Cyberbullying?"). Cyberbullying, unlike face-to-face bullying experiences, takes on the added dimension of being a virtual communication where the bully can assume any position or personality they choose. Therefore, the bully may be posing as the victim's friend, crush, or a stranger solely in order to further humiliate the victim. Furthermore, cyberbully provides anyone the opportunity to be a bully potentially without ever having to face their victims. The i-SAFE Foundation found that

- over half of adolescents and teens have been bullied online, and about the same number have engaged in cyberbullying.
- more than 1 in 3 young people have experienced cyberthreats online.

- over 25 percent of adolescents and teens have been bullied repeatedly through their cell phones or over the Internet.
- well over half of young people do not tell their parents when cyberbullying occurs ["Cyberbullying Statistics"].

Also, the Cyberbullying Research Center found that

- about half of young people have experienced some form of cyberbullying, and 10 to 20 percent experience it regularly.
- girls are at least as likely as boys to be cyberbullies or their victims.
- boys are more likely to be threatened by cyberbullies than girls.
- cyberbullying victims are more likely to have low self esteem and to consider suicide ["Cyberbullying Statistics"].

Using an example from popular media, this chapter will examine an unexamined facet of cyberbullying: parents who bully.

In season ten of *Law and Order: Special Victims Unit*, the episode "Babes" features a group of high school students responsible for the murder of a homeless man. As the crime details start to unravel, it is revealed that high school student Tina Bernardi became pregnant by a homeless man, Josh Galli, as part of a pregnancy pact between four friends. Alec Bernardi, Tina's brother, murdered the homeless man because he believed that Josh had raped his sister, when they did, in fact, have consensual sex. The ringleader of this group of young girls, Fidelia (played by Jessica Varley), is cocky and proud that she is pregnant, explaining to Detective Benson (Mariska Hargitay) that she is looking forward to being a MILF ("mother I'd like to fuck"). Disgusted by the pregnancy pact, and the influence that Fidelia has had on her own daughter, Tina, Peggy Bernardi (played by Debi Mazar) opts to instant message Fidelia under the screen name of the man who impregnated her, Dizzer. Eventually Fidelia is found dead, an apparent suicide by hanging. The original cause of her suicide points to Peggy Bernardi and her cyberbullying Fidelia into suicide. Although it is eventually discovered that Fidelia was murdered by her school boyfriend, the exchange and rationale behind Peggy Bernardi's virtual attack is a unique consideration to be discussed in this essay ("Babes").

As previously stated, research about children and adolescents bullying, as well as their motivations and rationale for bullying, has been prevalent. However, this understanding does not transfer into adults' rationale and motivation for participating in bullying behaviors. Although specifics of the definition of bullying vary by study and context, researchers agree that bullying is a social event or occurrence and typically results as a response to, or concern for, a particular group behavior, response, action, or belief (O'Connell, Pepler, and Craig; Fekkes, Pijpers, and Verloove-Vanhorick; Einarsen). In the case of "Babes," Peggy Bernardi admits, when confronted by detectives Stabler and Tutuola, that she wrote the instant messages, "Do you want me to admit that I wrote it? Okay, fine. I wrote it. Okay? But that little slut ruined this family. If it wasn't for her, my daughter wouldn't have gotten pregnant and my son wouldn't have made the mistake that he did" ("Babes"). Bernardi's response indicates a bullying reaction to a social issue. While Bernardi's thoughts are, at a surface level, accurate: Fidelia was a precipitator of this downhill slide; Bernardi is failing to attribute any of the responsibility of her children's actions to the children themselves. It is apparent that Bernardi feels that she is actually the victim in all of this, having now to deal with the ramifications of the behavior of both of her children, and a forthcoming grandchild. Per the research by Juvonen, Graham, and Schuster, a category exists of individuals labeled as "Bully-Victims," and are those who "both bully and get bullied" (1233), a category to which Bernardi most likely feels she belongs. Much of the research indicating rationale for bullying relies upon a comprehensive examination of bullies' lives, including history, childhood, adolescence, and their own bullying experiences. As the scope of this episode is limited to a present-day occurrence, a complete understanding of Bernardi's actions is unlikely. However, there is much to consider regarding her methods of bullying.

After Fidelia was found dead, her computer was searched in order to determine if anyone had talked to her electronically the evening of her death. Instant messages from screen name "Dizzer4ever" were found, originally leading the detectives to Dizzer, the man who impregnated Fidelia. However, with additional searching, the detectives found that these messages were actually sent from an Internet café, not an individual residence. Using ATM footage from next door to the café, the detectives identified Peggy Bernardi as the person who used the café; thus, the individual responsible for messaging Fidelia the night of her death. When being questioned in court, Bernardi indicated that the Internet café was convenient with the errands she was running that day. She denied that she used the Internet café in order to not have records of their conversation maintained on her home computer. The prosecutor asks Bernardi to read some of her messages aloud to the court.

> Dizzer4ever: OMFG. Ur a dumb whore. How dumb do you think that baby will be?
> FideliaV: Ur it's dad. Problee dumb like u.
> Dizzer4ever: Every1 hates u so stfu, LOL ["Babes"].

There are two unique considerations regarding this interaction between the bully and the victim. The first is that Bernardi chooses not to confront Fidelia face-to-face or in a public way. The second is that Bernardi chose to bully under the guise of someone else, a man with whom the victim had a personal relationship.

First let's examine the mode of bullying used—via instant messaging. Fidelia was a friend of the family's; she easily could have been invited to the Bernardi's house, whereby Peggy could have yelled at her, or embarrassed her in front of her friend Tina. Or, Peggy Bernardi could have showed up at school to ridicule Fidelia in front of all of her friends from school, as well as her school boyfriend. However, she opted to message her personally and have only a one-on-one dialogue with the victim. Perhaps Bernardi felt that if she confronted Fidelia in another way, Fidelia's parents would have found out and reacted negatively. If she confronted her in this seemingly "private" manner, though, Bernardi was able to be anyone she wanted, say anything she wanted, and make Fidelia feel bad about herself. In this exchange, Bernardi ridiculed Fidelia's intelligence and used name calling in order to shame her and her behavior. As is pointed out by the prosecutor, this language and inappropriate dialogue was used towards a pregnant, hormonal, emotional teenage girl. Not shown as chat conversation, but read by Bernardi, the final line that "Dizzer" said to Fidelia was "The world doesn't need you, slut. End it. End it now." The goal of this attack was to make Fidelia feel bad about herself, her choices, and ultimately, to forget the bond that the pregnancy pact brought to her, and to instead feel shame over her pregnancy. Bernardi is projecting her own shame of her daughter's pregnancy and her family's situation onto Fidelia, and wanted to make her feel how she felt about the situation.

Significant research has been conducted as to the difference between bullying technique between males and females. Male bullies have a tendency to act physically aggressive towards their victims, whereas females typically choose more emotionally-based, planned attacks. As indicated by O'Connell, Pepler, and Craig, "Girls may, therefore, be more likely to use indirect aggression—hostile acts where the perpetrator remains anonymous (Lagerspertz, et al.). Crick and Gropeter found that this type of relationship aggression is significantly more likely to occur among girls, while direct physical and verbal aggression are more likely among boys (441). Likewise, Fekkes, Pijpers, and Verloove-Vanhorick report that "boys were more often kicked, pushed or hit, whereas girls were more often ignored, excluded or had rumors spread about them" (87). Female bullies rely on these emotional attacks to not only have the initial sting of a physical attack, but to also have long lasting ramifications such as self-doubt or lowering the victims' self-esteem. Bernardi's attack on Fidelia is no different. As she indicated in her initial confession to detectives Stabler and Tutuola, as well as in court, Bernardi wanted Fidelia to understand and feel the pain that she caused to her family. This attack was entirely emotionally-based with an expected outcome of negative emotional repercussions. Bernardi felt that all of the turmoil and difficulty that was not only presently occurring, but that would occur, was Fidelia's direct responsibility ("Babes"). Therefore, utilizing an emotional attack on Fidelia would satisfy her quest to share the pain of the situation. Challenging Fidelia to commit suicide echoes Bernardi's own concerns that her life, and her children's lives, are forever changed as a result of this situation.

Also, Bernardi did not feel that her bullying of Fidelia was a crime. She refers to it in court as "a goof" ("Babes"). Although the goal of Bernardi's attack was to create panic, and to stir an emotional response in Fidelia, she did not fully consider or care about the ramifications of her actions. Perhaps this also correlates with the type of attack Bernardi launched on Fidelia. If Bernardi would have physically attacked Fidelia, there would have been physical scars and tangible danger presented to both Fidelia and her unborn baby. However, Bernardi seems to understand that a physical attack would have been too dangerous for both herself and for Fidelia. Bernardi can directly see the correlation between physical attack and the ramifications of that action. However, when chatting online, and using a pseudonym, the attack does not have such prominently direct correlations to negative repercussions, and therefore seems to be a valid way to express and share feelings, as well as garner an emotional response.

The second consideration of this situation is that Peggy Bernardi used a pseudonym under which to bully Fidelia. The pseudonym was not that of a friend, or anyone from school, but rather used Dizzer, the man who impregnated Fidelia. As indicated earlier in the show, Fidelia only met Dizzer at a party and did not have a relationship with him; she only had sex with him in order to become pregnant. However, this period of adolescence is associated with significant self-esteem issues as teenagers work to develop who they are and determine who they want to be. Dizzer was an older male with whom Fidelia had a personal relationship with. Even though they may not have been close, his words carry a lot of weight to such an impressionable teenager. Combine typically adolescent self-image and self-worth questioning with victimization via bullying, and Fidelia becomes an even weaker victim. According to Fekkes, Pijpers, and Verloove-

Vanhorick, "Victims usually have lower self-esteem than non-victims, are less assertive, tend to be more anxious, are more withdrawn, are physically smaller and weaker, and tend to have lower grades" (89). As is indicated by the snippets of the conversation given in court, Fidelia did not have much response to Dizzer's comments. She was not assertive and was withdrawing from the conversation in an almost pleading manner, asking Dizzer, "Why are you being so mean to me?" and only being further taunted by the situation ("Babes"). If Bernardi would have just called or contacted Fidelia and bullied her in her own name, it would have been easier for Fidelia to ignore and shrug off. This is evident by Fidelia's interaction with Detective Benson and her parents; she does not have a respect for adults and authority, and feels that she knows the best ways to take care of herself. By posing as Dizzer, a peer, and intimate friend, Bernardi is able to have a stronger negative impact on Fidelia even by using the same words. According to No Bullying: The Movement Against Bullying,

- nearly 20 percent of teens had a cyberbully pretend to be someone else in order to trick them online, getting them to reveal personal information.
- seventeen percent of teens were victimized by someone lying about them online ["Statistics"].

Bernardi posing as Dizzer in order to cyberbully Fidelia is a unique consideration to the phenomena because the perpetrator was not apparent.

Bernardi hiding behind Dizzer's fake screen name added weight to the force of the emotional blow that she gave to Fidelia. If Peggy Bernardi had met with Fidelia to discuss this out in the open, even if she made the same comments, it probably wouldn't have had the impact as it did coming from Dizzer. As was discussed earlier, Fidelia was proud of her pregnancy and did not back down from Detective Benson's questioning of her decision or concern over her pregnancy. In fact, Fidelia even turned the situation around onto Benson, exclaiming that the only reason Benson cared was because Benson was jealous of Fidelia's pregnancy. Fidelia asks, "So what's your story? ... Do you have kids? You're pretty old ... I bet you're jealous. Old chicks are totally jealous of me. Is that it? Did you wait too long? Tick tock." Benson tries to respond to Fidelia by explaining to her the challenges, social ramifications, and potential medical concerns of teenage mothers. When Fidelia becomes flustered by the statistics that Benson shares on developmental disabilities of babies of teen mothers, Fidelia's parents immediately step in and stop Benson from talking about it. This entire conversation even took place in front of Fidelia's parents, indicating that if Bernardi would have tried to have the dialogue with Fidelia, Fidelia would have most likely responded with the same nonchalant attitude she expressed with Benson. Instead, posing as Dizzer gave Bernardi the chance to cause the maximum amount of emotional damage in a single, short conversation with Fidelia.

Currently, there are limitations to research on adults that bully. Because the school environment plays such as significant role in adolescent bullying, that is where significant research time and money is invested. However, adult environments, including the workplace, are being researched and found to have many of the same bullying paradigms as elementary, middle, and high school. Once outside the realm of adolescence, bullying takes on a new term and a new definition: harassment. According to Einarsen, "Brodsky defined harassment as all those acts that repeatedly and persistently aim to torment, wear down, or frustrate a person, as well as all repeated behaviours that ultimately would provoke, frighten, intimidate, or bring discomfort to the recipient" (16). Furthermore, bullying/harassment in the workplace "often preys directly on the inadequacies of the victim's personality (Brodsky). This situation then seems to affect the mental and physical health of the victim quite dramatically" (19). In research regarding the causes of bullying/harassment in the workplace, there are three major causes identified including, "competition concerning status and job positions, envy, and the aggressor being uncertain about his/her self" (20). Peggy Bernardi's causes for bullying may have fit into any or all of these categories identified as to why adults bully in certain situations. However, also as indicated by Einarsen, "most people view their own behaviours and perceptions as legitimate and even moralistic, knowledge about the parties' assignment of blame and their accounts of both behaviours and perceptions are therefore of central importance" to understanding and evaluating the situation (20). Therefore, Bernardi has rationalized her behavior in her own mind and feels justified in her conversation with Fidelia. Perhaps, even, Bernardi feels that she is being a responsible parent by forcing Fidelia to take a critical view on the pregnancy pact, and the impact that this behavior will have on the remainder of her life.

Parents who bully and cyberbully pose a unique threat to the current infrastructure and paradigms of bullying information. One of the central themes to both research and public service announcements or presentations regarding bullying is that parents and teachers need to make themselves approachable for bullies and victims to talk to when they find themselves interested in, or involved with these situations. According to Stopbullying.gov, there are three options indicated for reporting cyberbullying: "Report Cyberbullying to Online Service Providers," "Report Cyberbullying to Law Enforcement," and "Report Cyberbullying to Schools." However, each of these suggestions exists with the implications that the adult receiving these bullying allegations will handle the situation in a professional and unbiased manner, thereby limiting or removing the victimization of any person. The situation that arose in *Law and Order: Special Victims Unit* episode "Babes" calls to mind the challenges of regulating individuals, information, and behavior that is increasingly complicated with the addition of technology. Critical assessment needs to continue of both depictions of bullying within popular culture, as well as documented research of situations happening in real life. Bullying Statistics explains,

> When you think of bullies, you often think of children terrorizing other children. However, it is important to note that even parents can be bullies. Bullying parents exist, and they can cause real problems in children's lives. Recently, there have been cases of adults bullying teenagers online. Additionally, some parenting styles can lend themselves to bullying. It is important to carefully consider your behavior with children, since it is possible that you are or could become a bullying parent ["Bullying Parents"].

Additional information on the Bullying Statistics website discusses parents who bully as parents who bully *their own* children, not necessarily parents who bully other children. Specifically with cyberbullying, this site explains,

> another form of bullying is cyberbullying. Some parent bullying is developing along these lines as they try and dominate others in an online social circle. Cyberbullying is becoming a real problem.... Indeed, cyberbullying is such a problem that there was a case in which an adult woman harassed a teenager so much that the teen went into depression and committed suicide.
>
> Some bullying parents use such tactics to control their children's lives online. Other parents think they are protecting their own children when they bully other kids. Indeed, in an effort to try and protect their kids, some parents go too far in trying to teach other kids a lesson and become bullies themselves ["Cyberbullying by Bullying Parents"].

As is indicated above, sometimes parenting styles can go too far, and actually step into the areas of bullying and harassment. However, it is interesting to consider parents that *choose* to bully their kids, or other kids. Perhaps these adults were bullied themselves when they were young, and feel that the opportunity has finally risen for them to move from victim to bully, or perhaps, as is the case with Bernardi, that she was actually trying to teach a lesson with her cyberbullying. Though she meant to express dismay and create a teachable moment with her conversation with Fidelia, Bernardi overstepped her boundaries and into the realm of bullying and harassing behaviors.

Although the research on adult and cyberbullying has increased tremendously in recent years, much more work needs to be done in these areas to better inform workplaces, supervisors, and systems of education about the possibilities and negative ramifications of these actions. Websites such as the Cyberbullying Research Center have made tremendous strides in making information about, and techniques of, cyberbullying more prevalent for anyone interested in the topic. Likewise, Stopbullying.gov has made the organization and design of their website user-friendly for individuals looking to report instances of bullying. As more research is conducted on these areas, the resources for bullies, victims, parents, teachers, and other support services will only be made stronger with this expanded understanding.

Works Cited

"Babes." *Law and Order: Special Victims Unit.* NBC. 11 Nov. 2008. Television.
Brodsky, Carroll M. *The Harassed Worker.* Toronto: Lexington, DC Heath, 1976. Print.
"Bullying Parents." Bullying Statistics. *Bullying Statistics,* n.d. 9 Dec. 2014. Web.
Crick, Nicki, and Jennifer Grotpeter. "Relational Aggression, Gender, and Psychological Adjustment." *Child Development* 66 (1995): 710–722. Print.
"Cyberbullying by Bullying Parents." Bullying Statistics. *Bullying Statistics,* n.d. 9 Dec. 2014. Web.
"Cyberbullying Statistics." Bullying Statistics. *Bullying Statistics,* n.d. 9 Dec. 2014. Web.
Einarsen, Stale. "The Nature and Causes of Bullying at Work." *International Journal of Manpower* 20 (1999): 16–27. Print.
Fekkes, M., F.I.M. Pijpers, and S.P. Verloove-Vanhorick. "Bullying: Who Does What, When and Where? Involvement of Children, Teachers and Parents in Bullying Behavior." *Health Education Research* 20.1 (2005): 81–91. Web.
Juvonen, Jaana, Sandra Graham, and Mark A. Schuster. "Bullying Among Young Adolescents: The Strong, The Weak, and the Troubled." *Pediatrics: Official Journal of the American Academy of Pediatrics* 112 (2003): 1231–1237. Print.
Lagersptz, K., K. Bjoerkqvist, and T. Peltonen. "Is Indirect Aggression Typical of Females?" *Aggressive Behavior* 14 (1988): 403–414. Print.
O'Connell, Paul, Debra Pepler, and Wendy Craig. "Peer Involvement in Bullying: Insights and Challenges for Intervention." *Journal of Adolescence* 22 (1999): 437–452. Print.
"Statistics." *Nobullying.* Nobullying, n.d. 9 Dec 2014. Web.
"What is Cyberbullying?" *Stopbullying.* U.S. Department of Health & Human Services, n.d. 23. August 2014. Web.

"Fire is catching!" and So Is Bullying

The Hunger Games

Katherine Lashley

Many people are familiar with the brutal elements of *The Hunger Games*. But how many fans recognize the games and their subsequent brutality for what the games really are: bullying? In the hunger games themselves, in the arena, the tributes bully one another in their efforts to injure and kill the other tributes. Adults bully children as the tributes are prepared by the adults for the games, and even after the games as the victors are threatened by the adults. Bullying occurs among the social strata as the upper classes bully the lower classes in their resources and governmental representation. The causes and effects of the different kinds of bullying in *The Hunger Games* point to the message of the novels and movies: bullying leads not only to emotional and psychological trauma, but to the trauma of an entire group and nation of people as the bullying is confronted. Such widespread and extreme bullying, if left unchecked, will spark and catch fire. Bullying results in more bullying as it leads to yet another form of bullying in order to halt the spread of the original bullying. As Katniss demonstrates, combating bullying is tough, though possible with the correct mindset and actions, which favors kindness over harsh words and damaging actions.

When it comes to bullying in literature, Joan Wickersham, writing for the *Boston Globe*, observes that "there's no category known as 'the bullying story,' and yet bullying is one of the great subjects of literature, and is often a pivotal experience in a character's moral awakening or disintegration." Wickersham is correct: there is little criticism on bullying and its emphasis in literature. Indeed, when it comes to *The Hunger Games*, bullying plays a pivotal role in how many of the characters act, especially Katniss. Because of the prevalence of bullying in *The Hunger Games*, this trilogy can be considered a "bullying story." Wickersham also observes the large amount of bullying in literature, from Jane Austen's *Emma* to Louise Fitzhugh's *Harriet the Spy*. Wickersham encourages teachers and readers: "If our goal is to create a culture that refuses to tolerate bullying, literature may be one of the most effective tools we have." Indeed, the critics Kristine E. Pytash, Denise N. Morgan, and Katherine E. Batchelor assert in their article, "Recognize the Signs: Reading Young Adult Literature to Address Bullying," that

> the stories within the pages of a book allow readers to wrestle with issues, to experience up close how words and actions shape and influence main characters and events. Readers see firsthand how a comment can cut, an action can damage, or a rumor can destroy [15].

These authors focus on the reading of young adult literature to help teachers more easily understand bullying so that they can notice it in their classes, schools, and students. The benefits of observing and discussing bullying in literature also holds true for students as well. When Pytash, Morgan, and Batchelor conducted their analysis, they asked English teachers to provide a list of novels that include bullying, yet *The Hunger Games* trilogy was not on the list, probably because the story does not take place within a classroom and because more varied and sophisticated forms of bullying are addressed. The list includes novels such as *The Absolutely True Diary of a Part-Time Indian* by Sherman Alexie, *Hate List* by Jennifer Brown, and *The Misfits* by James Howe. These novels, and others, show bullying—name calling through violence—in schools and how the teenagers deal with their friends, family, and schoolwork through the bullying. The researchers discovered that teachers were unaware of who can be a victim of bullying, especially if the student appears to be popular and if there appears to be nothing wrong. The researchers also discovered that certain forms of bullying, such as gossip, are easy to miss, yet need to be addressed. In addition to the list of novels and facts learned about bullying, a popular story such as *The Hunger Games* can also be used to instruct others—teachers, students, parents, and citizens—about the devastating effects of bullying.

Although the violence in the arena may appear to be simply violence, it actually stems from bullying. Sullivan states that "physical bullying is the most obvious form of bullying and occurs when a person is physically harmed, through being *bitten, hit, kicked, punched, scratched, spat at, tripped up*, having his or her hair pulled, or any other form of physical attack" (5). There is plenty of physical bullying within the Hunger Games themselves. The first instance of bullying is the blood bath that occurs within the first several minutes and hours of the games at the cornucopia. Once the tributes can move from their pedestals, they run for weapons and begin viciously attacking one another. Although Katniss does not participate in the first bloodbath, she still experiences the bullying when Clove throws a dagger at her that sticks in the backpack Katniss obtains. Katniss is forced by those stronger and faster than she is to retreat with only a small backpack and no weapons except the knife that was thrown at her. The bullying that she witnesses in the bloodbath indicates to her that if she wants to survive the violence, then she must distance herself from them. She realizes that she is certainly the victim in this situation and that she must minimize the bullying she witnesses if she is to survive.

Katniss flees from the other tributes partly because during the training that occurred prior to entering the arena, she did not make any allies; instead, she distanced herself from them and she allowed them to also maintain and increase this social distance and distrust of her. Her flight is caused by the gang of bullies—the allied career tributes—which leads to acts of bullying and being victimized, as noted by Sheri Hixon: "Peer rejection is associated with an individual's ability or inability to forge adaptive and cohesive social networks ... peer rejection appears to play a critical role for both bullies and victims" (259). The "Careers" keep her from reaching what could save her life: the bow and arrows. She sees them clearly in the cornucopia, but the bullies keep her from reaching the one weapon she could use to defend herself. The same gang of tributes bullies her further when they trap her in a tree. By calling her names, shooting arrows at her, and attempting to climb the tree to reach her in the high branches, they employ not only physical, but psychological bullying tactics.

One effective means of psychological bullying is in the form of Peeta, as he is allied with the careers who taunt Katniss. His presence with them and not with her weakens her resolve and trust in him:

> I will eagerly watch the night skies for signs of his death, if I don't kill him first.... Not only is Peeta with the Careers, he's helping them find me.... Is he saving that information [her skill with bow and arrow] because he knows it's all that keeps him alive? Is he still pretending to love me for the audience? What is going on in his head? [Collins 196–8].

This reminds a reader of the influences of peer rejection and the strength of social networks against an individual (Hixon 259). Because we know that Peeta was playing along with the careers and that he was doing so mainly to protect Katniss, this raises the question of the effectiveness of his actions. For several days, in Katniss's eyes, he had turned into a bully, something she did not approve. Of importance here, too, is the psychological damage done to Katniss by seeing him with the gang of bullies; she believed that he had turned on her and that he would not hesitate to kill her. In fact, she believed that he was with them in order to help them find her and kill her. Because she believes this, she is wary of trusting him again—if ever—until the rule change which enables there to be two victors from the same district. Despite the potential of two victors, she still mistrusts Peeta, wondering if he would attempt to kill her. It takes seeing him weak and injured in order to persuade her that he is not going to kill her. Nevertheless, she internalizes the doubt and hurt from his actions so much that when the rule change is reversed and there can be only one victor, she immediately turns her bow and arrow on him, ready to kill him before he can kill her.

After Peeta's mind and memories have been hijacked by the Capitol, he struggles to be nice, especially around Katniss, since the Capitol has trained him to kill her. As he acts more humane around her, he finds it easier to be around her without wanting to kill her. His change in temperament, even after the Capitol tortured him, is not only due to the healing treatments received. Indeed, the medical staff of the rebels did not believe that the damage done to Peeta could be reversed. Yet, Peeta overcomes this trauma due to his gentle nature before he was tortured. Throughout the first two novels, Peeta demonstrated kindness whenever he could: giving Katniss bread when she was starving, making her likeable to the audience of the games, saving her life in the arena, and forgiving her for her mixed feelings between him and Gale. Because of his genuine kindness, his original nature triumphs over the tortured Peeta. Since Peeta's original personality entails kindness and gentleness, he is able to recapture that part of himself after he has been tortured.

What may be surprising is that Katniss is not exempt from participating in bullying acts herself, even though she initiates words and actions to counter the negative consequences of bullying. Katniss exemplifies what we would term the bully victim: she is a bully in some situations, and yet a victim in others (Sullivan, Mark, and Sullivan 16). It is not until after Katniss volunteers as Tribute that she realizes that in order to survive—and to continue protecting Prim in the future—she would have to become vicious herself.

In the critical chapter, "'The odds have not been very dependable of late': Morality and Luck in the Hunger Games Trilogy" in the collection *The Hunger Games and Philosophy,* the author George A. Dunn does not necessarily write about Katniss in relation to bullying, yet he does note that Katniss's ordeals stem from her selflessness in the reaping (63). When she substitutes herself in Prim's place, she demonstrates a selfless act, which can lead the reader to believe that her later actions may always be selfless. However, the ordeals and trials she faces persuade her more easily to become a bully; she recognizes the contradiction that one effective way someone can protect another is through bullying. Katniss believes she has little choice but to resort to bullying and killing the other tributes if she wants to win. At first, Katniss believes that taking Prim's place as Tribute and going to the games in her stead will protect Prim from violence and hardships. Yet, Katniss, in her protective bullying mindset, later realizes that she is not protecting her sister from the control of the Capitol. This is when Katniss realizes the widespread severity of the bullying as the Capitol and its peacekeepers control the districts and the people within them. From Katniss' perspective, then, bullying for protection and survival does not work effectively, since the violent actions and words can trigger more bullying that can be even more dangerous.

Although Katniss experiences the negative effects of bullying, she still needs to be reminded of them. Haymitch reminds her that being likeable, not dislikeable as in the appearance of a bully, will help her more in the arena, since sponsors are more apt to support someone who is likeable. He guides her in certain situations, such as when she learns how to interact with the different Peeta who was tortured by the Capitol. Of course, Katniss' instincts are to be mean to Peeta, even though there is no need to be. After Haymitch tells her to be nice, she forces herself to remain calm and treat him nicely. Almost immediately, she experiences the benefits of her kind treatment to Peeta: he also treats her civilly; at least, he is not trying to kill her. Their stilted conversations and awkward encounters allude to the fact that when two people have engaged in damaging actions toward each other and other people, the civil, restrained actions can be hard to maintain at first. Since the inclination is automatically toward violence, it is tough for them to restrain themselves initially. Yet, after Katniss forces herself to be kind several times, the kindness comes more easily and naturally to her. Likewise with Peeta.

Also throughout the first two novels, Katniss occasionally abandons bullying for nurturing behavior. Wickersham uses Richard Wright's novel *Black Boy* to discuss the effect of forced violence and how it can lead to nurturance: "The bullying is intended to degrade and intimidate, but it also shocks the victim (and reader) into a sense of outrage and injustice." The same occurs with Katniss: the knowledge and experience of the games make her so outraged that she then strives for justice in response to them. In Katniss, her outrage actually takes the form of nurturance in some instances, as she cares for others in order to protect them from bullying. In the first novel, one of the first instances of nurturance occurs when Katniss volunteers to take Prim's place in the reaping. When she does this, she protects Prim from the horrors of the games. She teams up with Rue and tries to protect her in the games. She helps heal Peeta's injured leg and she is willing to eat the poisonous berries with him so neither one of them would have to kill the other. She saves the lives of innocent miners in *Mockingjay* when the rebels destroy the stronghold. She visits people in the hospitals to give them hope. Although she commits bullying actions, she also cares for others, demonstrating that she is capable of healing actions and not always of damaging actions.

However, since bullying comes more naturally to Katniss, she reverts to that mindset too easily and quickly. Even at the end of the trilogy, the negative thoughts of the past and future cloud her mind too quickly and it was this thinking that led her to revert to her bullying tactics. However, what keeps Katniss grounded in small, beneficial actions is Peeta, who balances her. We see that his kind, gentle nature influences her to act similarly. Katniss bullies Peeta quite frequently, and she is also juxtaposed with Peeta's kind actions. The comparison of their actions shows how beneficial Peeta's kind actions can be as opposed to how damaging her bullying actions are. Her mean nature comes quite naturally to her, which allows the reader to see the struggle she undergoes as she learns to be more gentle. His kind actions speak to her and overcome her desire to defend herself through bullying.

Even bullying committed by the government against Katniss leave her with physical and psychological damage. Both President Snow and Coin bully Katniss into doing what they want her to do. Because of the consistent bullying by these two powerful figures, she becomes defensive. Their constant bullying causes her to never really be able to trust the government or powerful figures ever again, and the psychological effects include nightmares and insecurity. President Snow bullies Katniss by threatening her family and friends for actions that are purely her own: "'And then there's her family to think of. Her mother, her sister, and all those ... cousins.' By the way he lingers on the word *cousins*, I can tell he knows that Gale and I don't share a family tree" (Collins, *Catching Fire* 23). In particular, he threatens her friend, Gale: "'Him I can easily kill off if we don't come to a happy resolution'" (Collins, *Catching Fire* 28). His threats become even more potent when he visits her in her own house when her mother and Prim are there as well. By telling her what she needs to do in order to keep her loved ones safe, he bullies her into pretending to be even more in love with Peeta in order to appease him and protect her family members and friends: "'Only you'll have to do even better [than pretending to be in love] if the uprisings are to be averted,' he says. 'This tour will be your only chance to turn things around.... Aim higher in case you fall short.... Convince me'" (Collins, *Catching Fire* 34–5). By bullying her, he takes away her agency and her ability to make her own decisions and operate on her own terms.

We can connect Snow's bullying of Katniss to that seen in the workplace, as noted by Tracy Whitaker: "These hostile acts include physical assaults and threats, sexual harassment, and verbally and emotionally abusive interactions" (115). Snow delivers physical assaults, threats, and verbally and emotionally abusive interactions against Katniss to force her to do what he wants her to do. Snow has a powerful relationship to Katniss (115) and it is his power over her that encourages him to continue bullying her. Also, his immense control over her life and the lives of her friends and family conveys to her that she apparently does not have a choice in being bullied by him. Indeed, for a time, she believes that this bullying relationship is the way it should be because he is the president and she is a citizen. When she believes that there is no way to fight back, she does not fight; instead, she succumbs, allowing President Snow to bully her by forcing her to succumb. Obviously for Katniss, this bullying relationship is not ideal, which gives her the hope and initiative to find a way to rebel against him.

The victim's loss of agency is vital, for without agency, the victim remains a victim, even when the bullying temporarily subsides. When it comes to dealing with Snow, Katniss does not have agency, which means that she is bullied into doing what he wants her to do. She recognizes that she is a player in his games and politics and that there is nothing she can do about it. This conclusion causes her to react against him by agreeing to join the rebels. In response to a tyrannical government, the idea of a political resistance seems promising, until she realizes just how steeped in politics and orders the rebels are under Coin. Bouncing from one gang of bullies to the next is an unfortunate side effect of losing agency at the hands of one bully and trying to regain agency. With the rebels, Katniss finds herself just as embroiled in the games and politics and the subsequent loss of agency forced upon her. Therefore, Katniss's apathy (when she is with the rebels and neglects her duties by doing nothing) and her brash actions in warfare are her attempts at regaining her agency. When Katniss joins the fight by shooting guns and arrows, she leaves the realm of bullying and enters an area that is both characterized by violence and agency. She regains her agency once again by forming her own special mission to kill Snow, though she ends up dragging her team in with her. Her violent and rash actions highlight the point that when the victim takes back agency, it is mostly done through violence; there is little diplomacy.

Since the most common contemporary forms of bullying occur in schools and online, it is easy to overlook another type of bullying that can occur: abuse among social strata. When an imbalance of power occurs among social classes, it affects more than the children; it affects everyone, and it also implicates everyone. Wickersham once again writes on bullying by those in control, using George Orwell's novels as examples: "Orwell's two dystopian novels, 'Animal Farm' and '1984,' are allegories of 20th-century politics, in which society itself, or the state, is the bully, using ruthless tactics to terrorize and crush individuals." President Snow, the government of Panem, and even President Coin demonstrate bullying against the people. The analysis of the government as bully is extended by Sheri Hixon who adds the connection of social class: "Across the life span, social status appears to play a role in the development and pervasiveness of bullying behaviors and the determination of whether an individual may become a bully or a victim. Those with lower social status are most vulnerable to becoming a victim, compared to aggressive/bullying individuals" (260–1). The lower classes in Panem become the victims and the upper classes become the bullies. Within the novels, it is no surprise that the people in the Capitol practice bullying against the districts. Capitol citizens enjoy more jobs related to fashion and entertainment while the districts provide what is needed in order to survive—food, clothing, energy. Many of the people in the districts resent the Capitol's demands, especially when they see the lavish lifestyles of the Capitol people. The citizens in the districts know they are being taken advantage of, and apart from some rebellious talk and acts (such as the likes of what Katniss and Gale do when they poach game and when Gale curses the government) there is nothing much that can be done.

The Capitol and government even create isolation and suspicion among the districts so that no one district would trust the other. President Snow does this by making sure that the districts do not interact with one another by erecting walls and fences. The children of the districts are forced to kill other children who represent their respective districts. Neither the children in the arenas nor the adults in everyday life trust one another or collaborate with one another against the Capitol. Susan Dominus observes that the children who commit murder in the Hunger Games are created by the adults: "Young people, even murderous ones, are for the most part innocents, creations of adults' cruelty or victims of adult weakness in the face of power" (33). Although these murderous and bullying children are created and influenced by the adults who are bullies themselves, the young people do not have to imitate them. Indeed, Katniss and Peeta demonstrate that it is possible to break free from the bullying tradition.

In *Mockingjay*, Katniss and her team hide in Tigress' shop, and they see the poorer sections of the Capitol; they see the refugees, families, and children who flee their homes because of the damage done by the fighting. Without explicitly stating it, Collins shows the lower classes of the Capitol—these people who struggle to survive even in the well-to-do areas. Yet the effects of such widespread bullying occur when President Coin tells the few surviving victors of the previous Hunger Games about a last Hunger Games: "'What has been proposed is that in lieu of eliminating the entire Capitol population, we have a final, symbolic Hunger Games, using the children directly related to those who held the most power'" (Collins, *Mockingjay* 431). Coin wants to use the children from the Capitol populace because the Capitol population suppressed the districts and never had to lose their children to the brutality of the games. When the rebels and people in the districts want the Capitol's children to pay for their parents' misdeeds, this is a reversal of the bullying that the Capitol did to the districts. If Coin and her government were allowed to go through with this, then Panem would see more of the same kind of widespread bullying that trickles down to the people, the tributes, and the children at home. Fortunately, Katniss sees Coin's strategy for what it is: more of the same bullying that has already been occurring. Now, one can debate whether or not Katniss' shooting Coin was the best way to stop her and her plans for a supposedly final Hunger Games. Yet, Katniss' decisive and violent action of killing Coin prevents another Hunger Games and the bullying that would have resulted from it. The history of the games and the people's struggles for freedom reminds those living in the present what can happen when bullying is left to grow, and also when people forget the past occurrences of bullying, and especially when they answer one form of oppression with another.

The Hunger Games is more than a tale of violence, love, and sacrifice; it is a cautionary tale about the dangers of bullying, for as the bullying increases, it affects more people, more age groups, and more social classes. Bullying itself is seen as both the cause and the effect, especially as those who are bullied believe that for a while, the only recourse to action they have is to seize the chance to bully back or bully someone else. This occurs because the bully removes the victim's agency and powers. Yet through the portrayals of Peeta and Katniss, we are shown the kinds of actions that can finally break the cycle of bullying: the ethics of care. These two characters practice love, care, and self-sacrifice to reveal that it is possible to break from the cycle of violence and to exist without bullying. Thus, when the Hunger Games are defeated, bullying is defeated.

Will readers and viewers accept the bullying presented as natural and expected, or will they recognize the deadly effects of it? Critics Susan Shau Ming Tan, Vivienne Muller, and Tom Henthorne write about the influence of the simulations on the audience: they conclude that audience members themselves have difficulty in separating the real from the unreal. Sometimes viewers have difficulty discerning the real violence that occurs in everyday life and is shown on the television and news, from the simulated violence that occurs in TV shows, movies, and video games. They assert that the simulated violence can become the norm for some people, which means that when real violence is witnessed, the viewer may interpret it not as real violence that deserves action, but as the fake violence that is performed for entertainment. Indeed, Andrew Shaffer applies the term "schadenfreude"—gaining pleasure from viewing someone else's pain—to the citizens of the Capitol because they enjoy seeing the children suffer in the games (80). We can extend Shaffer's application of schadenfreude to the actual, real audiences of the books and movies. Of importance is that the audience recognizes the bullying in the novels and movies for what it is: bullying that has serious consequences. The use of simulation needs to be related to real life with the audience learning to recognize bullying and its negative effects in school and the workplace.

Unfortunately, a recent incident in real life is now associated with *The Hunger Games*. On May 23, 2014, Elliot Rodger killed three roommates, and then killed several more people and injured others in a drive-by shooting in Isle Vista, California. His violent acts are now associated with *The Hunger Games*, as he is the son of Peter Rodger, who was an assistant director for *The Hunger Games* movie. We can see that his violence was rooted in bullying, as he felt ostracized by others, especially girls, and he used videos on YouTube in order to share his bullying mindset. Unfortunately, his bullying and violence echoes the awful effects of bullying seen in *The Hunger Games* (Dorell and Welch).

Although there is this unfortunate connection between the drive-by shooting and *The Hunger Games*, this real life tragedy can actually help readers, teachers, and students to turn to young adult literature in order to analyze how it addresses bullying and other inequalities. Young readers, especially, can relate to the characters and see themselves in the good, caring, beneficial, and sacrificial actions of Katniss and Peeta. While a number of readers will recognize the violence and brutality in *The Hunger Games*, they will also notice the humanity and morality present within the characters, and it is this humanity that persuades readers that even in the midst of violence, people can still find their humanity and then reveal it to others through caring for them and even sacrificing their lives for others. The characters prove that instead of violence dictating their lives and becoming or remaining bullies, like a number of murderers and bullies today, in real life people have the ability to change. Readers can learn that they can be like Katniss who struggles between caring and bullying mindsets and actions and yet who ultimately overcomes her violence in order to demonstrate care. Like Katniss, readers can realize that they can stop their violent actions and that they do not have to be bullies.

Collins mentions that inspiration for this trilogy came from watching reality TV shows such as *Survivor* and actual footage from the war in Afghanistan. Images of reality and simulation blended together presenting an image of confusion based in violence and bloodshed. What was real and what was not real? This echoes Peeta's "real or not real" game. Yet this reality and absence of reality in *The Hunger Games* has led to the very real image of bullying. Whether based in fact or fiction, bullying has very real consequences that should not be ignored. Instead of parting with the slogan associated with the games and the trilogy itself—"May the odds be ever in your favor"—we should remember Katniss' message: "Fire is catching! And if we burn, you burn with us!"

Works Cited

Collins, Suzanne. *Catching Fire*. New York: Scholastic, 2009. Print.
_____. *The Hunger Games*. New York: Scholastic, 2008. Print.
_____. *Mockingjay*. New York: Scholastic, 2010. Print.
Dominus, Susan. "'I Write about War. For Adolescents.'" *New York Times Magazine*. April 20, 2011. *MLA International Bibliography*. Web. 3 Jan. 2014.
Dorell, Oren, and William M. Welch. "Police Identify Calif. Shooting Suspect as Elliot Rodger." *USA Today*. Gannet Satellite Information Network, Inc. May 25, 2014. Web. 26 May 2014.
Dunn, George A., and Nicolas Michaud, eds. *The Hunger Games and Philosophy: A Critique of Pure Treason*. Hoboken: John Wiley & Sons, 2012. Print.

Henthorne, Tom. *Approaching The Hunger Games Trilogy: A Literary and Cultural Analysis*. Jefferson: McFarland, 2012. Print.

Hixon, Sheri. "Psychosocial Processes Associated with Bullying and Victimization." *The Humanistic Psychologist* 37 (2009): 257–70. Web. 27 Feb. 2014.

Muller, Vivienne. "Virtually Real: Suzanne Collin's *The Hunger Games* Trilogy." *International Research in Children's Literature* 5.1 (2012): 51–63. *MLA International Bibliography*. Web. 6 Jan. 2014.

Pytash, Kristine E., Denise N. Morgan, and Katherine E. Batchelor. "Recognize the Signs: Reading Young Adult Literature to Address Bullying." *Voices from the Middle* 20.3 (2013): 15–19. National Council of Teachers of English. Web. 15 April 2014.

Shaffer, Andrew. "The Joy of Watching Others Suffer: Schadenfreude and *The Hunger Games*." *The Hunger Games and Philosophy: A Critique of Pure Treason*. Eds. George A. Dunn and Nicolas Michaud. Hoboken: John Wiley & Sons, 2012. Print.

Sullivan, Keith, Mark Cleary, and Ginny Sullivan. *Bullying in Secondary Schools: What It Looks Like and How to Manage It*. New York: Sage, 2005. Print.

Tan, Susan Shau Ming. "Burn with Us: Sacrificing Childhood in *The Hunger Games*." *The Lion and the Unicorn* 37.1 (2013): 54–73. *ProjectMUSE*. Web. 3 Jan. 2014.

Wickersham, Joan. "The Literature of Bullying: Our Books are Full of Disturbing Stories of Cruelty in its Starkest Form." *Boston Globe*. Boston Globe Media Partners, LLC. Sept. 20, 2013. Web. 15 April 2014.

Queerness and Bullying in Popular Culture

Kylo-Patrick R. Hart

Unfortunately, and undeservedly so, queerness in its various forms has long attracted bullies and bullying behaviors. "It's always open season on gay kids" (154), explained Eve Kosofsky Sedgwick in the early 1990s, and that reality has continued relatively unabated to the present day for LGBT young people as well as their peers who are otherwise perceived as being queer (sexually or otherwise, and whether or not that is actually the case). Once regarded primarily as an unpleasant rite of passage during childhood and/or adolescence, bullying in the early twenty-first century has been taken more seriously than in the past, and it has received a growing amount of media attention (Cloud par. 6). Bullying has also resulted in the creation and dissemination of a growing number of noteworthy representations of queerness and bullying within which the bullied individuals ultimately stand up strongly against their tormenters.

This essay explores the topic of queerness in relation to the phenomenon of bullying as it is represented in two media representations of the current millennium: the feature-length film *The Mudge Boy* (2003, directed by Michael Burke), about a teenage boy who is struggling to make sense of the world around him following the unexpected death of a parent, and the FOX television series *Glee* (2009–present), about the daily challenges experienced by a small group of high school students who are members of a competitive show choir. One of the common themes foregrounded in both of these media offerings is that the bullies' own latent homosexual tendencies are what motivate them to feel so threatened by the otherness of their surrounding young males and to lash out at them in such disturbing and deleterious ways. Another is that queerness (in the sexual orientation sense) does not always manifest itself in blatant or stereotypical ways.

Representing Queerness and Bullying in *The Mudge Boy*

The Mudge Boy tells the story of Duncan Mudge (played by Emile Hirsch), a 14-year-old farm boy who experiences a bland daily existence while continuing to live with his stoic father, Edgar (played by Richard Jenkins), in the aftermath of his mother's untimely death. Clearly a "mama's boy," Duncan is a bit lost in the world without the parent who was most special to him, so he develops a close "friendship" of sorts with the deceased woman's favorite chicken, which follows him around like a puppy, shares meals with him indoors, and occasionally sleeps in the boy's bed. He also regularly places this chicken in the basket of his mother's old (women's) bicycle and rides around town with it, which makes him the object of derision for a group of local male teens who ride around constantly in a red pickup truck.

Just minutes into the film, Edgar walks into the chicken shed to discover his son with his favorite bird's entire head in his mouth, an action (which visually resembles an individual engaged in the act of fellatio) taught to him by his mother that can be utilized to calm a chicken. Although the man does not comment explicitly on what he has just seen, his palpable disapproval nevertheless makes Duncan very self-conscious. This development apparently serves to explain why, the next day, Edgar breaks the necks of two chickens right before the eyes of Duncan and Juster (played by John D. Alexander), Edgar's part-time worker, as well as why Edgar reacts so awkwardly when Juster asks why Duncan doesn't help out more on the farm and subsequently refers to the boy as "a funny kid." At this point, it has become readily apparent that Duncan is a "queer" character in this story world—in the sense of being identifiably unique, atypical, strange, odd, or somewhat weird—a perception that is solidified moments later when Edgar glimpses him wearing nothing but his underwear and his mother's old, furry black dressing gown one morning before they head to church. Perhaps unsurprisingly, it is not long before Edgar expresses that he expects his son to work harder at the farm and encourages the boy, when the working days are done, to spend increasing amounts of time with the "normal" boys in town.

Feeling increasingly alone and "defenseless in the hard world of men—men like his stern and distant father, and the beer-swilling local kids who haunt the back roads ... [and appear to be] in basic training for a lifetime of alcoholism and wife-beating" (Ebert par. 1), Duncan finds some comfort in quiet moments spent with Perry Foley (played by Tom Guiry), an attractive local teen who is nicer to him than the other small-town boys with whom Perry regularly associates. During their first on-screen interaction alone together, Perry broaches the topic of sex with animals when he, referring to the cow Duncan has just been petting, jokingly informs the boy that she will "suck your dick if you let her"; their conversation is unexpectedly interrupted when Perry's verbally abusive father arrives. Before their interaction concludes, however, it becomes evident that Duncan is touched when Perry refers to him as "my friend" and refers to Duncan's fowl companion as a "nice chicken."

Days later, their next interaction centers on (heterosexual) sex with humans, as Duncan is sent to retrieve Perry in a church bathroom and finds his friend feeling up a girl. Shortly thereafter, when Duncan and Perry are alone in a barn, Perry takes out his penis and urinates right in front of his friend, commenting on how big his own sexual organ is and bragging that most girls are unable to tolerate its size. When he is done, he asks Duncan if he has ever had sex with a girl and seems unsurprised that he has not; to let him know what he is missing, Perry proceeds to share the graphic details of one of his own recent sexual encounters. All the while, it is clear that Duncan feels a bit uncomfortable with what he is hearing and yet is simultaneously intrigued. That night in his own bed, for example, while reflecting upon Perry's detailed descriptions of rubbing and pinching someone else's nipples, Duncan pleasures himself by playing with his own nipples until his father unexpectedly enters his bedroom.

As the days and weeks progress, Duncan is invited to spend increasing amounts of time riding around with the local boys (including Perry) in the red pickup truck, not necessarily because they particularly enjoy his company, but rather because he has money to buy them beer and they find him to be a continual source of amusement. During this same period, it also becomes quite clear that Perry is drawn to Duncan's queerness, which he (perhaps erroneously) concludes to be of the sexual orientation variety because he seems to be experiencing queer feelings of his own. As Jeff Bush has noted:

> Duncan, for example, is read as gay but he never defines himself as gay, or queer, throughout the [entire] film. In it, Duncan and Perry are attracted to each other but in a very asymmetrical way. We get a strong sense that Perry is repressing his [true] sexuality, or his queerness. Duncan, however, is simply a confused and rather maladroit teenager, which is exacerbated by his mourning the death of his mother.... People think he is "queer" simply because he looks, dresses, and talks differently than everyone else. The odd connection between Perry and Duncan exists because Perry is attracted to Duncan's queerness,

which he misrecognizes as sexual queerness. Perry reads the strange and disparate aspects of Duncan's character as the collectivized identity of a possible kindred (gay) spirit. He mistakenly projects a gay identity upon Duncan that he, himself, is repressing [191].

As a result, Perry's next interaction with Duncan leads the pair to a local train bridge, atop which Perry strips immediately to his underwear and instructs Duncan to do the same. When his friend hesitates, Perry pushes him into the water below before jumping in himself; the playful splashing between them reveals the bond of affection they have recently developed. Once done swimming, the two climb into the metal area below the tracks of the bridge, both clad only in their wet underwear, and they huddle together closely as some of the other boys arrive and toss Duncan's bicycle into the water below.

When a train passes overhead, Duncan, still in very close proximity to his friend, first admires Perry's hairy armpit and chest before reaching up to touch his bicep; Perry recoils instantly, but then regains his hypermasculine composure and says, while grinning, "It's like a rock, huh?" He then immediately departs to retrieve Duncan's bike. Walking home together, Duncan shows Perry the chicken graveyard that he and his mother created. Continuing to bond, Duncan then reveals one of his deepest secrets—which Perry promises never to share with anyone else—by becalming his chicken right in front of Perry's eyes. In what he hoped would be a moment of acceptance, Duncan feels betrayed when Perry responds, about the secret Duncan's mother previously shared with him, "Your Mom was a weirdo too, huh?" Although Perry apologizes for this comment, he nevertheless jokes that Duncan is a little bit weird. However, he becomes alienated by the extent of Duncan's weirdness (or perceived queerness) seconds later during this interaction when Duncan asks if Perry would like to becalm the chicken, too. It is evident in this sequence, as Jeff Bush notes, that "Perry refers to Duncan's idiosyncratic behavior as 'weird' but reads it as 'queer' (as in 'gay'), while Duncan is drawn to Perry because Duncan feels that Perry has all the masculine qualities he feels would impress Edgar and gain his love" (193).

That intimately awkward swimming and bonding experience marks a turning point in Duncan and Perry's relationship. Perry's conflicting sexual feelings are revealed at a late-night outdoor party, during which he intentionally makes out with a girl in front of Duncan (in order to reassert his heterosexual exterior) yet then physically attacks a nearby male who makes fun of the "chicken boy" moments later. His masculine bravado lauded by his surrounding peers, Perry goes on to claim the "prize" for his actions:

an end-of-the-evening blowjob from another guy's girl; however, he isn't really into it until he notices the drunken Duncan viewing their interaction from afar and gazes directly into the boy's eyes as she continues.

When the girl departs prematurely, the still-horny Perry accompanies Duncan back to the Mudge's garage, where, after Duncan thanks him for being nice, Perry commands him to put on his dead mother's wedding dress. "It's just the two of us—who cares?" Perry reassures him, casually smoking a cigarette while emphasizing that he doesn't think it would be weird. Recalling his father's request that Duncan stop wearing his mother's old clothing items, Duncan hesitates momentarily but then complies. Once he zips up the back of the dress, Perry roughhouses with Duncan, ultimately pushing him to the floor and demanding that he suck his penis. When Duncan uses too much teeth and hurts him, Perry slaps him violently across the face, bends Duncan over, makes him spread his legs, and proceeds to engage in rough anal intercourse. "Feels just like a pussy," he emphasizes just prior to ejaculating, unable to see the shock and tears on Duncan's face. When they are done, Perry makes small talk and Duncan asks him not to mention what has occurred to his father. Unfortunately for Duncan, Edgar notices the lights on and enters the garage to discover the two boys together before Duncan is successfully able to remove the dress.

Edgar refuses to talk to his son after what he has just witnessed, and he proceeds to burn his wife's remaining clothing items so that his son can no longer wear them (although Duncan retrieves the black dressing gown from the burning pile to his father's dismay), as if hoping that the boy's queerness will simultaneously go up in smoke (Stein par. 3). Desiring some sort of compassion (or at least companionship), Duncan knocks on Perry's bedroom window in the night and invites him outside to talk. After climbing into the cab of Perry's father's truck, Perry declares that he and Duncan "can't do nothin' no more [because] it ain't right." Perry proceeds to explain that such behavior is "queer" and states that he, himself, is not "queer." Nevertheless, seconds later Perry finds himself engaged in a somewhat violent kiss with Duncan, followed by a longer and more tender one. These kisses trigger a self-loathing moment of homosexual panic in Perry— "You're a fuckin' faggot, Dunc—stay the fuck away from me," he states— a reaction made all the worse when Perry goes back indoors and gets beaten up by his drunken father, who senses that his son has been up to no good. It is at this instant that Perry transforms from Duncan's friend into Duncan's bully, with additional bullying assistance being provided by the local boys who had just previously been allowing Duncan to hang out with them.

As would be expected in this sort of narrative trajectory, it is during the film's climax that Duncan stands up powerfully to Perry and his male minions. Exiting the town's small grocery store and returning to his bike, he finds that his chicken has disappeared from its basket and begins to look around for her. Hearing some clucking on the side of the store, he turns the corner to find three of Perry's peers tossing the chicken back and forth, threatening to injure it, as Perry dispassionately looks on. Duncan looks to Perry for help, but his former friend, seriously bruised on his face and torso from his father's most recent beating, glares at Duncan coldly and calls him a "faggot." Boldly, Duncan stares him down and confidently declares, "I'm not a faggot." Just as it appears that Perry is going to break the bird's neck, he tells the others to let Duncan go and returns the chicken to him. Although relieved, Duncan is not willing to simply slink away from these bullies. Instead, he boldly stands up to them once again by reiterating, "I'm not a faggot, Perry." This comment enrages Perry and his friends, who refer to Duncan as "fudge boy" and tell him to show them how he sucks a dick. Betraying the boy's secret, Perry orders Duncan to use the chicken and "suck it like your mother showed you." They are all clearly amused as Duncan inserts the chicken's head into his mouth as if it were a penis—that is, until he bites down very hard, staring directly at the group of them, and decapitates the bird using his teeth. His direct eye contact with Perry immediately thereafter suggests that this symbolic castration, one of the most blatant in the history of U.S. cinema to date, is indicative of what might happen to Perry if he ever attempts to bully or sexually assault Duncan again in the future.

Early in *The Mudge Boy*, when a fellow churchgoer emphasizes that Duncan is the spitting image of his recently deceased mother, Edgar is not at all pleased because he, too, notices the striking resemblance and fears that his "soft" son's "queerness" may actually be emergent homosexuality. When all is said and done in the film, however, Duncan comes across as being just another unique individual who "defines himself in accordance with his own notion of pleasure and stands outside the drive to categorize that marks and defines our existence, heterosexual and homosexual" (Bush 186) and "brings something fresh to a story that Tennessee Williams and William Inge told often, about the fate of those constitutionally unable to conform to small-town life" (Stein par. 5). In contrast, it is the emergent bully Perry—the "town tough who likes to brag about his sexual conquests [and whose] bravado is a cover-up for his scary feelings toward Duncan" (Stein par. 4)—who is truly wrestling with the complexities of his sexual orientation in this courageous and compelling work. It is implied that his increasingly aggressive ways are the result of being raised by a verbally and physically abusive father, and his adolescent confusion is mirrored in the appearance of Duncan's beloved fowl friend, which everybody refers to as "she" but more closely resembles a rooster; as Roger Ebert states, "This may be a reference to the sexual uncertainty that uncoils during the film" (par. 2)—"Perry is trapped in a maze of macho acting-out and baffled by his own behavior" (Ebert par. 6).

Representing Queerness and Bullying in *Glee*

Although bullying is a prominent theme in many episodes of *Glee*, the present discussion of the contents of this television series will focus primarily on the powerful storyline within which the openly gay high school student/glee club member Kurt Hummel (played by Chris Colfer) is bullied relentlessly by a fellow student, the football player Dave Karofsky (played by Max Adler), because of his sexual orientation during the program's second season. In contrast to the adolescent males in *The Mudge Boy*, Kurt is an openly gay male, and he is the only such student attending his Lima, Ohio-based William McKinley High School as this season begins.

Glee's queerness and bullying storyline kicks off in the episode "Never Been Kissed" (Episode 6). While walking down the school hallway with his fellow glee club member Tina (played by Jenna Ushkowitz), Kurt is unexpectedly thrown into a locker by Karofsky, who approaches the two from behind, glares at Kurt momentarily, and walks off. Later that day, Karofsky repeats the same action as Kurt walks through the hallway alone, which motivates Kurt to stand up immediately to Karofsky by shouting, "What is your problem?" His bully, apparently unfamiliar with his various victims responding in any way, is shocked to find Kurt talking back to him and threatens to introduce him to "the fury" (his preferred nickname for his fist). Will Schuester (played by Matthew Morrison), the glee club's director, witnesses the tail end of this interaction and takes Kurt aside, expressing his concern and noting Kurt's atypically angry and belligerent reaction. In response, Kurt points out that his teacher, like so many other people at the school, is too quick to allow homophobia to continue unchallenged.

As the episode continues, Kurt heads to the nearby Dalton Academy to spy on his own school's glee club competition. While there, he meets the club's openly gay student leader, Blaine Anderson (played by Darren

Criss), and learns that the school has a zero-tolerance harassment policy. As their conversation continues and Kurt speaks of the "Neanderthal" who is making his life a living hell, Blaine admits that he encountered similar behavior at his last school, which led him to transfer to Dalton. However, because he regrets having run away from the bullying problems he personally faced, Blaine advises Kurt to refuse to be the victim by confronting Karofsky, calling him out, and educating him that prejudice is the end result of ignorance.

Accordingly, when Karofsky slams Kurt into a locker the next time, Kurt chases his bully into the nearby locker room. "I am talking to you!" Kurt exclaims. "The girls' locker room is next door," Karofsky sarcastically responds. After Kurt asks what Karofsky is so afraid of, the athlete expresses that he does not want Kurt sneaking around to peek at his "junk." Acknowledging the ridiculous nature of the widespread heterosexual male misconception that all gay men are seeking to molest and convert them, Kurt emphasizes that Karofsky is not his type: "I don't dig on chubby boys who sweat too much and are gonna be bald by the time they're thirty." This statement enrages Karofsky, who clenches his fist next to Kurt's face. Continuing to defend himself while simultaneously enlightening his tormenter, Kurt defiantly adds, "Hit me 'cause it's not gonna change who I am. You can't punch the gay out of me any more than I can punch the ignoramus out of you. You are nothing but a scared little boy who can't handle how extraordinarily ordinary you are!" Seconds later, when Karofsky grabs Kurt's face and kisses him (and proceeds to initiate a second kiss before the shocked Kurt pushes him off), it becomes clear that Karofsky's own latent homosexual tendencies are what motivate him to feel so threatened by Kurt's queerness.

Before this episode concludes, Blaine accompanies his new friend Kurt to confront Karofsky on campus yet again. When Karofsky first glimpses them together, he refers to them as "lady boys" and asks if Blaine is Kurt's boyfriend before he pushes through them and shoves Kurt out of the way. Karofsky denies that he kissed Kurt, and he snaps when Blaine says that he seems to be confused and is not alone. "Do not mess with me," Karofsky orders as he charges Blaine and pushes him violently. Undeterred, Kurt pushes Karofsky off of his friend and demands, "You've got to stop this!" Karofsky departs immediately thereafter, looking scared. As a result, like in *The Mudge Boy*, this storyline is noteworthy because it represents the victim standing up quite strongly to his bully. In contrast to the film, however, it does not suggest that this courageous act will instantly result in an end to such bullying activity. Instead, during the final minutes of "Never Been Kissed," Karofsky slams Kurt into his locker harder than ever before. Falling to the floor, Kurt is left to wonder what the future will bring in this regard.

As the season continues, Kurt—with help from his various friends and faculty members (as well as his eventual boyfriend, Blaine)—continues to bravely battle this deleterious bullying situation while at the same time revealing the harmful impact of such actions on their receivers. In "The Substitute" (Episode 7), Karofsky refers to Kurt as "homo" and winks at him, and he threatens to kill Kurt if he ever tells anybody else (besides Blaine) what happened between them in the locker room. In "Furt" (Episode 8), Kurt boldly stands up to Karofsky once again, staring him directly in the eyes and telling him that he doesn't want him anywhere near him. As the episode continues, however, the emotional toll of this bullying on Kurt becomes increasingly evident, as he finds himself unable to concentrate and his fear level escalates: "I feel like I'm in a horror movie where this creature follows me around, terrifying me," he explains. Because Karofsky cannot be expelled without more seriously assaulting Kurt, several of the glee club girls ask their football-player boyfriends to confront Karofsky and defend Kurt, which they do after Karofsky initiates aggression and throws the first punch. Shortly thereafter, Karofsky gets expelled from McKinley High, which gives Kurt greater peace of mind. However, when the school board overturns the expulsion, Kurt's father (played by Mike O'Malley) and his new stepmother (played by Romy Rosemont) decide to use the money they had saved for their honeymoon to enroll Kurt as a student in Dalton Academy.

In "The Sue Sylvester Shuffle" (Episode 11), Karofsky and several of his football-player pals are forced to become part of the glee club for an entire week and perform in an upcoming halftime show if they want to be allowed to play in a championship game. Early in this episode, Kurt's stepbrother, Finn (played by Cory Monteith), points out the hypocrisy associated with Karofsky calling everybody "gay" all the time when he never seems to have a girlfriend himself, and glee club diva Rachel (played by Lea Michele) refers to Karofsky as a "known homophobe" while in his presence. As it continues, although Karofsky emerges as a talented singer and dancer, he loses interest in taking part in the upcoming halftime performance when a member of the hockey team says that his glee club participation has "turned Karofsky gay," fearing that he may soon become the victim of vicious rumors or bullying himself. In "A Night of Neglect" (Episode 17), when Kurt returns to McKinley High with Blaine to support their friends at a benefit concert, Karofsky intentionally seeks them out and says that they are "spreading [their] fairy dust all over the place"; he also refers to Blaine as a "butt boy" and to both of them as a "couple of queers." Once again, however, Kurt and Blaine stand up to him, emphasizing that the three of them know what's *really* going on with him.

Karofsky's bullying behavior begins to change for the better in "Born This Way" (Episode 18), after the closeted-lesbian glee club member Santana (played by Naya Rivera) blackmails him into becoming her gay "beard" and prom date by threatening to reveal his true sexual orientation if he refuses. In addition, because Santana would like them to be voted prom king and queen, she pressures him into starting an anti-bullying group, called the Bullywhips, with her at McKinley High. Seeing no viable alternative, Karofsky goes along with her plans. In part, this requires him to apologize to the members of the glee club for everything he has done to them over time, and especially what he has done to Kurt. (Although it is clear that he is simply reciting a speech that Santana wrote for him and he has memorized, this is the first moment when his character begins to take a step in the right direction, as he indicates that he no longer wants to be one of the world's bad people who might cause others to commit suicide as a result of being bullied.) "I want Kurt to feel safe to come back," he states, adding that he plans to reach out to Kurt personally to make amends. When they meet, Kurt indicates that he will return to McKinley only if Karofsky is willing to start a local chapter of Parents, Family and Friends of Lesbians and Gays (PFLAG) with him, because Karofsky needs to be educated in order to overcome his ignorance. Karofsky reluctantly agrees, and Kurt reunites with his friends by re-enrolling at his former school.

The second-season queerness and bullying storyline concludes in "Prom Queen" (Episode 20), in which Karofsky is shown taking his commitment to protecting Kurt and other students from bullies quite seriously. One afternoon, while walking Kurt to his French class, Kurt tells Karofsky that he no longer hates him (like he did when he was bullying him) and realizes how miserable he is wresting with his own sexuality. This causes Karofsky to tear up, and he offers Kurt a sincere apology for how badly he has treated him in the past. Kurt takes Blaine as his date to the McKinley High Junior Prom and, in accordance with their prior arrangement, Karofsky attends as Santana's date. When it is announced that Karofsky has been voted king of the prom, Santana incorrectly assumes that she has been voted queen, as she desired. In what was intended to be a cruel joke, write-in voting results have instead selected Kurt as "prom queen." His immediate response is to walk out of the auditorium; however, after

Blaine comforts him in the hallway and inspires him stand up to those who voted for him, Kurt decides to reenter the auditorium in order to get coronated. "I'm gonna show them that it doesn't matter if they are yelling at me or whispering behind my back—they can't touch me. They can't touch us, or what we have," Kurt boldly declares. Upon receiving his crown and scepter from the school's principal, Kurt quips, with a slight smile, "Eat your heart out, Kate Middleton." The widespread applause that results is an indicator that such cruel treatment of others will no longer be tolerated. Sticking with tradition, the prom king and queen are then invited to enjoy the first dance together. "Now's your moment," Kurt says to Karofsky. "Come out; make a difference." He is disappointed, however, when Karofsky says that he can't and walks off the dance floor. In what otherwise might have been an incredibly awkward moment, Blaine walks onto the floor and asks Kurt to dance with him.

From beginning to end over the course of the second season, therefore, this bullying storyline does a very impressive job of reflecting the complexities involved with successfully reducing bullying behaviors in a school environment as part of "one teen series that is authoritative in its representation of gay teens" (Dhaenens 304). It effectively demonstrates that "bullies are often simply callous people who do bad things without considering how far they can reverberate" (Alston 55), and it provides cautionary learning opportunities for "would-be bullies [to] see the guilt and remorse that comes from making someone's life feel worse" (Alston 55). With regard to its overall representational approach and real-world relevance, series creator Ryan Murphy has emphasized:

> You've seen [Kurt] thrown in Dumpsters, you've seen him get slushied. We wanted to do a storyline where the abuse pushed him to the edge and he was like, "That's it, I'm not going to take it anymore," and fight back. It's a big story … and it has tentacles that touch on all the characters. Right when we finished writing this, that's when there were these front-page stories about teen suicides from bullying, so it took on an extra, added significance [Itzkoff par. 4].

Concluding Observations

When it comes to the topic of queerness and bullying, statistics reveal that gay, lesbian, and bisexual young people in the United States attempt suicide at a rate that is four times greater than that of their heterosexual peers (West et al. 49). Accordingly, it is important that both *The Mudge Boy* and *Glee* intentionally explore complex bullying phenomena that, when left unchecked, frequently endanger or even cut short the lives of too many children and adolescents who are forced to encounter inhospitable daily environments (West et al. 50). In doing so, these media offerings effectively reveal the range of consequences that regularly stem from repeated bullying attacks, which include absenteeism, depression, health problems, helplessness, loneliness, negative self-concept, and withdrawal, among many others (Cooper and Nickerson 526–527).

Significantly, *Glee*'s queerness and bullying storyline did not wrap up entirely neatly at the end of the series' second season. Acknowledging that bullying is a persistent problem that is difficult to eradicate and frequently experienced in cycles, during the program's third season Karofsky finds himself the victim of bullying at his new high school, to which he transferred so that he could continue to play football without having to worry about rumors surfacing about his sexual orientation during his senior year. Unfortunately for him, after one of his teammates sees him talking to Kurt at a restaurant on Valentine's Day and concludes that Karofsky must also be gay, Karofsky enters a locker room to find the word "fag" spray-painted across his locker, and he subsequently becomes the target of relentless cyberbullying as a result of this assumed sexual orientation. Entirely distraught and uncertain what else to do, he attempts suicide. When Kurt visits him in the hospital as he recovers, Karofsky apologizes to him once again for his past behavior by emphasizing how strong Kurt is—although Karofsky made Kurt's life hell for several months, Karofsky himself found it impossible to endure similar treatment for even one week. In response, Kurt helps Karofsky to envision a bright future in ten years with a great job, loving partner, and beautiful child, and the two agree to be friends. This resolution, too, is noteworthy, because it reveals that there is always hope for bullies to reform and to one day be forgiven by the individuals they have hurt.

Both *The Mudge Boy* and *Glee* demonstrate clearly that, although bullying is sometimes regarded as one of the less obvious forms of abuse in contemporary society because its effects are readily apparent to victims yet frequently relatively invisible to the surrounding public at large, such incidents of peer-to-peer interaction that are intended to be harmful—including the issuing of threats, instances of name-calling, and various forms of physical violence such as pushing, kicking, and punching—can no longer simply be ignored as they have in the past (Bush 190; Cooper and Nickerson 526; Garby 448). At least in part, that is because bullying activities that start out as being simply pesky or relatively innocuous have repeatedly been shown to become much more elaborate, violent, hateful, and hurtful over time (Itzkoff par. 6); in addition, recent studies have demonstrated that bullying trends tend to continue unabated without intentional intervention by parents, teachers, and others, so raising awareness about the realities of modern-day bullying is regarded as an important priority in decreasing the frequency of bullying activity (Cooper and Nickerson 537). Furthermore, both of these media offerings perform an additional valuable public service by demonstrating that bullies themselves frequently face challenging familial and social realities of their own, which can in turn produce a host of related negative consequences including loss of confidence, difficulty regulating their emotions, and inadequate coping abilities (Cooper and Nickerson 527).

A primary goal of the bullying [story lines] in this film and television series is to emphasize that the individual who is perceived as being different and therefore bullied as a result is frequently an innocent victim—his only "offense" is being "the kind of [confident] person who, by being completely and mysteriously on his own [cultural] wavelength, causes the uncertain people around him to insist loudly and with growing unease on how certain they are of themselves" (Ebert par. 8). Another is to show viewers the truth about what is really going on in today's world of childhood and adolescence, even when their resulting on-screen developments are emotionally excruciating and/or uncomfortable to watch, so that they will begin to talk about bullying and, even more ideally, feel compelled to take action in order to combat it (Bush 185; Itzkoff par. 14). For many of their viewers, both *The Mudge Boy* and *Glee* certainly succeed in achieving these very important objectives. And while doing so, rather than communicating the age-old message that the daily lived realities of bullying victims will remain an "uphill struggle for anyone who is a bit [different or] strange" (Bush 195), they instead inspirationally reveal that the recipients of such harmful acts can effectively emerge as happy, self-assured individuals who are able to stand up powerfully against their tormentors and cause their circumstances to improve (Dhaenens 304).

Works Cited

Alston, Joshua. "The Bully Pulpit." *Newsweek* 1 Nov. 2010: 55. Print.
Bush, Jeff. "The Post-Queer Dystopia of *The Mudge Boy* (Michael Burke, 2003)." *New Cinemas: Journal of Contemporary Film* 10.2–3 (2012): 185–196. Print.
Cloud, John. "The Myths of Bullying." *Time* 12 Mar. 2012: 40–43. EBSCOHost. Web. 4 June 2014.
Cooper, Leigh A., and Amanda B. Nickerson. "Parent Retrospective Recollections of Bullying and Current Views, Concerns, and Strategies to Cope with Children's Bullying." *Journal of Child and Family Studies* 22.4 (2013): 526–540. Print.

Dhaenens, Frederik. "Teenage Queerness: Negotiating Heteronormativity in the Representation of Gay Teenagers in *Glee*." *Journal of Youth Studies* 16.3 (2013): 304–317. Print.

Ebert, Roger. Rev. of *The Mudge Boy*, dir. Michael Burke. RogerEbert.com. 25 June 2004. Web. 4 June 2013. http://www.rogerebert.com/reviews/the-mudge-boy-2004.

Garby, Lisa. "Direct Bullying: Criminal Act or Mimicking What Has Been Learned?" *Education* 133.4 (2013): 448–450. Print.

Itzkoff, Dave. "Ryan Murphy Brings a Bullying Story to 'Glee.'" NYTimes.com. 9 Nov. 2010. Web. 2 June 2014. http://artsbeat.blogs.nytimes.com/2010/11/09/ryan-murphy-brings-a-bullying-story-to-glee/?_php=true&_type=blogs&_r=0.

Sedgwick, Eve K. *Tendencies*. Durham: Duke University Press, 1993. Print.

Stein, Ruthe. Rev. of *The Mudge Boy*, dir. Michael Burke. SFGate. 4 June 2004. Web. 4 June 2014. http://www.sfgate.com/movies/article/FILM-CLIPS-Opening-today.

West, Isaac, Michaela Frischherz, Allison Panther, and Richard Brophy. "Queer Worldmaking in the 'It Gets Better' Campaign." *QED: A Journal in GLBTQ Worldmaking*, Inaugural Issue (2013): 49–86. Print.

Swatch Dogs and Plastics
The Codification of Female Bullying

Kasey Butcher

"It's one thing to want someone out of your life, but it's another thing to serve them a wake-up cup full of liquid drainer," Veronica Sawyer says, resisting a plan to kill her best friend. Although female bullies had been portrayed in films such as *Carrie* (1976), *Heathers* (1988) emerged as the first popular film to focus primarily on female bullies. Over the course of the 1990s and early 2000s, psychologists and educators increasingly studied bullying behavior between girls, noting the tendency toward passive-aggression or relational and hierarchy-based bullying. Many works including Rachel Simmons's *Odd Girl Out* (2002) and Rosalind Wiseman's *Queen Bees and Wannabes* (2002) as well as the film *Mean Girls* (2004) examined and depicted the gendering of aggression and the effects it had on girls' lives and relationships. These works not only sought to shed light on the politics of female aggression, but also to analyze how to cope with the rules of what *Mean Girls'* Cady Heron calls "girl world." In articulating these rules and norms of girls' relationships, parenting books, psychological studies, and popular entertainment often reinforced the commonality of female bulling, even while providing ways to resolve conflicts. By examining film and television representations of microaggressions between girls including the above, *Jawbreaker* (1999), *Veronica Mars* (2004–7), *Friday Night Lights* (2006–10), *Gossip Girl* (2007–12), and *Pretty Little Liars* (2010–), I argue that the representation of high school female bullying has become increasingly codified, based on predictable patterns, in a way that makes the signs of bullying easy to spot, but also an expected part of young women's experiences. I further assert that, although some works playfully subvert the rules, the persistent representation of adolescent female hierarchy makes it hard to imagine an alternative, thus portraying this aggression as inevitable rather than a problem worth addressing.

The Psychology of "Mean Girls"

The "mean girl" or female bully is a popular subject of works on adolescent relationships and psychology. Particularly during the 1990s and 2000s, studies of adolescent aggression increasingly focused on gender differences in the expression of aggression. Researchers found that starting between the ages of four and six, girls were punished more than before for aggressive behavior and boys were punished less often for the same behavior. Furthermore, girls were told to be quiet three times more than boys were, socializing girls to be quieter and less assertive. Findings like these led researchers to focus on how girls express aggression differently from boys, rather than on a different frequency of aggression for girls and boys (Lipkin 92). Following, studies about girls' aggression centered on relational aggression including "behaviors such as excluding another child from a play group or as a form of retaliation, intentionally withdrawing friendship as a way of hurting or controlling a child, and spreading rumors about a child to persuade her peers to reject her" (Ringrose 410). According to Jessica Ringrose, through representations of "mean girls," "complex phenomena, ranging from friendship to bullying to suicide to murder were brought together into a single sensationalized narrative about girls' aggression" (409). Furthermore, such aggression was so shocking because of how it casts light on the fissures in cultural constructions of girls as both submissive and independent (408). In this way, mean girl narratives put pressure on larger gendered ideologies. Ringrose and Marina Gonick argue that these discourses not only normalize a universal idea of girlhood and girlhood experiences, they also reify ideas that aggression is aberrant, or dangerous, when expressed by girls and women (Ringrose 419, Gonick 397). It is further worth noting that while these constructions of "good girls" or proper femininity tend to assume the norms of white culture, they affect girls differently depending on racial backgrounds. For example, researchers found that African American girls were less affected by the imperative to be perfect, perhaps as a side affect of being under-represented in popular culture. Conversely, they were more affected by the norm that girls should be quiet because they were more likely to be perceived as loud when asserting themselves (Lipkin 94–96). These differences in girls' experiences are also reflected in popular representations of mean girls, which largely focus on cliques of middle or upper-class white girls.

The representation of relational aggression in girls' friendships tends to follow a contradictory discourse. On one hand, girls are portrayed as in crisis or danger, as in "Opheila" narratives following Mary Pipher's *Reviving Ophelia* (1994). On the other hand, if good girls are often used to represent what is pure or virtuous in a culture (as in Shirley Temple or Eva from *Uncle Tom's Cabin*), the mean girl becomes symbolic of cultural disorder or moral panic. As Gonick argues, both of these narratives depend upon girls' vulnerabilities (Gonick 396). Further, through the intense focus on hierarchy and the sometimes arbitrary rules of girls' cliques, Gonick asserts that in parenting and popular psychology texts, "girls' friendships are presented as almost cult-like organizations that separate children from their families and their parents' influence" while also structuring girls' relationships in terms of power and control (396). The hierarchical power dynamics inherent in girls' relational aggression may reflect the way that girls relate to the world more broadly, stemming from how girls are constructed as powerless in the larger culture (Okamoto 284).

The news media narratives about teen girl bullies tend to criminalize girls' bullying through heightened attention to girls' roles in cases of bullycide, such as the 2009 Phoebe Prince case.[1] Emily Ryalls asserts that these portrayals, even in severe cases such as Prince's, reify ideas that boys are physically aggressive and girls are passively aggressive in such a way that there is "no normal use of aggression by girls" (477). She argues that media portrayals of mean girls amplify the dangers associated with activities that are also constructed as normatively feminine, such as gossip, so that it is "made to appear extremely dangerous when shown to be capable of leading another girl to kill herself" (477). While discussions of relational aggression focus on relatively common passive-aggressive behaviors that may be hurtful, but not dangerous, such as ignoring or gossiping, when these behaviors escalate to harassment, the line between hurtful and harmful can be blurred by the taboos on girls' aggression. For example, Elline Lipkin observes how, after years of being socialized not to be aggressive, many girls turn to writing for release: "diaries—meant to be secret, silent receptacles that no one is supposed to read—were the only place girls felt they could legitimately unleash their rage" (92). Yet, diaries can easily become weapons as well, when they become public or when they are used to put other girls' down. For example, in *Mean Girls*, the "burn book" the Plastics share is made public, inciting a riot. In *Pretty Little Liars*, the theft of Alison's diary makes her friends' secrets vulnerable.

Like Ringrose, Ryalls argues that this scrutiny on girls' bullying is symptomatic of a desire to control white, middle-class femininity. Even as relational aggression is constructed as a normal part of girlhood, it is also pathologized: "In popular accounts, girls' indirect aggression/repression (lack) is normalized, but it is also infused with the implication that it might very easily slip into outright violence (excess)" (Ringrose 417). The tension here between bullying as "girls will be girls" and bullying as girls gone bad illuminates how mean girl discourses help construct a particular type of acceptable girlhood.

Alongside the attention paid to relational aggression by parenting and psychology texts, mean girls are arguably staple characters in popular media for and about teenagers. In the films and television shows I examine below, ranging from the cult classic *Heathers* to more recent productions such as *Gossip Girl*, I analyze the way that depictions of mean girls increasingly focus on a "queen bees" and "wannabes" structure, popularized by Wiseman's book and Tina Fey's *Mean Girls*. Even texts that aim to subvert traditional gender ideologies start from a place that assumes relational aggression and associated hierarchies are normal in girls' friendships. This rhetoric makes it hard to make serious strides in addressing aggression and the roots of why girls bully—including repression, lack of control, social pressures, etc.—because it portrays harmful behaviors as rites of passage.

Heathers and *Jawbreakers*

When *Heathers* was released in 1989, it stood out not only because of its dark sense of humor, but also because it foregrounded the relationships between young women in its satire. Although the twisted romance between Veronica (Winona Ryder) and J.D. (Christian Slater) compels much of the plot, at the heart of the film is the conflict between Veronica and her friends, the Heathers—Heather Chandler (Kim Walker), Heather McNamara (Lisanne Falk), and Heather Duke (Shannen Doherty). For these reasons, *Heathers* has become a benchmark for films that followed and helped establish a pattern for portraying female-female aggression with Heather Chandler as the queen bee, Wiseman's term for the most dominant or clearest leader of a clique, and Heather Duke as the wannabe, a girl who looks up to and emulates the leader. Veronica provides commentary on the border of the group, one foot in with the in-crowd and the other longing for her childhood friendship with nerdy Betty Finn.

Additionally, while other films, such as *Grease*, included a makeover "creating" a popular girl, *Heathers* depicts how power and particular standards of physical beauty are intrinsically linked in clique dynamics so that the makeover becomes a site for constructing a certain type of girl as a leader, while also cementing the power of the girl who performs the makeover. While Veronica's makeover does not happen in the film itself, it is referenced by Heather Chandler in a threat meant to keep Veronica in line: "You were nothing before you met me. You were playing Barbies with Betty Finn. You were a Bluebird. You were a Brownie. You were a Girl Scout Cookie."

After *Heathers*, throughout the 1990s, many movies involved bullying in their plots, but the bullying dynamic varied considerably. For example, in the makeover[2] films such as *She's All That* (1999) and *Never Been Kissed* (1999), the victims of bullying or social isolation were made-over and then accepted, even if only temporarily, into the popular clique. In these scenarios, the bullying is out-group bullying with girls (and boys) picking on nerds or other people outside of their friend group, but remaining relatively friendly within the clique. For example, in *Never Been Kissed*, Josie (Drew Berrymore) is bullied by the popular kids both in high school and when she returns to high school as an undercover reporter. Once she is made over by her once-popular brother, Rob (David Arquette), she can join the clique. The popular kids are nice to each other and to made-over Josie, but they exclude and play tricks on the mathletes and other unpopular students.

Occasionally, relational aggression spills out into physical violence, as in *Cruel Intentions* (1999) and *Carrie* (1976, 2013). In *Jawbreaker* (1999), three popular girls accidentally kill their best friend when prank kidnapping her for her birthday. *Jawbreaker* is often compared to *Heathers* because of its murderous plot and snappy dialogue and to *Carrie* because of its violence. In many ways the film, which is so indebted to *Heathers'* legacy, mirrors the commentary, but revs up the dialogue of its predecessor. For example, while Heather told Veronica, "You were nothing before you met me," queen bee Courtney (Rose McGowan) tells newly made-over Fern/Violette, "I made you and I'm God. That's all you need to know." While in *Heathers* aggression was shown to be both an issue for young women and men (J.D. clearly has homicidal tendencies and the jocks are both bullies and date rapists), in *Jawbreaker* the narrative focuses more intently on the aggression between young women, depicting a world in which, as Detective Cruz (Pam Grier) puts it, "some of the sweetest candies are sour as death inside." Through both visual and scripted cues, the girls themselves are portrayed as jawbreakers, sugary sweet and dangerous. In this way, the film constructs the adolescent women as desirable, sexualized, and potentially lethal if the borders of their aggression and sexuality are not kept.

In addition to satirizing the norms of good girls and bad girls, the film also directly comments on the social politics of high school. For example, Courtney tells Fern, "I'm not sure we've officially met, what with the cruel politics of high school and all." Fern asks Detective Cruz, "This is high school, Detective Cruz, what is a friend anyway?" which is reprised in voiceover as the final line of the film. Yet, even through the heightened reality and melodramatic plot of *Jawbreaker*, the social politics underlining the bullying and murder are depicted as normal or common experiences. When Fern introduces the "Flawless Four" in the opening monologue of the film, she notes, "You know them, they went to your school," gesturing to how every school supposedly has a clique of pretty, perfect, mean girls sitting at the top of the rigid social hierarchy.

These films demonstrate a trend in the 1980s and 1990s of portraying bullying in a variety or relationships. While girls were often bullies in passive-aggressive ways, the narratives around bullying did not solely focus on the power structures of popular girls. Furthermore, with the exception of black comedies such as *Heathers* and *Jawbreaker*, mean girls were usually the antagonists of the films, given less screen time and character development than the protagonists, usually an unpopular young man or woman. Through the various depictions of bullying and the secondary role of the bullies themselves, teen films placed less emphasis on the politics of relational aggression than later representations would.

From Swatchdogs to Plastics

In the early 2000s, following the increased scrutiny of relational aggression noted above, and the release of Simmons's *Odd Girl Out* and Wiseman's *Queen Bees & Wannabees*, teen movies in general, and bullying stories specifically, started to follow a more regular focus on mean girls and the social hierarchies within female friendships. These narratives reflected the growing body of work on relational aggression, using the politics of girls' power structures in plots that dramatized girls' struggles while also glamorizing the popular or mean girls. Placing the emphasis on the mean girls puts telling stories that girls can relate to and learn from in tension with normative discourses that reinforce gender and beauty norms so that often films do both at once, making it difficult to parse the helpful from the potentially harmful.

Mean Girls is the most famous example of this genre of teen films, and has been thoroughly examined by critics and scholars (Gonick; Meyer et al.; and Okamoto et. al). An important shift that *Mean Girls* makes compared to the previous films above is the central role of specific rules and of romantic relationships in structuring girls' relationships and their relational aggression. Following the specific rules about proper dress ("On Wednesdays we wear pink"), keeping secrets about, from, and for each other, and not interfering with each other's love interests is central to the plot of the film, both in structuring the Plastics' clique and in Cady's (Lindsay Lohan) sabotage of Regina (Rachel McAdams). Through these rules and relationships, girlhood is constructed around norms of heterosexuality and girls as objects of the male gaze (Meyer 16–18). Nonetheless, through screenwriter Tina Fey's satire of the rules of girlhood and the way she portrays the suppression of aggression (shown through Cady's imaginings of girls breaking into animalistic fighting) in favor of passive-aggression and sabotage, the film critiques the very norms it relies on and ultimately reinforces.

In *Mean Girls*, there is a distinct shift away from bullying members outside of the clique to focusing on aggression within a friend group as "girls recognize that maintaining popularity requires the support of unpopular girls, popular girls (particularly as they grow older) tend to act nice around their peers and instead direct their meanness and aggression towards the members of their own clique" (Meyer 8). Whereas *Heathers* and *Jawbreaker* stood out before because of their focus on relational aggression, after *Mean Girls*, aggression between friends became a prevailing narrative in teen entertainment. Coinciding with, and following, the success of *Mean Girls* is a trend of focusing on the gender politics of girls' relationships in a hierarchical way that reinforces what Cady Heron calls the rules of "girl world."

For example, over the course of three episodes during its first season, *Friday Night Lights* (2006–12) depicted the bullying of Lyla Garrity (Minka Kelly), a pretty, popular, prim captain of the Dylan Panthers cheerleaders. After her boyfriend, quarterback Jason Street (Scott Porter), was paralyzed during a football game, Lyla slept with his best friend and teammate Tim Riggins (Taylor Kitsch). When Jason finds out, he punches Tim in the face, making their falling-out public. As a result, both Tim and Lyla are ostracized at school. The manifestation of their bullying, however, takes distinctly different trajectories, putting their experiences in contrast and conversation with each other, as evidenced even by the episode title "It's Different for Girls." All of the backlash against Tim is direct and physical. His teammates call him out for his transgression and break the windows out of his truck while he sits inside (1.9, "Full Hearts"). Although he is temporarily cut-off from the social life of the team, a good performance on the football field is all he needs to get back on the inside. By comparison, Lyla's suffering lasts much longer. Prompted by Jason's teammates, the other girls at school and on the cheerleading squad verbally harass her and call her a slut. The situation escalates so that in practices her teammates purposely drop her, weakening her performance as a cheerleader not only through verbal abuse, but also through passive-aggressive physical threats. At a football game, the major public event around which the TV show is built, after Riggins is injured on the field Lyla is publicly taunted, as girls in the crowd ask her if Riggins prefers boxers or briefs and then throw a bottle of water at her, prompting her to run off the field ("Full Hearts").

Even after Riggins is socially accepted back into the team, Lyla continues to be harassed at practice and in school. When shaken by having "Slut" written on her locker, Lyla struggles to hold a liberty[3] and a teammate quips, "I guess Tim Riggins banged the balance right out of her" ("It's Different for Girls"). Riggins notices Lyla's isolation and tries to help, sitting with her at lunch. Lyla asks him, "What're you doing? Don't you know you're sitting with the school slut?" When he protests, she counters, "It's different for girls. You can sleep around all you want and people think you're cool" ("It's Different for Girls"). After a website is started to advertise what a slut she is, Lyla contemplates quitting the cheerleading squad. Quickly, Lyla's bullying is resolved, not through intervention by an adult or through any recourse to justice, but through her own determination not to give up. Instead of quitting the team, she shows up late to their cheerleading showcase and checks in: "Lyla Garrity.... Yeah, I'm the one with the website."

While *Friday Night Lights* handles the bullying situation with the nuance that the show tackled other issues from abortion to racism, the basic premise remains: the football players are actively aggressive and the cheerleaders are passive-aggressive. And while the aggression on *Friday Night Lights* is less passive than the sabotaging used in *Mean Girls*, Lyla is still punished for transgressing norms of adolescent sexuality by cheating on her boyfriend with his best friend. Furthermore, the adults, however well intentioned, cannot do much for Lyla and the tidy ending of the story in which Lyla bolsters her courage and shows up for her team reinforces the idea that bullying is just part of high school life and something that girls can deal with and move on from.

Relational aggression plays a much more central role to the plot of *Gossip Girl* (2007–13), the CW drama focused on wealthy teenagers in Manhattan. In *Gossip Girl*, as in *Mean Girls*, the social dynamics of the Upper East Side cliques revolve around a queen bee and her best friends, whose relational aggressions focus on secrets, lies, and boyfriends. Although the plots grow more complex as the seasons progress, at the start *Gossip Girl* focuses on Blair Waldorf (Leighton Meester) and her bullying of her former best friend, Serena van der Woodsen (Blake Lively), after Blair finds out that Serena slept with her boyfriend, Nate Archibald (Chace Crawford). For much of the series, in fact, maintaining appearances and sexual propriety motivates a lot of the aggression between the friends. Over the first three episodes, Blair bullies Serena through taunts, exclusions, and threats, culminating in the third episode "Poison Ivy," when she publicly outs Serena for a drug problem she does not have, in front of representatives from Ivy League colleges.

While much of *Gossip Girl* sounds like a pretty typical bullying plot, aside from the enormous trust funds and lavish lifestyles, the twist that the series puts on these expected rules is the presence of Gossip Girl, an anonymous and seemingly all-knowing gossip blogger. Within the world of the show, Gossip Girl functions as an anonymous bully, telling people's secrets and creating an all-seeing presence to be feared while also allowing teens, girls in particular, to lash out at each other by leaking information to Gossip Girl's website or Twitter feed. For the audience, Gossip Girl serves as narrator, bridging the gap between the world of the show and the audience at home. Often, this relationship works through voiceovers that serve as commentary for the audience and, presumably, for the Gossip Girl readers within the show. For example, in "Poison Ivy," Blair says to Serena, "Brown doesn't offer degrees in slut," and Gossip Girl interjects, "Spotted: Serena running late and dressed down by Blair." Gossip Girl also provides a narrative arch to the episodes, providing foreshadowing or commentary that helps structure how the audience interprets the events of the episode. In "Poison Ivy," when Blair and Serena reconcile at the end of the episode, Gossip Girl wonders if the armistice will last, observing "we all know a nation can't have two queens." Gossip Girl's commentary often relies on tropes of teenage hierarchy to make her quips, such as in positioning the two friends as "queens" in a way that references the expected "queen bee" discourse about popular teenage girls. Therefore, even in the heightened soap opera plots of *Gossip Girl*, the narrative relies on expected patterns of relational aggression and expected social structures for teenage friendships.

Even works that play with the rules or subvert them start from a place of acknowledging and establishing the rules for girls and their relationships. For example, *The House Bunny*, which focuses on the bullying of a sorority of outsiders, the Zetas, by a pretty and popular sorority makes fun of beauty and dating norms for much of the film as Shelley (Anna Faris), a former *Playboy* bunny becomes the Zeta's housemother. Shelley makes the girls over in an attempt to get them the pledges they need to keep their house from being sold to the mean girl sorority. While most of the film focuses on the friendship and growing self-esteem of the Zetas, the mean girl narrative creates the conflict in the plot not only through the threat of losing the house, but also as a consequence of the girls' makeovers. Even though Zeta girls Natalie (Emma Stone) and Mona (Kat Dennings) regularly joke about beauty norms, once they become the pretty and popular girls they start to judge potential pledges based on their looks and other superficial qualities. Mona yells at Shelley, "Before you got here we were all individuals and you turned us into a bunch of stupid bimbos." Even though the film seems to send a message undermining relational aggression and the rules of girl world focused on policing the body, the explicit connection between the girls' popularity and their "mean girl" attitudes reinforces the importance of attractiveness in structuring social dynamics among young people, particularly young women.

Focusing on social class and gender norms, *Veronica Mars* (2004–07), which aired starting the fall after *Mean Girls* was released, features a heroine who uses her skills as a private investigator to bring bullies and criminals to justice. Veronica (Kristen Bell) is frequently bullied herself, particularly by the people who used to be her friends, the rich and popular '09ers. While Veronica uses her skills as a PI to bring down local criminals and help students who are bullied, extorted, or otherwise victimized by their classmates, much of her dynamic with the '09ers still relies largely on "mean girls" tropes as the cases Veronica solves largely stem from relational aggression. For example, in "Like a Virgin" she finds out who was behind the a scandal involving an online "Purity Test" and the leaking of fake answers exposing popular and chaste Meg Manning to scrutiny and bullying. While Veronica spends much of the series with one foot on the outside and one on the inside of the popular clique, her position allows her to critique the rules of girl world even as the show still presents them as normal, if corrupt.

Another series that takes a note from *film noir*, *Pretty Little Liars*

(2010–) uses the mysterious history of a mean girl, Alison DiLaurentis (Sasha Pieterse) as the backdrop for a psychological thriller about the threats, blackmailing, and other bullying of Aria Montgomery (Lucy Hale), Spencer Hastings (Troian Bellisario), Emily Fields (Shay Mitchell), and Hanna Marin (Ashley Benson) after Alison's murder. While the girls are harassed by an unknown assailant (or group of assailants) who goes by "A," the way the girls investigate their situation largely revolves around investigating Alison, the secrets she kept, and the ways that she pitted her friends against each other or controlled them by holding information— such as Emily's sexual orientation or Aria's father's infidelity—over their heads. While the series deviates from the normal mean girls plot through the loyal and typically non-aggressive friendship between the four surviving friends and through its thriller-based plot, the girls' problems still ultimately stem from the secrets, lies, and bullying by Alison before her death and the way "A" has taken up her blackmailing after her death. Further, the narrative of the first three seasons ultimately revolves around the revenge of Mona who was bullied by Alison in a narrative more akin to 1990s bullying stories. After Alison's death, however, Mona befriends Hanna and becomes one of the popular girls. Her plots as "A" then take on the quality of relational aggression, blending the makeover narrative and subverting it while still upholding the expected politics of mean girl cliques established by the mean girls discourses.

Conclusion

While mean girls and other bullies have long been a key feature in teen movies and television shows, after the huge success of *Mean Girls* and the popular books *Odd Girl Out* and *Queen Bees and Wannabes*, bullying narratives in film and television shifted from the diverse portrayals of bullying and bullies in the 1990s to a more consistent focus on aggression between friends, particularly between female friends. Further, this aggression follows a predictable, hierarchical pattern that is structured around norms of beauty and romantic relationships. These narratives also move the popular "mean girls" from secondary characters to the center of the plot, both making the popular girls more relatable than they used to be, and reifying the idea that the aggression depicted in their relationships is normal. Furthermore, bullying is often presented as a phase to be worked through or something normal without presenting realistic coping strategies *or* it is presented in such an extreme way that it doesn't resonate with real experiences. These dynamics make addressing relational aggression or proving girls with healthier models of coping with aggression difficult to achieve by codifying the rules of "girl world."

NOTES

1. In January 2010, Phoebe Prince, a 15-year-old girl who had immigrated to Massachusetts from Ireland, killed herself after she was taunted and harassed at school for weeks. After her death, six of her classmates were prosecuted for their involvement in bullying her. While their sentences included probation and community service, the case also lead to stricter anti-bullying legislation at the state level.

2. It is worth noting, also, that while 1996's *Clueless* focused primarily on young women's lives and included a makeover plot, the film did not include bullying within its social dynamics. Even Cher (Alicia Silverstone) and Dionne's (Stacy Dash) makeover of Tai (Brittney Murphy) was done out of misguided friendship as Tai was a new kid in school, but not a socially isolated one. Still, the power to make someone over remains a central trope for demonstrating power in teen relationships and the power Tai gains through her makeover causes tensions between her and Cher, a queen bee.

3. A cheerleading move in which one girl is hoisted in the air, balancing on one leg with her arms raised in a V-shape. It is a fairly basic position for high school cheerleaders.

WORKS CITED

"Full Hearts." *Friday Night Lights*. Writ. Aaron Rahsaan Thomas. NBC. December 5, 2006. Television.
Gonick, M. "The 'Mean Girl' Crisis: Problematizing Representations Of Girls' Friendships." *Feminism & Psychology* 14.3 (2004): 395–400. *CINAHL Plus with Full Text*. Web.
Heathers. Dir. Michael Lehmann. Perf. Winona Ryder, Christian Slater. New World Pictures, 1988. DVD.
The House Bunny. Dir. Fred Wolf. By Karen McCullah Lutz and Kirsten Smith. Perf. Anna Faris, Colin Hanks, and Emma Stone. Columbia Pictures, 2008. DVD.
"It's Different for Girls." *Friday Night Lights*. Writ. Andy Miller. NBC. December 12, 2006. Television.
Jawbreaker. Dir. Darren Stein. Perf. Rose McGowan, Rebecca Gayheart. Crossroads Films, 1999. DVD.
"Like a Virgin." *Veronica Mars*. Writ. Rob Thomas and Aury Wallington. CW. November 23, 2004. Television.
Lipkin, Elline. *Girls' Studies*. Berkeley: Seal, 2009. Print.
Mean Girls. Dir. Mark Waters. Perf. Lindsay Lohan, Tina Fey. 2004. DVD.
Meyer, Michaela, Danielle Stern, and Linda Waldron. "Interrogating Mean Girls: Feminist Implications Of Mediated Representations Of Alternative Aggression." *Conference Papers—National Communication Association* (2008): 1. *Communication & Mass Media Complete*. Web.
Okamoto, Scott K., and Meda Chesney-Lind. "Girls And Relational Aggression: Beyond The 'Mean Girl' Hype." *Family & Intimate Partner Violence Quarterly* 1.3 (2009): 281–286. *Criminal Justice Abstracts with Full Text*. Web.
"Poison Ivy" *Gossip Girl*. Writ. Felicia D. Henderson. CW. October 3, 2007. Television.
Pretty Little Liars. Writ. I. Marlene King and Maya Goldsmith. CW. Television.
Ringrose, J. "A New Universal Mean Girl: Examining The Discursive Construction and

Social Regulation of a New Feminine Pathology." *Feminism & Psychology* 16.4 (2006): 405–424. *CINAHL Plus with Full Text.*

Ryalls, Emily. "Demonizing 'Mean Girls' in the News: Was Phoebe Prince 'Bullied to Death?'" *Communication, Culture & Critique* 5.3 (2012): 463–481. *Communication & Mass Media Complete.*

Simmons, Rachel. *Odd Girl Out: The Hidden Culture of Aggression in Girls.* New York: Harcourt, 2002. Print.

It Gets Better
(When You Come Back from the Grave and Kill Them All)

Bullying and the Horror Film and the Indeterminacy of the Monster

Fernando Gabriel Pagnoni Berns,
Mariana S. Zárate *and*
Canela Ailen Rodriguez Fontao

Bullying is a recurrent topic in horror cinema since the opening of *Carrie* (Brian de Palma) in 1975. And as this problem increases in our current times, the presence of bullying is more visible in scary films, one of the most beloved genres for teenagers. In films such as the aforementioned *Carrie, Terror Train* (Roger Spottiswoode, 1980), *The Pit* (Lew Lehman, 1981) or *Tormented* (Jon Wright, 2009), the bullied kids are represented as monsters who kill their student companions in revenge for all their suffering. Other films represented them as victims-turn-heroes: *Return of the Living Dead Part II* (Ken Wiederhorn, 1988), *The Burning* (Tony Maylam, 1981) or *A Nightmare on Elm Street Part II: Freddy's Revenge* (Jack Sholder, 1985). Finally, a third group of films has bullied kids represented as hybrids between the above mentioned categories: in *Christine* (John Carpenter, 1983), *Let Me In* (Matt Reeves, 2010) or *Fido* (Andrew Currie, 2006), the bullied kids have as companions supernatural beings that help them against the bullies.

What do all these different groups of films have in common? A link between bullying and horror film appears with the notions of the abject and the Other. Both theoretical tools are, as Robin May Schott (2014) argues, very useful today in the analysis of the anxieties of exclusion born in childhood and adolescence, stages in which the formation of identity is crucial (21). Historically, these notions are frequently used to analyze horror films, since the anxieties from a particular society are embodied in an abject monster considered as an Other, which must be destroyed to the status quo to resumes (Wood 31). Now, what goes under discussion is how good it is in fact the restored status quo to begin with or which proper order is reestablished when, for example, Carrie dies after her ordeal at the prom night.

Many of these films end by avoiding possible restoration of a peaceful order, and that may be for two reasons. First, because bullying is that much inserted and accepted in society as a natural occurrence and is not viewed as unusual to begin with. The status quo has bullying as an integral part of society. Then, there is something very wrong in our status quo. Second, because the position of the abject/monster as an Other is constantly shifting in bullying. While for the bully, the Other is the person who must be attacked, for many, the abject Other is the bully. Thus, there is a permanent shift which demonstrates what a complicated situation bullying may be; it is a societal shift that horror films portray through metaphors. This chapter's aim is to analyze a large corpus of horror films to demonstrate first: that representation of bullying in the horror film has followed the historical conceptualizations of this phenomenon and second, that bullying is represented in our contemporary horror cinema as a mobile social activity rather than a static phenomenon.

Slasher Films: From Mobbing to Bullying

The "slasher" films are a great starting point to begin the analysis, since this sub-genre was the first one to introduce (even in a limited way) the problematic of bullying. It should be noted that slasher films were the first horror sub-genre starred exclusively by teenagers and with an eye on an audience composed mostly by teenagers (Jerslev 188), so it is not surprising that issues typical from the adolescent stage make its appearance.

The slasher film took over the horror genre in the eighties and theaters were flooded with masked serial killers who mutilated promiscuous teenagers (Prince 351) to the point that very few horror movies released in the eighties were not part of this cycle (Shary 182). Coincidentally, the first studies upon the phenomenon of bullying begin at the end of the 1970s and first years of the 1980s in Scandinavian and British countries (Sanders 2). In these first studies, bullying was called "mobbing," and, not coincidentally, bullying as mobbing was seen in the slasher films from the eighties.

In order to discuss mobbing, we will use Schott and Søndergaard's two paradigms of bullying (2). The concept of mobbing fits into paradigm one. Peter-Paul Heinemann first introduces the term mobbing in 1969 (Schott and Søndergaard 2) and it was subsequently developed for the Norwegian psychologist Dan Olweus. Mobbing refers to group violence against a deviant individual, "which occurs and stops suddenly" (Schott 22). From the perspective of this first paradigm, bullying is understood as an act of violence by an individual with marked personality issues, such as aggressiveness, impulsivity and little empathy with the other. His victim is usually insecure, passive and weak (Schott 28), thus a perfect target to suffer from repetition of abuse (Schott 27). In brief, these are two fixed and antagonistic positions. Thus, bullying would be understood as a phenomenon that depends on the personality traits of the involved participants. This paradigm one explores the aggressor's abusive family history, and mobbing is result of individual problems rather than a social phenomenon. The aggressor is born of aggressive or dysfunctional families, while the passive victims are born into households with overprotective parents, especially mothers (Schott 28). In the definition of mobbing, the group violence is exerted upon some "deviant" subject. The boy—since the concept of mobbing "was based chiefly on research with boys" (Taki 152)—is a deviant male, a weak, queer subject who in his own passivity calls the attention of aggressive males.

Slasher films are of great necessity to understand this first definition of bullying as mobbing since this sub-genre is full of aggressive males and weak, deviant boys. This sub-genre is repeatedly based on the story of a group of teenagers who are serially murdered by a masked psychopath, who usually is guided by a desire for revenge against those who caused him some kind of humiliation in the past. Carol Clover has also raised the presence of the "Final Girl" (35) as essential in the genre. This unique character is the only one in the entire film with some psychological profile developed, and a highly conservative behavior. She is the massacre's only survivor and she represents moral values. Those who choose to engage in sex or vices (drugs, smoke, drink), typically die, but the "Final Girl" remains. This cycle of films are based on a system of punishments on those who do not respect traditional moral rules.

The film *Prom Night* tells the story of how four children playing in an abandoned building, intimidate little girl Robin Hammond (Tammy Bourne), causing her a fall from a window that kills her. The four children make a pact of silence and swear to never confess the crime. Six years later, in a prom night attended by Robin's siblings, Kim (Jamie Lee Curtis) and Alex (Michael Tough), the four children, now teenagers in their graduation night, are ruthlessly murdered, one by one, by a masked killer, which eventually turns out to be Robin's little brother, Alex. In this film, the murderer is not necessarily someone who suffered bullying (i.e., bullying is not explicitly the focus), yet it contains many elements that demonstrate school mobbing among peers.

For example, the film opens with an abuse of power exerted upon a little girl who is alone (she is the last one in joining the game). The four kids stalk and oppress little Robin as if they were an animal pack, a mob of aggressive kids cornering a weak victim in an asymmetrical relationship of power. As was mentioned as characteristic of mobbing, the violence begins and stops suddenly. The audience does not known if Robin was suffering harassment prior to her final day, or this act of mobbing was only a circumstantial explosion of aggression. Beyond Robin's death, there is a bully in the school: Lou (David Mucci) who is an abusive student who kisses Kim by force and attacks Alex, who reminds viewers of the victim's description on paradigm one, since the main attribute of Alex is weakness. It is possible to understand with this example, that even in a film that is not engaged with the prototypical psychopath who wants revenge from past attackers, we can find elements that clearly references to bullying by means of weak victims (one who is a very deviant subject since he is in fact revealed as the killer) and children aggression produced by a mob in an act of violence that is only momentary.

Another deviant victim appears in the slasher *Terror Train* (Roger Spottiswoode, 1980). In this film, a group of teenagers make a practical joke on a shy classmate named Kenny (Derek McKinnon) and make him to believe that Alana (Jamie Lee Curtis), a popular girl, wants to have an intimate encounter with him. Alana reluctantly accepts to participate in the joke, but the results are horrible and Kenny loses his sanity. Years later, in a fraternity party held in a running train, Kenny returns to take revenge on everyone involved in the joke. Alana, the only one who feels guilt over the past misdemeanor, is the film's final girl.

Here, the previously described characteristics of mobbing are remarkably noticeable. Again, this film depicts a unique act of aggression upon a weak, deviant victim. Kenny is a passive victim who will only take an active role when he turns into a sadistic serial killer. Then, the victims of bullying (or mobbing) are indeed deviant in a double way: they are weak, effeminate men since they are not aggressive, and a serial killer lurks within all them.

One of the most complex cases, which brings us closer to the tipping point where the boundaries of the first paradigms starts to blur, is the film *The Burning* (Tony Maylam, 1981). This slasher film offers some rather curious and innovative twists to the otherwise predictable genre. The film begins telling what happened in the Blackfoot camp where some teenagers plan to make a joke to a concierge named Cropsy (Lou David), but the joke gets (as always) out of control and ends up causing a fire. Cropsy is horribly burned and scarred. Many years later, Cropsy returns to exerts revenge upon his now teenager tormentors, who are now working in another sleepaway camp.

The Burning presents a very interesting character, Alfred (Brian Backer), a boy with a remarkable role in the film. On one hand, he undergoes continuous abuse by one of the characters, Glazer (Larry Joshua), but nevertheless Alfred systematically stalks his bully, exposing a homoerotic desire. Every time Glazer furtively leaves the sleepaway camp, Alfred surreptitiously follows him, presumably to see him making love with girls. But if it is girls that Alfred wants to watch, he could follow his female companions rather than his bully. In fact, Alfred is captured watching Glazer's girlfriend when she is taking a bath. But Alfred answers to the sleepaway camp's authorities that he does so to "scare her away" (away from the camp? From Glazer?).

Moreover, the abused Alfred will take, within the narrative, the role of the Final Girl. Somehow the girl who reaches the ending of the slasher films represents socially accepted moral values. In this case, Alfred represents a big change. He is a victim of bullying, and, therefore is seen through the prism of weakness and insecurity that frames paradigm one and the concept of mobbing, but at the same time, he can not necessarily be seen as fully "innocent" since he is not entirely passive. He is continuously looking for troubles, spying girls to scare them or following his tormentor with no discernible purposes than a homoerotic attachment. He is branded as perverse (deviant) by his companions and suspected of the murders.

While he is a survivor and has the role of the final girl, a homosexual inclination is also insinuated, which is clearly not morally acceptable or desirable in the 1980s. The Final Girl embodies positive values, and while Alfred does not have sex or use drugs, all the characters from the film branded him as queer and sinister. But although he is classified as perverse for his companions, the film presents him as the Final Girl, the real hero. In *The Burning*, these paradigms begin to change; a contradiction is shown in the way of conceiving a phenomenon (an abused boy) that obviously begs to be rethought. Alfred is the victim, but he is not passive as the guidelines of paradigm one suggest. He is deviant (for the decade, at least) but the film main hero. He is not suffering from some kind of mobbing, but from continuous harassment. Fixed dynamics start to move, at least, in this early slasher. The clearly conservative moral structure of slashers here is breached. In fact, maybe this film is the starting point for imagining bullying within the horror genre in a different way.

A Tale of Two *Carries*

Analyzing the theme of bullying in cinema requires inevitable focus on an iconic film of the seventies, both for its subject and for its memorable visual display: Brian De Palma's *Carrie* (1976). Continuing the division between paradigm one and two suggested by Schott and Søndergaard, we will analyze the way in which the dynamics of bullying arises in this film and in its remake *Carrie* (Kimberley Peirce, 2013), in light of what the authors call paradigm two. Paradigm two supposes a shift in the understanding of the problem of bullying. In this sense, it is necessary to include in studies of bullying not only the analysis of the personality of those involved (bully-victim), but also the social environment and cultural, technological and psychological forces involved in the act. If the paradigm one starts from the question of what types of family's characteristics create an aggressive boy, paradigm two emphasizes the social dynamics that not only include the binomial victimizer/victim (understanding the phenomenon in terms of individual violence), but other subjects in the school and social environment (teachers, principals, media).

The opening sequence of both *Carrie* films exposes how the topic of bullying will be addressed. There are very few differences found in terms of composition and progression of the story, but those that indeed exist pose different paths at the time of analysis.

The first scene of De Palma's film presents a Carrie (Sissy Spacek) unable to follow her mates in a physical education class and so she is insulted. This scene appears in Peirce's film displaced by an introductory sequence in which a young and pregnant Mrs. White (Julianne Moore) gives birth without being fully aware of her situation. Seeing that her "cancer" as she defines it, is in fact a baby, she decides to kill her, but the attempt is contained by the baby Carrie's powers. In the subsequent scene, Carrie (Chloë Grace Moretz) is a teenager suffering the ridicule of her companions. This shows us that Carrie is not only a victim of school's abuse, but also of a monstrous mother.

The infamous shower scene is similar in both films. It chronicles the discovery of young Carrie having her first menstruation and her ignorance about what is really taking place within her body. The mocking of her companions ("Plug it up!") will put her in a situation of total helplessness, which will only ends with the help of the gym teacher. If the incident in the shower in De Palma's film remains contained within the space of the bathrooms, in Peirce's film the use of cell phones and video recording allows audiences to think about the issue of cyberbullying. Carrie's exposure in this situation is total; not only is she mocked by her physically present classmates, but also all those absent can see her pain displayed online.

In both films there are subjects trying to prevent violence against Carrie. In the original version, the gym teacher (Betty Buckley) is central. The remake keeps this character (now played by Judy Greer), but includes new ones; throughout the film, different characters help Carrie in different ways. Clearly, the remake is telling its audience that around a bullied kid there are many people ready to help. For example, in the scene immediately following the birth of Carrie, during the games in the school's pool, Carrie makes a mistake and she expects mock or aggression from her classmates. But rather, they only smile at her. They seem to be not that cruel, at least, until the menstruation scene arrives. This is a key difference in respect at the same scene in the original film. In the original movie, Carrie is chastised by her classmates because her lack of skills for sports. Moreover, other characters, in the remake, offer their help to Carrie, such as the boy in the library, helping her to enhance the image in her computer. However, she seems to be unable to perceive this help.

In De Palma's film we come to the final scene, the bloodbath of the prom night, as a result of an almost silent tension that develops slowly and gradually throughout the film. Carrie is embarrassed by her teacher, insulted by her peers, mocked by her neighbor, and denied by the school's principal. Simultaneously, Carrie's response to the violence that is exerted upon her is presented as an almost unconscious impulse, through the use of her telekinetic powers. In De Palma's film, the violence comes out of her body as a burst, an unconscious eruption of power upon the school system in general, without distinction of any kind. She cannot distinguish between the ones that had tried to help her of those that always hurt her. Her gym teacher (who attempted to help her along the way) is punished along with the rest. In this final moment, Carrie resembles those kids who, exhausted their hopes of a better day, choose to engage in a murderous spree that make no distinction between victims.

In Peirce's remake things happen in a slightly different way in the prom night scene, but unwittingly altered the problematic of the film and even end up contradicting its implicit intention of work as an "anti-bullying pamphlet." Throughout this version of the film, we see the development of Carrie's powers as she tries to manage them. Facing ridicule, Carrie reacts by making full use of her telekinetic powers. Anger and rage are used consciously, and she selectively removes from danger those who had helped her (her teacher). In this regard, it is clear that Carrie intends to pursue her main bully, Chris (Portia Doubleday) and her boyfriend while they escape in the car. Carrie chooses with cold premeditation and sadism to kill her. She takes her time and enjoys watching Chris' face going through the car's glass. By this point, Carrie is now in full control of her power and uses it sadistically, turning her into another deviant subject, while in the original film, the killing of Chris is quickly and obeys more to Carrie's sorrow than powerful sadism.

Carrie marks the blurring of the distinctions between the two paradigms. The De Palma's film is one of the first in present bullying in cinema. Here, it is not mobbing being depicted; there is not any sudden group violence, but rather, continuous harassment in school. Bullying appears to be a social problem within the frame of the scholar institution which does not know how to contain the problem. But Carrie White is, in fact, the passive deviant victim created by bad mothers (especially in the remake), while her tormentors are too many and too different one from another to simply correspond all of them to bad parents. Paradoxically, is the remake, which tries to present the idea that in school harassment were more than bullies and victims in its insistence upon the presence of people ready to assist Carrie, which can relates more strongly with paradigm one: the opening scene establishes Carrie as product of a monstrous mother, underlies that the bullies have parents that neglected their offspring and gives an highly negative image of Carrie as a vengeful monster. The first Carrie displays an ambiguity in the figure of the monster in a more successful way to the point that Carrie is conceptualized as a victim more than a monstrous deviant creature.

The rigid binaries composed by bullies and bullied is the basis of paradigm one. Kids are aggressive or passive according to their upbringing at home. Instead, paradigm two will make as its central point the idea that the categories are fluid and that the problem of bullying is social in origin, rather than individual aggression. It is possible to see this in the horror films that engage explicitly with bullying as a social activity that goes beyond the simplistic binarism of victim/aggressor.

Abjection and the Other as a Shifting Categorization

Julia Kristeva in her book *Powers of Horror* (1982) identifies that we first experience abjection in the point of separation from the mother when the child (who is a being without any borders) enters the symbolic realm, which produces a revolt against that which gave us our own state of being. The self is threatened by something that is not part of us in terms of identity and non-identity. Abjection, then, is all about the creation of boundaries that divide oneself from otherness. Kristeva says: "The abject has only one quality of the object and that is being opposed to I" (1). The abject is "what one spits out, rejects, almost violently excludes from oneself" (McAfee 46) to constitute subjectivity. But rejected does not means erased. What is abject and dangerous for the proper construction of identity it is not something that disappears, but something that "hovers at the periphery of one's existence, constantly challenging one's own tenuous borders of selfhood" (McAfee 46), thus a threat to our existence since it, the abject, is always there, menacing with pulverizing our borders-of-the-self.

Horror cinema has the abject as primal figure in the embodiment of the monster, an impure creature whose existence puts the fabric of normalcy into danger. The monster is unclassifiable, and society must have everything classified to preserve the status quo. Monsters are metaphors of the anxieties of a concrete society in a concrete time. The final kiss of the heterosexual couple at the end of horror films is the sign that marks the return to hegemonic normalcy. The monster is an alternative from that normalcy, and it must be obliterated. Even Kristeva equals abject with monster (11). Thus, abjection and horror cinema goes hand by hand.

In paradigm two appears one of the factors which cause bullying: the anxiety of social exclusion, meaning, the fear in childhood and adolescence of being excluded/abjected from social circles. The fear of being invisible in High School leads to many teens to engages directly or indirectly (as observers or reinforces) in practices of bullying if that helps them gain popularity among their peers. There is a shift from someone who is in risk of being converted in abject, i.e., expelled from the popular circles, to someone "weaker," a more proper victim (a shy kid, a tomboy girl, a foreign student) who is collectively framed as abject. As Dorte Søndergaard argues, "the target of bullying is someone under pressure to assume an abject position" (67). This person is transformed into the Other, and with this action, turned into a monster; some creature that must be expelled to keep normalcy.

Here we find many ties with horror cinema, which always have an abject creature that embodies Otherness and disrupts order (Wood 29). Thus, the monster must be destroyed to resume status quo (Langford 159).

The kid suffering bullying is, also, some abject element that the bully felts put in risk his or her identity and for that, must be chastised. The abjection takes place with the rejection, maybe even obliteration, of some Other, and this practice pervades bullying practices (Søndergaard 68). Abjection, for Judith Butler, is the way the dominant order excrementalizes its dispossessed; it is, as she writes in *Gender Trouble*, the "mode by which others become shit" (134). Here appears the idea of shifting in the categorization of what is abject. For the bully, the kid whose presence is a (unconscious) threat (for whatever reason that maybe even the bully probably cannot put into words) must be expelled. But for parents, school's directives and, surely for the bullied kids, what is abject and must be expelled because its monstrous nature is the bully. In brief, for the bullies, their victims are Others, abject monsters. For many others, the monsters are the bullies. They, as antisocial beings, are the excrement of society.

This shift is mirrored in horror cinema, but only when the practice of bullying is a main thread in the film. If not, horror cinema has a very well defined monster. But when bullying is central to the story, define with exactitude who is the real monster of the story is hard to point. If we take the most classic of bullying horror films, *Carrie*, we find that it is not that easy to define who the real monster is. Carrie herself? Her mother, for mistreated her? Carrie's peers? Sue Snell? Society in general for allows that this violence upon a shy girl takes place? To complicate things further, with the passage from paradigm one to two, the binary category of bully/bullied open up to many variations. Sometimes, the bullied kid, in turn, practices bullying with some other kid. Moreover, the binary game of opposites between oppressors/oppressed as the only way of understanding the practice of bullying is open to some other categories, as assistants of bullies, reinforcers of bullying (with laughter or indifference), outsiders who withdraw without taking sides and defenders of the victims (Schott 35).

We have already seen how the different versions of *Carrie* work in terms of bullying, and how the newest version tries to establish the idea that not everyone in a school are potential bullies but rather potential helpers. Let's now examine participants of bullying in other films. *Tormented* begin with a requiem for Darren Mullet (Calvin Dean), a high school kid who kills himself after suffering many acts of bullying through his years as a student. This opening scene resonates strongly with all the cases of suicides of teenagers that take their own lives at the prospect of endure even more public humiliations or exclusion in their schools. The eulogy is given by Justine Fielding (Tuppence Middleton), to whom this duty was given because she is a good student. But even when she spokes in the church about what a good fellow Darren was, the true is that Justine has many problems to even recall who the kid was. That way, and taking into account that Justine is the film's main female character, *Tormented* is a horror film narrated from the point of view of those who invisibilize the practice of bullying, thus reinforce it.

Justine is a complex character. She is not the most popular girl in school but her circle is not that of the school's misfits. This way, she is a fluid character who can move from one group to another. In the beginning of the film, Justine is invited to join the most popular school group, composed by snobs and bullies. This social circle includes the schoolmates that had terrorized Darren. Justine accepts and for that, she gradually leaves aside her previous girlfriends, two shy girls, even when nobody explicitly asked her to do so. To define herself as a popular girl she must expel that what is abject, which threatens the formation of her new identity; in this case, her prior circle of friends. At the end of the film, she is punished for making such a "betrayal."

Darren returns from the dead to take revenge on those who humiliated him and in the last scene, Justine is blamed for the killings committed by the boy's ghost. In the final scene Justine is led to a patrol car while her teammates and school authorities watch in amazement. This resonates with any real scene image taken from TV's news where spectators can see a student arrested after school violence. For spectators and the people affected, the perpetrators of the school massacres are monsters, but Justine, as the (alleged) killer, could blame as responsible for the actual slaughter to another monster: the killer ghost. Since *Tormented* is a horror film, the monster here is literal, but outside the movies, the kids who decide to end their humiliation through killing sprees can also note that the monsters are others than themselves, the bullies and the school as an institution that allows them to continue their practice of harassment. As was noted in respect to the Columbine massacre, "if Harris and Klebold were monsters, they were made that way by the school" (Larkin 201).

Justine is a monster in a triple way: for the media and the common people, because she killed her classmates. But she was a monster for Darren too, since she never assisted him when he was molested, thus working indirectly with the practice of harassment. And Justine is a monster for the audience, too. In the film's climax, Justine not only learns that her boyfriend Alexis (Dimitri Leonidas) also abused Darren, but, to her surprise, she did not even notice that Darren Mullet was being abused literally in front of her. To the audience then, she is reconfigured as monstrous because her school days were spent in a state of selfishness that prevents her from observing practices of bullying.

The opening scene of Justine reading a eulogy on behalf of Darren resonates at the end with irony, given that she contributed to his ordeal indirectly. Or directly, since her incapacity of see bullying as a practice outside of the common life of school reinforce this practice. Here it is possible to see how complex are both framing someone as monstrous in the practice of school bullying and how these social activities have more figures that only those of bullies/bullied. The complexity that surrounds the various participants in the practices of bullying can be seen in *The Final* (Joey Stewart, 2010). In the film, a group of students who suffer daily bullying decide drug their aggressors at a party, and later keep them captives in an isolated house to subject them to various kinds of physical tortures. The film is notable for the way it negotiates the representations of abused and abusers. Typically, there would be two clearly defined spheres: attackers and attacked. But a character embodies the passage from a sphere to the other. Kurtis (Jascha Washington) is a student who has never exercised bullying upon his peers and, therefore is left out of the revenge. However, Kurtis talks with the "popular circle of students" too, and for that, he works more like a bridge between the two worlds. Although both groups want to establish a dichotomy of "us/them," Kurtis operates smoothly within both groups without problems in his identity and what is more interesting, without putting the identities of the groups into risk. Thus, even with his mobility, he is not abject.

Both groups considered as Others (monstrous) the opposing group, confirming the mobility of the points of view at the moment that someone is depicted as abject in the practice of bullying. As Ravi (Vincent Silochan), one of the bullied kids says about Kurtis, he must be leaved out of the vengeance plan because "he's not one of them" clearly differentiated between "us/them." But Kurtis did go the party and the avenging group has in their hands a problem: the different members do not decide whether kill or not Kurtis. *The Final* is effective in submitting alternatives. First, because Kurtis does not respond to any binary system of "them/us," "good/bad." Second, because the outcasts do not know what to do with him once he is captured with the bullies just because he goes to the party where them where drugged. Some will want to release him, while others will decide that there is no difference at all, that Kurtis, if not an outcast, is part of the social system that oppresses them, and for that he must die. Unlike the new *Carrie*, who can clearly distinguish between good and bad people, the abused characters from *The Final* respond more to the antisocial pain that afflicts children who have experienced bullying, a fear and anger born from the idea that "nobody cares" and thus, this anger is directed to nobody in particular rather than just certain people.

Moreover, *The Final* begin with a flashforward of one of the bullies carrying the scars and disfigurations that she will gain during the film. She is observed and mocked by people. The irony is obvious: is she now the abject, the monstrous Other that society marginalizes as a pariah because of her horrid appearance, but she was a monster before in her daily harassment of her classmates that she considered, in turn, abject monsters.

Conclusions

Horror films illustrate in an interesting way the shifting nature of the categories in the problematic of bullying. This is not casual, since bullying and horror cinema engages with notions of the Other and abjection. Both categories are, in fact, inseparable from both, bullying practice and horror cinema. This way, horror films articulates with the real horror of bullying and social anxieties. Horror movies with bullying as a central trope deny a return to the status quo. With the exception of slasher films, since the nature of this cycle is "conservative law-and-order ideology" (Simpson 123), all the examples mentioned here end on a dark note. Both *Carrie* movies present a horrid nightmare as the final scene. *The Final* ends with Kurtis returning to college permanently damaged, while the killer ghost of *Tormented* is seen in the final shot as a presence still haunting the school even when all Darren's tormentors are dead.

If the end in horror films marks the re-instauration of some presumably good status quo, bullying as a social practice is so present in our actual daily life that it is not, in fact, any proper status quo to which return.

Bullying and harassment will continue until all the social actors and institutions decide to attack this problem in a coordinate way. If not, bullying will continued to be a game of spot who the monster is and who the victim and not the complex social problem that bullying is, a problem that requires everybody to get involved.

WORKS CITED

Butler, Judith. *Gender Trouble: Feminism and the Subversion of Identity.* New York: Routledge, 1990.
Clover, Carol J. *Men, Women, and Chainsaws: Gender in the Modern Horror Film.* Princeton: Princeton University Press, 1992.
Jerslev, Anne. "Youth Films: Transforming Genre, Performing Audiences." *International Handbook of Children, Media and Culture,* edited by Kirsten Drotner and Sonia Livingstone. London: SAGE, 2008. 183–195.
Kristeva, Julia. *Powers of Horror: An Essay on Abjection.* New York: Columbia University Press, 1982.
Langford, Barry. *Film Genre: Hollywood and Beyond.* Edinburgh: Edinburgh University Press, 2005.
Larkin, Ralph. *Comprehending Columbine.* Philadelphia: Temple University Press, 2007.
McAfee, Noëlle. *Julia Kristeva.* New York: Routledge, 2004.
Prince, Stephen. *A New Pot of Gold: Hollywood Under the Electronic Rainbow 1980–1989.* Berkeley: University of California Press, 2000.
Sanders, Cheryl. "What Is Bullying?" *Bullying: Implications for the Classroom,* edited by Cheryl Sanders and Gary Phye. San Diego: Elsevier/Academic Press, 2004. 2–18.
Schott, Robin May. "The Social Concepts of Bullying: Philosophical Reflections on Definitions." *School Bullying: New Theories in Context,* edited by Robin May Schott. Cambridge: Cambridge University Press, 2014. 21–46.
_____, and Dorte Marie Søndergaard. "Introduction: New Approaches to School Bullying." *School Bullying: New Theories in Context,* edited by Robin May Schott. Cambridge: Cambridge University Press, 2014. 1–18.
Shary, Timothy. *Generation Multiplex: The Image of Youth in American Cinema After 1980,* rev. ed. Austin: University of Texas Press, 2014.
Simpson, Philip. "Whither the Serial Killer Movie?" *American Horror Film: The Genre at the Turn of the Century,* edited by Steffen Hantke. Jackson: University Press of Mississippi, 2010. 119–141.
Søndergaard, Dorte. "Social Exclusion Anxiety: Bullying and the Forces That Contribute to Bullying Amongst Children at School." *School Bullying: New Theories in Context,* edited by Robin May Schott. Cambridge: Cambridge University Press, 2014. 47–80.
Taki, Mitsuru. "Relations Among Bullying, Stresses, and Stressors: A Longitudinal and Comparative Survey Among Countries." *Handbook of Bullying in Schools: An International Perspective,* edited by Sahen Jimerson, Susan Swearer, and Dorothy Espelage. New York: Routledge, 2010. 151–162.
Wood, Robin. "An Introduction to the American Horror Film." *Horror: The Film Reader,* edited by Marc Jancovich. New York: Routledge, 2002. 25–32.

Bullying, Quidditch and the Golden Snitch

Harry Potter and the Philosopher's Stone

Chantelle MacPhee

A bully belittles and berates a victim in order to feel empowered, in control. The way in which the aggressor controls the victim may vary: manipulation, innuendo, lies, gossip. This sense of power is intoxicating as the bully becomes ever more enraptured by the actions and reactions of his or her victim(s). If the victim responds, then he or she begins to lose control and the aggressor may become even more domineering. The victim's self-worth is attacked, effaced, regarding his or her own importance or role in the community with family, friends. David Farrington, in his article, "Understanding and Preventing Bullying," defines bullying as "physical, verbal, or psychological attack or intimidation that is intended to cause fear, distress, or harm to the victim; an imbalance of power, with the more powerful child oppressing the less powerful one" (384). In *Harry Potter and the Philosopher's Stone*, J.K. Rowling appears to address this issue quite substantially. Harry Potter is the victim of bullying from Dudley, Aunt Petunia, Uncle Vernon and Draco Malfoy. However, as the novel progresses, Quidditch becomes the metaphor for the bullying.

The moment J.K. Rowling's *Harry Potter and the Philosopher's Stone* opens, the narrator tells us that "if there was one thing the Dursleys hated even more than his [Harry's] asking questions, it was his talking about anything acting in a way it shouldn't, no matter if it was in a dream or even a cartoon—they seemed to think he might get dangerous ideas" (24). For his relatives, Harry represents all that is strange and odd about the wizarding world. Harry has no idea he has magical powers, but he certainly understands that he is ignored by his aunt, uncle and cousin. Harry is anything but respected. Potter is trying to survive by being quiet. Anytime he says something, Harry's relatives make clear that his thoughts and opinions are not valued. Harry's Aunt Petunia, Uncle Vernon and cousin Dudley do not want to learn about anything that is strange or outside their realm of existence. They judge Harry and his parents harshly because they are different. For Aunt Petunia and Uncle Vernon, the wizarding world is strange, and being the sister of a witch is not something Petunia is particularly proud of but jealous. Moreover, Harry's parents were not just killed. They were murdered by Voldemort, and Harry is now the most popular wizard alive unknown to him. Harry's popularity and abuse frighten him. He knows nothing about his parents nor his powers. The moment Hagrid arrives to take Harry to Hogwarts, he learns that bullies occupy both worlds, but the wizarding world he will join—Albus Dumbledore, Professor McGonagall, Hagrid, Ron and Hermione, in particular—teaches Harry how to overcome his fears, loneliness and low self-esteem without using magic as the salve for all wounds. Harry learns to use his intelligence to outthink and outmaneuver his opponents, just as he does in Quidditch. Harry quickly becomes a fearless opponent who searches for the golden snitch ever aware that he is the seeker, both metaphorically and literally throughout the series of novels.

Harry's famous escape from Lord Voldemort, or He-Who-Should-Not-Be-Named, the death of his parents, and his identity as a wizard is silenced by Aunt Petunia and Uncle Vernon as quickly as Harry arrives on their doorstep. They rewrite Harry's past and hide it from him, at least until Hagrid arrives some eleven years later, only to imprison him in a daily existence of bullying by the very people who should be nurturing and teaching him. As a victim, Harry longs to be away from the Dursleys. He does not even know who he is, nor can he remember how the car accident, which claimed the life of his parents, occurred:

> He'd lived with the Dursleys almost ten years, ten miserable years, as long as he could remember, ever since he'd been a baby and his parents had died in that car crash. He couldn't remember being in the car when his parents had died. Sometimes, when he strained his memory during long hours in his cupboard, he came up with a strange vision: a blinding flash of green light and a burning pain in his forehead. This, he supposed was the crash, though he couldn't imagine where all the green light came from. He couldn't remember his parents at all. His aunt and uncle never spoke about them, and of course he was forbidden to ask questions. There were no photographs of them in the house [27].

Yet, Petunia's and Vernon's silence on Harry's past merely intensifies Harry's desire to know who he is and who his parents were.

Ten years after Harry is placed with his aunt and uncle, Harry is living in the "cupboard under the stairs" (20), from which there appears to be no escape, at least not for a muggle (non-magic person). He can only open the door when it is not locked from the outside. His very movements are restricted by his aunt and uncle while Dudley, their child, is coddled. Harry becomes Dudley's punching bag so often that Harry uses sellotape to hold his glasses together. Potter is the quintessential victim of bullying because he lacks an identity and a sense of place in the Muggle world. He has no idea the wizarding world exists: "He had no friends, no other relatives— he didn't belong to the library so he'd never even got rude notes asking for books back" (30). Everything changes, however, when Harry begins receiving letters "addressed so plainly there could be no mistake:

Mr. H. Potter
The Cupboard under the Stairs
4 Privet Drive
Little Whinging
Surrey [30].

For Harry, even his birthday is not celebrated with the pomp and circumstance of Dudley's. Harry's "were never exactly fun—last year, the Dursley's had given him a coat-hanger and a pair of Uncle Vernon's old socks" (36) while Dudley receives the number and type of presents he demands. Harry's lack of importance and place in the family, however, will contribute to his eventual love for Hogwarts, a place where he has more friends and receives more presents than he has in his entire life to this point. When Hagrid bursts onto the scene, the green light that pervades Harry's long-forgotten memories is identified and defined. Hogwarts will become Harry's journey of self-discovery and help him develop from a shy, young boy in the early novels into the hero of the wizarding world in the final one.

Of course, none of this would be possible without Quidditch—a sport at which Harry is a natural. Quidditch is a magical game that parodies Harry's struggles with others. This game is a reinvented form of soccer (football) that involves physical contact, teamwork, and various players who have responsibilities assigned to their particular role in the game. There are seven players on each team. Three of these players are called Chasers. They are similar to the forwards in soccer. To score, the Chasers much use the Quaffle—a red ball—and throw it back and forth between them as they aim for the three golden poles with hoops on the end of each pitch (think soccer) where they can score. If the quaffle goes through one of the hoops, then a goal is tallied. One player on the team is the Keeper, similar to the goalkeeper in soccer. The keeper's job is to fly around the hoops and prevent the opposing team from scoring. Two black balls are called the Bludgers. Players on the team hit the bludgers with a bat, as these balls are meant to knock off players on the opposing team. The two Beaters on each team try to keep the opposing team's bludgers from knocking their players off their brooms. The last member of the team is the Seeker whose job is to catch the Golden Snitch—the fourth ball. The Golden Snitch is the most important ball of the game. It is extremely fast and difficult to see. The Seeker must catch it, and to do so the Seeker must weave around the bludgers, the quaffle, the Keeper, the Chasers and the Beaters. There is only one Golden Snitch to chase. Once caught, the team wins an extra 150 points. In a typical Quidditch match, the Seeker is often fouled.

In Quidditch, Harry is able to address his daily struggles to fit in, to excel at something that the corresponding bullies in each world do not—Petunia, Vernon, Dudley, and Draco. The reader has hope that Harry can overcome obstacles in both worlds because he has an innate ability to fly. He is so famous in the wizarding world and a pariah in the muggle world that Harry has to learn to weave in and out and around those individuals who thrive on his failures, on attacking him in every way. In essence, the game teaches him to challenge himself and break the physical and emotional shackles that have imprisoned him for so long. After all, not only is he the youngest seeker in history, he is also a very talented young boy at finding the golden snitch and catching it to win the game. The Golden Snitch, at least in this first novel, becomes the metaphor for Harry's obstacles.

The moment Harry decides to go with Hagrid to Hogwarts School of Witchcraft and Wizardry, his entire world undergoes a metamorphosis. At the moment Harry grabs a broom and becomes a Seeker, his world begins to change. Harry begins to narrate his own life. He discovers who he is. He is no longer alone, forgotten and despised for his unique traits. Hagrid initiates this removal of the impermeable clouds that engulf Harry about his past when he tells him:

> You-Know-Who killed 'em. An' then—an' this is the real myst'ry of the thing—he tried to kill you, too. Wanted ter make a clean job of it, I suppose, or maybe he just liked killin' by then. But he couldn't do it. Never wondered how you got that mark on yer forehead? That was no ordinary cut. That's what yeh get when

a powerful, evil curse touches yeh—took care of yer mum an' dad an' yer house, even—but it didn't work on you, an' that's why yer famous, Harry. No one ever lived after he decided ter kill 'em, no one except you, an' he'd killed some o' the best witches an' wizards of the age—the McKinnons, the Bones, the Prewetts—an' you was only a baby, an' you lived [39–40].

Coupled with this fame, Harry learns that his parents provided for him financially. Once Hagrid takes Harry to Gringotts to retrieve some of the money left him by his parents to pay for his schooling, Harry begins to rewrite his past, to identify with others who have a similar plight. He learns to join others, to become a team member, a friend, and loyal. Harry, for example, is unable to refrain from standing up for Hagrid when Malfoy (the wizarding antagonist through much of the novel) meets Harry for the first time in Diagon Alley, unaware he is the famous boy who survived He-Who-Should-Not-Be-Named. Potter believes Hagrid is brilliant and tells Draco such right after Draco tells Harry, "I heard he's [Hagrid's] a sort of savage—lives in a hut in the school grounds and every now and then he gets drunk, tries to do magic, and ends up setting fire to his bed" (62). Harry's response is based on the fact that Harry interprets Draco's comments as ones to which he has been a victim all of his life. Harry is no longer a silenced victim; rather, he has begun the first steps to healing and developing a voice.

Of course the moment Harry begins to develop so, too, does Draco's presence in the novel. While Harry is the Seeker in this story, Draco is definitely the opposing Seeker who even assumes the role of a Beater. While on the train to Hogwart's, Draco arrives at Harry's car and proceeds to teach Harry, "You'll soon find out some wizarding families are much better than others, Potter. You don't want to go making friends with the wrong sort. I can help you there" (81). Harry's response indicates a spirit that no longer is the passive, lonely victim of bullying. "'I think I can tell who the wrong sort are for myself, thanks,' he said coolly" (81). Thereafter Draco tries to warn Harry about the importance of associations: "You hang around with riff-raff like the Weasleys and that Hagrid and it'll rub off on you" (81). Nonetheless, Harry ignores these comments. Harry is seeking love, friendship, companionship—something he has not had. After all, ten years of his aunt's, uncle's and Dudley's persistent bullying have taken their toll. The moment Harry returns home briefly after purchasing his school supplies, his world is not the same. From the moment he meets Hagrid, Potter's quest to discover who he is and who his parents were begins. This is first evident when Harry returns home from Diagon Alley. Aunt Petunia, Uncle Vernon and Dudley are "half terrified, half furious, they acted as though any chair with Harry in it was empty" (67). Rather than take advantage of this newfound power, though, Harry stays in his room and reads so he can learn as much as he can about the world in which he was destined to be a part. He does not enact revenge. Instead, he immerses himself in books.

Once Harry arrives at Hogwarts, Harry discovers who he is. Once Harry begins asking Hagrid about Quidditch, the sport becomes the metaphor for Harry's life and teaches him to fight back to overcome his insecurities:

> It was as Harry dodged another Bludger which went spinning dangerously past his head that it happened. His broom gave a sudden, frightening lurch. For a split second, he thought he was going to fall. He gripped the broom tightly with both his hands and knees. He'd never felt anything like that.... Harry tried to turn back towards the Gryffindor goal posts; he had had a mind to ask Wood to call time out—and then he realized that his broom was completely out of his control. He couldn't turn it. He couldn't direct it at all. It was zig-zagging through the air and every now and then making violent swish movements which almost unseated him [139].

As Harry learns Quidditch and becomes more adept at it as the seeker, Harry learns to adapt to his opponent, defend himself and his team and overcome his challengers as a player and wizard—a rather famous one— who will continue to learn and develop as a player and a wizard. His newfound talent, of course, also unleashes jealousy from Draco Malfoy, the counterpoint to Harry. Draco begins most certainly as the smug, overconfident, repulsive young boy in the first book as he repeatedly attempts to compete with Harry and his reputation. When Harry wins a Quidditch match, by catching the Golden Snitch, Draco, "jealous and angry goes back to taunting Harry about having no proper family" (143). Draco fails to see that Harry is not disturbed by this comment. Harry learns the value of teamwork. When he unites with his friends and their talents, success is inevitable. While Harry excels, Draco falters. The Golden Snitch, a symbol for every obstacle Harry will face in the book series, is not only caught in the first game, but it is swallowed. The Golden Snitch can be caught. Obstacles can be overcome. The game is over, but only for this obstacle. The Mirror of Erised and the Philosopher's Stone are next.

Nowhere is Harry's success at teamwork more evident than when Ron, Hermione and Harry battle the troll in the dungeon. Harry cannot leave Hermione in the bathroom when he knows danger is lurking. Instead, he and Ron arrive to rescue her from the troll, but not before "Ron pulled out his own wand—not knowing what he was going to do he heard himself cry the first spell that came into his head: '*Wingardium Leviosa!*'—the spell in which Hermione had recently told Ron to swish and flick his wand and to pronounce the word with emphasis on the third syllable (130). From that moment on, "Hermione Granger became their friend. There are some things you can't share without ending up liking each other, and knocking out a twelve-foot mountain troll is one of them" (132). This camaraderie will only develop further in the novel when these friends try to solve the mystery of Nicolas Flamel and the Philosopher's Stone while also escaping the three-headed dog, Devil's Snare, catching the key to unlock the door and playing a game of chess.

In all instances, what Harry learns in Quidditch helps him overcome his adversaries in this novel. When Harry stands before the Mirror of Erised, Albus Dumbledore warns him of the dangers of idleness. If Harry forgets to focus on what is important and becomes consumed by the Mirror of Erised, the game is over. Harry will not win the game—the desire to keep the Philosopher's Stone in good hands. Without teamwork, Harry cannot defeat the three-headed dog, the Devil's Snare, unlock the door or win a game of chess. He needs his friends as much as they need him. After all, each obstacle is a riddle that Harry and his friends need to solve to progress. The Golden Snitch, or the Philosopher's Stone, is only as invisible as the Seeker who desires it but does not wish to use it.

In essence, from the time that Draco Malfoy attacks Ron for being poor, a Weasley, and Harry defends him, Harry and Ron are friends, and Draco and Harry become adversaries. While bullying takes a wide range of forms, the coercive behaviors associated with bullying can be classified into two categories: physical and verbal. Physical bullying includes hitting, pushing, holding, and hostile gesturing. Verbal bullying includes threatening, humiliating, degrading, teasing, name-calling, put-downs, sarcasm, taunting, staring, sticking out the tongue, eye rolling, silent treatment, manipulating friendship, and ostracizing (see Clarke & Kiselica; Remboldt). If anything, Harry is bullied by Draco Malfoy and Dudley Dursley but he only remains a victim as long as he does not react. As in Quidditch, if the Seeker fails to participate, to be an active seeker of the Golden Snitch, then he or she will fail. Harry's fear of being assigned to Slytherin house dissipates when he, for the first time, verbalizes his desire to be assigned to any house but Slytherin to the Sorting Hat. At the same time, J.K. Rowling makes it clear in the story that Harry has spunk, character. He will definitely stand up for those individuals who have similar issues of insecurity, acceptance and a desire to excel and make their own mark in the world. The belittled and berated Harry is no longer the victim. As the narrator makes clear, in Quidditch, the Golden Snitch is the most important ball of the entire group. Its speed and difficulty in being seen are what make it so valuable. Harry is virtually invisible but quickly learns how to outmaneuver and out play the others: "You've got to weave in and out of the Chasers, Beaters, Bludgers and Quaffle to get it before the other team's Seeker, because whichever Seeker catches the Snitch wins his team an extra hundred and fifty points, so they nearly always win. That's why Seekers get fouled so much. " (125). The remaining novels in the series will certainly show us a Harry Potter who will continue to fight his insecurities and his adversaries. After all, the Quidditch game has only begun.

Works Cited

Clarke, E.A., and M.S. Kiselica. "A Systemic Counseling Approach to the Problem of Bullying." *Elementary School Guidance and Counseling* 31 (1997): 310–315.

Farrington, David P. "Understanding and Preventing Bullying." *Crime and Justice* 17 (1993): 381–458.

Ma, Xin. "Bullying and Being Bullied: To What Extent are Bullies Also Victims?" *American Educational Research Journal* 38.2 (Summer 2001): 351–370.

O'Sullivan, Sheryl. "Books to Live By: Using Children's Literature for Character Education." *The Reading Teacher* 57.7 (April 2004): 640–645.

Remboldt, C. *Solving Violence Problems in Your School: Why a Systematic Approach Is Necessary*. Minneapolis: Johnson Institute, 1994.

Rowling, J.K. *Harry Potter and the Philosopher's Stone*. London: Bloomsbury, 1997.

"Carrie White burns in hell"
Re-Evaluating Carrie *in the Post-Columbine Era*

Don Tresca

Eric Harris. Dylan Klebold. James Holmes. Adam Lanza. Elliot Rodgers.

These names are synonymous with some of the deadliest, most shocking mass murders in recent memory. And they each have one thing in common. They were outsiders, men who felt bullied, belittled, and victimized, and they lashed out at their persecutors in the darkest, most violent ways they possibly could, inflicting injury and death to the guilty and innocent alike. They are the monsters of the late-twentieth and early-twenty-first centuries, condemned by the media and the public alike in equal measure. Although bullying has been around for decades (if not centuries), rarely has a bullying victim taken such drastic and deadly action to end their torment. But these men do have their literary forbearers, among them Carrie White, a young high school girl with a terrible secret power, one that will help her gain a bloody vengeance against those who tortured and humiliated her, both at school and at home.

Carrie's story is told in Stephen King's 1974 novel *Carrie*, his first full-length published work, and then subsequently explored in two feature films, one by Brian De Palma in 1976, and the other by Kimberly Peirce in 2013. Each of these works explores Carrie's tale from slightly different perspectives to answer some very complex questions: Is Carrie justified in her actions? How are we in the audience to view Carrie's actions? (with empathy? horror?) In the end, is Carrie a victim, or a monster, or perhaps even a little of both? Only through a detailed examination of the texts (the novel and both films) are we going to find our answers.

Stephen King's original novel begins with the shower scene, in which Carrie has her first menstruation. King's first words of description of her appearance make clear both her unattractiveness and her isolation from her peers; he describes her as "a frog among swans" (4). As the physical description continues, his words become more negative, suggesting Carrie's low opinion of herself and how she is viewed by her classmates:

> She was a chunky girl with pimples on her neck and back and buttocks, her wet hair completely without color. It rested against her face with dispirited sogginess.... She looked the part of the sacrificial goat, the constant butt, believer in left-handed monkey wrenches, perpetual foul-up, and she was.... They stared. They always *stared* [Ibid, italics in original].

Even Sue Snell, the character the novel holds up as the one girl in the school who sympathizes with Carrie, initially cannot help but ridicule her when Carrie panics upon discovering the menstrual blood coming from her: "You big dumb pudding" (7). Then the taunting and bullying really begins, as Carrie is pelted with tampons and sanitary napkins as the girls chant "PER-iod" and "Plug it *up*" (6–7).

Along with the humiliation, Carrie's first period is accompanied by the rising of her long-dormant power of telekinesis. At first, she uses the power instinctively, without even realizing she is doing anything (such as shattering a light bulb in the girl's shower and knocking over the principal's ashtray in his office). Her first conscious use of her power occurs soon afterwards; however, on her way home when she causes a little boy who has been taunting her to fall off his bicycle. Realizing the incredible gift that she has been given, she begins to do research at the library on telekinesis and discovers that the talent is a scientific phenomenon, as opposed to the demonic power her religious zealot mother claims it to be.

Meanwhile, Chris Hargensen, the ringleader of the girls who bullied Carrie so relentlessly in the gym showers, has been denied entry into the upcoming senior prom dance as punishment for her actions while one of the other girls who participated, Sue Snell, convinces her boyfriend, Tommy Ross, on whom Carrie has a crush, to ask Carrie to the prom instead of her in order to assuage her guilt for her actions. While Sue atones, Chris plots revenge with the help of her boyfriend, Billy Nolan. The two of them plan a horrible practical joke: to arrange for Carrie to be voted Senior Prom Queen and then, at the moment of her coronation, dump a bucket of pig's blood on her from the overhead rafters. Both Sue's plan to give Carrie a magical night of happiness and Chris' plan of bloody vengeance succeed, although the results are something neither of them would dare imagine. Being humiliated beyond measure at the moment of her seeming acceptance drives Carrie into a murderous rage, culminating in the unrestrained release of her telekinetic powers. She uses her abilities to burn down the school (with most of the students still trapped inside) and then makes her way through town, leaving a trail of death and destruction as she makes her way back home to the arms of her mother, who has become so convinced that her daughter has been possessed by a demon that she plans to murder her. Betrayed by the one person she believed would protect her, Carrie kills her mother by telekinetically stopping her heart and then, wounded from her mother's knife attack, dies in the arms of Sue, who has tracked her down in an effort to save her.

King's own feelings about his literary creation have been very ambivalent throughout the years since the novel's publication. Initially, he empathized immensely with Carrie, claiming "there's a little bit of Carrie White in me" ("An Evening with Stephen King" 16) and that he felt she was "justified [in her actions] because she had been driven mad by all the teasing" (Grant, "Interview" 86). In his book on horror, *Danse Macabre*, King stated that, in his opinion, *Carrie*'s popularity as both novel and film could be attributed to the fact that "Carrie's revenge is something that any student who ever had his gym shorts pulled down in Phys Ed or his glasses thumb-rubbed in study hall could approve of. In Carrie's destruction of the gym ... we see a dream revolution of the socially downtrodden" (174). However, two similar but disparate incidents of school-violence seemed to have changed King's opinion of his characterization of Carrie.

On December 1, 1997, Michael Carneal concealed three guns on his person and took them with him to school at Heath High in West Paducah, Kentucky. He opened fire in a student prayer group, killing three and injuring five, and then immediately surrendered. During the investigation of the shooting, law enforcement found a copy of King's 1977 novel *Rage* written under the pseudonym Richard Bachman in Carneal's school locker. *Rage* was a novel similar to *Carrie*, but without the supernatural overtones, focusing on Charlie Decker, a high school senior who murders his algebra teacher and holds the rest of his classmates hostage at gunpoint.[1] While most of Carneal's friends and family stated that his primary motivation for his actions was bullying (he had been humiliated when a gossip column in the school newspaper insinuated that he was gay and stated in a school essay the he felt other students at the school "mocked and slaughtered my self-esteem" [Glaberson A17]), some suggested the novel had, at least, inspired Carneal to carry out his rampage.[2] Then on April 20, 1999, Eric

Harris and Dylan Klebold murdered a total of twelve students and one teacher (and injured twenty-four other students) at Columbine High School in Columbine, Colorado, becoming the deadliest school shooting in American history.

Although his work was not cited as a source of inspiration for Harris and Klebold in the same way it was for Carneal, King seemed to take the Columbine shooting much closer to heart and his view of Carrie White as a character seems to have been colored by his perceptions after that incident. In his memoir *On Writing*, published in 2000, one year after the Columbine shootings, King makes several comments about his characterization of Carrie that are seemingly at odds with his earlier statements. While discussing the genesis of the writing of Carrie, he claims that "I didn't much like the lead character. Carrie White seemed thick and passive, a ready-made victim.... I just didn't care" (76). He repeats twice more in subsequent pages that "I never liked Carrie" (77, 82) and refers to her directly as a "female version of Eric Harris and Dylan Klebold" (82), darkening Carrie's motivation and actions by comparing them directly with those of the Columbine shooters. His earlier claims of Carrie's "justified" actions and "dream revolution of the socially downtrodden" are forgotten, allowing her to lumped with the real-life mentally-ill mass murderers of innocent young people. Instead of claiming that he identified with her directly as he had in earlier interviews ("An Evening with Stephen King" 16), now he says simply that he "pitied her" (*On Writing* 82), but that he actually aligns himself more with her classmates "because I had been one of them once upon a time" (Ibid).

In 1976, many years before the recent spate of mass shootings, a time when King still viewed Carrie White in a much more sympathetic light, Brian De Palma released his cinematic vision of Carrie's story. The most immediately obvious change between King's novel and De Palma's film is Carrie's appearance. Instead of the overweight, pimply teenage girl of King's novel, De Palma's Carrie (Sissy Spacek) is skinny and pale with stringy hair. She is plain, but not unattractive. Her physical looks do not really set her apart from the other girls in her peer group. But her physical characteristics do: downward cast eyes, stuttering speech, conservative plain clothing. De Palma begins his film differently than King begins the novel. Carrie's status as an outsider and victim of bullying are established immediately in the opening scene, a volleyball game in the girls' gymnasium, which does not appear in King's original text. She is withdrawn and desperately trying not to draw attention to herself. Her hair hangs in her face, and she stands in the corner with her eyes cast down. When the ball is hit to her and she misses it, costing her team the game, she is immediately ridiculed by the other girls who push violently past her as they enter the locker room. One girl, Norma (P.J. Soles), even hits her in the face with her baseball cap.

During the shower scene itself, she is even further isolated by the camera. All of the other girls are shown in frame together, a large and cohesive group, while Carrie is framed completely alone. This framing mechanism becomes almost threatening as the scene progresses as Carrie emerges from the shower, small and frightened, believing she is bleeding to death. Instead of getting sympathy from the other girls, she is subjected to even more ridicule that becomes progressively violent when they begin throwing the tampons and sanitary napkins, surrounding her like a pack of animals. The rapidly moving camera and the swift intercuts as well as close-ups of the bullies and long shots of Carrie herself, emphasize the mob mentality at work as well as Carrie's terror and isolation (Warren 110–111). Carrie's victimization at the hands of her tormenters in the shower room, her palpable fear, and her childlike misunderstanding of the cause of her bleeding combine to shift the audience's sympathetic focus to Carrie, especially as subsequent scenes with the school principal (Sydney Lassick) (who cannot even be bothered to remember Carrie's name), her mother (Piper Laurie) (whose mental and physical abuse of Carrie in their first scene together is particularly horrible), and her English teacher (Stefan Gierasch) (who ridicules Carrie for her critique of her classmate Tommy Ross' [William Katt] poem) show that she has no allies—peers and adults alike shun her and treat her with abuse, derision, and indifference. Even Miss Collins (Betty Buckley),[3] the sympathetic gym teacher who saves Carrie from the attack in the showers, admits she was initially disgusted by the sight of Carrie in the showers and understood the other girls' reaction to her.

De Palma also establishes early on Carrie's lack of control over her powers. Her first powerful flashes of ability (the blown lightbulb in the shower room, the principal's ashtray, the boy on the bicycle [Cameron De Palma]) are responses to teasing or indifference and are accompanied by screaming violins.[4] The musical cues and Carrie's reactions suggest that Carrie is just as startled by the incidents as everyone else in the scene is. She us utterly powerless over everything in her life (her family, her social life, her sexuality, and her body and the psychic rage it wields as a powerful defensive force [Newland 6]). Therefore, when prom night comes, De Palma and the audience are much more sympathetic to Carrie. She cannot be held responsible for her actions. In the film, the bullies are the ones truly responsible for everything that occurs. They are the ones who ignite Carrie's explosive fury. Spacek plays up Carrie's lack of control through her trance-like body movements and facial expressions. De Palma's Carrie cannot control her power's destructive momentum once her emotions overcome her (Newland 6). She merely stares outward, and the power surges forth, claiming guilty and innocent alike.

In this respect, the death of Miss Collins is significant. Miss Collins is the one teacher understanding of Carrie's plight. She punishes the other girls for teasing Carrie and seeks to protect her by questioning Sue and Tommy about their motives regarding Tommy's inviting of Carrie to the prom. She even tells Carrie that she is beautiful and advises her on how to wear her hair and what makeup to use to accentuate her features. But she dies just the same during the prom, crushed under the weight of a suspended basketball backboard that drops and seemingly cuts in her in two. The fact that Miss Collins dies despite her efforts to protect Carrie from the bullying both suggests Carrie's lack of control (she indiscriminately kills both those nice to her and those mean to her) and signifies the collateral damage that occurs during such mass murder rampages, the innocent victims whose only seeming crime is being in the wrong place at the wrong time.[5]

When Carrie returns home, she removes the traces of her murderous rampage—her prom dress, her makeup, the pig's blood—and she becomes a child again, searching the house and crying out for her "Momma." But her mother, the woman to whom she should be able to seek for comfort and protection, betrays her, literally stabbing her in the back. This action leads to Carrie's final fall from innocence, symbolized by her tumble down the stairs. After killing her mother by impaling her with various kitchen implements (including butcher knives and a potato peeler) in a manner reminiscent of the cruciform figure of Christ in her prayer closet, Carrie cradles her mother's body in grief. With her mother's death, Carrie has pushed her isolation as far as possible. She has killed everyone who has touched her life, dissolving all social bonds until there are literally no groups left. At that moment the final disaster strikes: the house itself, a continuing image of security for Carrie, disintegrates (Collings 38–39), collapses in on itself, crushing her. The house collapse is significant because it, again, shows Carrie's lack of control over her abilities. Here, the telekinesis seems to respond directly to Carrie's misery and, no doubt, suicidal thoughts and merely responds in kind by destroying the house. Carrie dies as she lived, a victim of powers beyond her control.

By 2013, when Kimberly Peirce released her own vision of Carrie's story, reports of mass school killings, such as Columbine, Virginia Tech, and Sandy Hook, were well-documented national tragedies. Peirce was very cautious about the material:

> It was vital to me in light of all of [the real-life tragedies such as Sandy Hook and Columbine] that this was a superhero-origin story. Carrie was discovering her powers as the movie went along and she never had mastery of them. And when those powers come out, she's not in control of them, and she immediately starts looking for the culprits. And that's really important because I knew that we needed a sense of justice and a sense of good old-fashioned revenge [Enk 6].
>
> I wanted to make sure she doesn't have actual control ... because I thought that if she had actual control, then she could be more liable for what she does at the prom. And I think in a post–Columbine world, it was really essential that it was something she was figuring out [Raynaldy 13].

However, if such was truly Peirce's intention, it must be said that she fails at the execution of her concept. Unlike De Palma's Carrie, Peirce's Carrie (Chloe Grace Moretz) is shown in complete control of her powers prior to the prom massacre. Peirce includes two scenes (neither of which appears in De Palma's film) which show her in total control. The first is the scene in her bedroom where Carrie flexes her power to levitate first books and then her bed. Here Carrie musters easy control over the power, only losing concentration when she fears discovery by her mother (Julianne Moore). Later, when she finally confronts her mother and reveals her power to her, she is easily able to grab her mother in a telekinetic grip and lift her off the floor. She revels in her newfound power, slyly smiling when she is able to move the flag outside her class window just by thinking about it. That she is able to gain command of her powers so early in the story changes the meaning of the film dramatically compared with the earlier versions. Instead of a story that attempts to coax the audience to empathize with its weak and pitiful main character, only to have them root with horror at her actions at the story's end, here we get something more akin to an empowerment story, a tale of a bullied girl who is suddenly gifted with a terrible weapon with which to obtain her revenge on those who tormented her (Turner 5).

The prom sequence begins in Peirce's film almost identically to De Palma's film, with many lines of dialogue transferred verbatim from one film to the other. However, when Tommy (Ansel Elgort) and Carrie are voted prom king and queen and take their place on the stage and Chris (Portia Doubleday) and Billy (Alex Russell) dump the pig's blood onto Carrie, the sequence of events change abruptly, transforming the final elements of Carrie's narrative from one of a sympathetic victim of circumstance inadvertently unleashing her fury to one of a tormented girl wielding her dark weapon of destruction on those she blames for her victimization. It is a fine line, but one that clearly shows the change in attitude within America in the post–Columbine era when the bullied who seek deadly retribution are seen by the media and the general populace as every bit the monster the bullies themselves are. Peirce, in an effort to pull her version of Carrie back from the precipice of monsterdom and back into more sympathetic territory, does attempt to justify Carrie's actions by suggesting that the impetus for Carrie's murderous rage is not her degradation over the pig's blood and the broadcast of the video of her humiliating moments in the girls' shower, but is instead Tommy's death caused by the bucket containing the pig's blood falling from the rafters and striking him on the head. For Peirce's Carrie, knowing the innocent boy who treated her like an equal at the detriment to his own popularity was senselessly killed by the bullies who sought to play one final horrible trick on her sends her over the edge, especially because in her mind everyone is laughing about the tragic situation. It is for this reason she truly decides to punish them all (Shultz 35).

But Carrie's vengeance represents the ultimate overkill. Unlike De Palma's version of the prom massacre, in which Spacek appears to be in a trance and does little to indicate conscious manipulation of her power, Peirce's film shows that Carrie is one hundred percent conscious of what she is doing and in complete control. Moretz uses physical movements and facial expressions to indicate that she is moving objects with deliberate intent and with an ecstatic bloodlust. The visual dichotomy between the fragile and helpless girl in the shower video playing on the screen surrounding Carrie and the vicious and powerful girl on the stage gleefully raining death and destruction down on the heads of her tormentors reveals the post–Columbine message of the film with perfect clarity: This is what happens when a bullying victim is pushed too far, a sharp warning to bullies that the easy target of their "harmless" hazing just might snap and come back seeking bloody vengeance (Shultz 48; Sodaro 6). While it appears she primarily targets specific individuals who were involved in the bullying (such as Tina [Zoe Belkin], Nicki [Karissa Strain], and Lizzy [Katie Strain]), she does endanger many of her classmates who were never involved in the bullying and other individuals who are clearly shown being nice to her (such as Tommy's friend George [Demetrius Joyette] and his date Erika [Mouna Traore][6], The only person Carrie consciously saves is Miss Desjardin (Judy Greer), whom she grabs in a telekinetic choke-hold and throws onto the stage and off the water-soaked floor before releasing the power cables to electrocute everyone.

Carrie's rescue of Miss Desjardin again demonstrates her control over herself and her powers throughout the prom scene. She has the presence of mind to save the one person who has been kind to her and attempted to protect her from the bullies, and she knows full well what she intends to do (drop live electrical power cords into the water on the floor of the gymnasium) and what the consequences of that action would be (the death of everyone touching the floor at that moment). But Carrie clearly cares nothing about any of the prom-goers at this point (beyond Miss Desjardin) and murders them all without any hesitation, cementing her status within the film as monster rather than sympathetic victim.[7]

The most crucial scene that truly cements the difference between the two films in relation to their stance on Carrie's status as victim or monster is the death of Chris and Billy in the car crash. In De Palma's film, Carrie is walking down the street from the school to her home when Chris (Nancy Allen) and Billy (John Travolta) approach her from behind. Billy clearly intends to run Carrie down with his car and speeds up as he gets closer to her. Suddenly, as he is about to strike her, Carrie becomes aware of the car's presence and turns her head towards it. She forces the car to swerve away from her, causing the car to flip and explode in a ball of flame, killing Chris and Billy. However, since Billy was clearly attempting to murder Carrie, a claim could be made that Carrie's actions in the scene were justified, a moment of self-preservation. The same cannot be said for Carrie's actions in the same scene from Peirce's film. Although Billy deliberately tries to run Carrie down with his car in the scene, he does so because she is standing in the roadway before them, facing the car rather than walking away from it.[8] Instead of causing the car to swerve and flip as in the original film, Carrie releases a wall of telekinetic force in front of herself just before the car reaches her, causing the car to smash and critically injuring (or possibly killing) Billy in the process. Chris survives the crash and attempts to escape the vehicle. Even though the car is disabled, Carrie remains and uses her power to lift the car into the air. She locks eyes with Chris for a moment, and the look in her eyes is pure evil. She then uses her power to throw the car into the gas pumps of a nearby gas station, forcing Chris face-first through the windshield. The impact does not kill Chris, and Carrie continues to stare at her for a moment and then turns to walk away, simultaneously using a nearby sparking power cable to ignite the gasoline and blowing up the car and the gas station. As in the scene of the prom massacre, Carrie's actions in this scene are calculated and completely in control. Rather than reacting in pure self-defense as Carrie did in De Palma's film, she takes steps to ensure that Chris, her primary tormentor, suffers before killing her in a deliberate and cold-blooded fashion. This Carrie is not the innocent girl undergoing a psychotic break which causes her to lose control. Here, Carrie is a monster of pure vengeance raining down destruction on those she believes deserve death for their treatment of her.

Carrie's monstrous actions in Peirce's 2013 film clearly align her with the dark evil of the real-life mass murderers who have focused their rage against others they believed belittled and bullied them their whole lives. Young men like Eric Harris, Dylan Klebold, and Elliot Rodger were, seemingly at times, victims of horrible cruelty and persecution. But did the acts perpetrated on them justify murder? Even if the ones they had murdered were the individuals responsible for the cruelty? Perhaps at one time, when King's novel and De Palma's film were released, such vengeance would have been seen as justified. Now, in the post–Columbine age, with real victims (in some cases, as in Sandy Hook, child victims) with real families and potential futures cut short seen daily in the media, that vengeance seems excessive and unjustified (especially when innocent victims are involved, which is frequently the case in such situations). While Peirce's intent may have been to create "a culprit narrative in which justice is clearly being served" (Russo 6), the truth is in this day and age, audience are no longer able to separate the fantasy they see on the screen from the daily reality going on around them. Carrie White and her real-life counterparts truly "burn in hell" from what their actions have wrought, and the shocking final image of a shattering tombstone in Peirce's film reveals a truth terrifying to conceive. Until the bullying ends, the tormented will never truly rest until they have their tragic vengeance, punishing the innocent and guilty alike for their pain.

Notes

1. The primary difference between *Carrie* and *Rage* lies in the protagonist's motivation. While Carrie is clearly motivated by the bullying she endured to lash out, Charlie's justification for his actions is much murkier, with Charlie himself admitting that he does not understand what has compelled him to commit the murder (Bachman 38).
2. After the West Paducah shooting, King requested to his publisher that *Rage* be allowed to fall out of print to avoid "inspiring" any further incidents of school-related violence. The publisher agreed. *Rage* is King's only novel to have gone out of print.
3. De Palma changes this character's name from Miss Desjardin, as it appears in the novel and in Peirce's 2013 film version, to Miss Collins. No explanation has ever been given as to the reason for the change.
4. The screaming violins are an homage to Bernard Herrmann's score of Alfred Hitchcock's *Psycho* (1960), as is the name of the school, Bates High.

5. Such "collateral damage" is seen frequently in mass killings by individuals who are seeking retribution for some alleged bullying or other mistreatment. Despite Eric Harris' claim that the Columbine shooting was his "revenge on people for mistreating him" (Langman 7), he did not just shoot the "white hats" (the school athletes who wore white baseball caps to indicate their status), whom he blamed for the bullying, but other students as well. In fact, "none of the people he shot had ever bullied him" (Ibid.). Likewise, Elliot Rodger's rampage through the streets of Isla Vista in May 2014, motivated by Rodger's frustration in being rejected by women, resulted in the deaths of six people, only two of which were women, neither of whom, it appeared, had ever had any contact with Rodger prior to the shooting (Alcindor 14).

6. Although the exchange between Carrie and Erika is extremely brief (only a few lines are exchanged between the two), film scholar Cynthia Fuchs believes the scene between the two is one of the most crucial to the film because it suggests "what Carrie's life might have been like had she lived among peers who hadn't abused her for years" (1). It gives Carrie a glimpse into that other life, one that is almost immediately snatched away in subsequent events. This may be why we in the audience never learn the fates of George or Erika. Carrie, in her madness, may have killed them along with the rest because Erika dared to give Carrie hope even for that brief period and, for Carrie, that moment of hope is the cruelest element of the final trick played on her (Fuchs 8).

7. This monstrous status is further intensified in a very brief throwaway moment in the film when Carrie is leaving the high school after setting fire to the gym with her classmates still inside. In keeping with King's original novel (154–155), Carrie sabotages the various fire hydrants nearby (causing them to explode rather than merely unscrewing the lug nuts as she did in the novel) in a blatant attempt to delay firefighters from putting out the fires and potentially saving lives. It is a calculated act of coldness and cruelty that further removes Carrie from sympathetic status.

8. A brief moment earlier in the scene suggests that Carrie is following Chris and Billy, no doubt in order to kill them for what they did to her at the prom.

WORKS CITED

Alcindor, Yamiche. "Victims of Santa Barbara Rampage Mourned." *USA Today Online* (May 26, 2014). http://www.usatoday.com/story/news/nation/2014/05/25/victims-of-santa-barbara-killings/9567357/.
Bachman, Richard (Stephen King). *Rage*. In *The Bachman Books*, by Stephen King. New York: Signet, 1996. 1–111.
Carrie (1976). Dir. Brian De Palma. Wr. Lawrence D. Cohen. Perf. Sissy Spacek, Piper Laurie, Nancy Allen, and Amy Irving. Beverly Hills: MGM Home Entertainment, 2004.
Carrie (2013). Dir. Kimberly Peirce. Wr. Lawrence D. Cohen and Roberto Aguirre-Sacasa. Perf. Chloe Grace Moretz, Julianne Moore, Portia Doubleday, and Gabriella Wilde. Beverly Hills: MGM Home Entertainment, 2014.
Collings, Michael R. *The Films of Stephen King*. Mercer Island, WA: Starmont House, 1986.
Enk, Bryan. "Did *Carrie* Do Enough to Separate Fantasy from Recent Tragedies?" *Yahoo! Movie Talk* (October 18, 2013). http://movies,yahoo.com/blogs/movie-talk/carrie-director-faced-challenge-separating-fantasy-recent-tragedies-003846836.html.
"An Evening with Stephen King at the Billerica, Massachusetts Public Library." *Bare Bones: Conversations on Terror with Stephen King*. Eds. Tim Underwood and Chuck Miller. New York: McGraw-Hill, 1988. 1–24.
Fuchs, Cynthia. "Carrie's Mother Loves Her, and So Proceeds to Save Her by Destroying Her, Slowly." *PopMatters* (October 18, 2013). http://www.popmatters.com/review/175942-carrie-high-school-hell-again.

Glaberson, William. "Finding Futility in Trying to Lay Blame in Killings." *New York Times* (August 4, 2000). A17.
Grant, Charles L. "Interview with Stephen King." *Bare Bones: Conversations on Terror with Stephen King.* Eds. Tim Underwood and Chuck Miller. New York: McGraw-Hill, 1988. 79–88.
King, Stephen. *Carrie.* New York: Doubleday, 1974.
_____. *Danse Macabre.* New York: Berkley, 1981.
_____. *On Writing: A Memoir of the Craft.* New York: Scribner, 2000.
Langman, Peter. "Columbine, Bullying, and the Mind of Eric Harris." *Psychology Today Online* (May 20, 2009). http://www.psychologytoday.com/blog/keeping-kids-safe/ 200905/columbine-bullying-and-the-mind-eric-harris.
Newland, Christina. "Screen Women: Brian De Palma's *Carrie.*" *Kubrick on the Guillotine* (September 20, 2013). http://kubrickontheguillotine.com/2013/09/20/ screen-women-brian-de-palmas-carrie/#comments.
Raynaldy, Romain. "*Carrie* Updated to Troubled America." *Rappler* (October 18, 2013). http://www.rapler.com/entertainment/movies/41645-carrie-2013-remake-kimberly-peirce.
Russo, Tom. "Why Remake *Carrie?*" *Boston Globe Online* (October 12, 2013). http://www.bostonglobe.com/arts/movies/2013/10/12/why-remake-carrie/ wRo78WImtEcKfUyRQaCmeN/story.html.
Turner, Kyle. "The Cruelty of Growing Up: *Carrie.*" *The Movie Scene* (November 8, 2013). http://moviescene.wordpress.com/2013/10/22/the-cruelty-of-growing-up-carrie/.
Warren, Bill. "The Movies and Mr. King." *Fear Itself: The Horror Fiction of Stephen King.* Eds. Tim Underwood and Chuck Miller. San Francisco: Underwood-Miller, 1982. 105–128.

Dauntless Bullying in Veronica Roth's *Divergent*

Katherine Lashley

Permeating the dystopian novel *Divergent* by Veronica Roth is a large amount of bullying and violence. The bullying is present in order to reflect back to readers their own potential situations and to recognize the damaging effects of bullying. *Divergent*, the first novel of the *Divergent* trilogy, recounts how the young woman, Tris, leaves her faction of Abnegation (which focuses on gentleness) and joins the Dauntless faction—the toughest people in the *Divergent* world and among the factions. The *Divergent* world is divided into five factions—Abnegation, Dauntless, Amity, Candor, and Erudite. In the Dauntless faction, Tris and the other initiates learn how to fight, throw knives, shoot guns, and strategize in battle. The tough, war-like culture of Dauntless fosters bullying that runs rampant as Peter and other initiates bully Tris several times and as another young male, Al (one of Tris's friends and also an initiate) also experiences the effects of bullying and is driven to suicide. Although *Divergent* is a dystopia, set in a post-collapse city where the government and social structures have changed, the bullying described throughout this first book indicate that dominant power structures and stereotypes of gender and sexuality still exist, and that for the characters, the key issue they must deal with is the age-old problem of bullying and violence.

Bullying in School

A number of young adult dystopias are set within various radically charged political and social structures, yet *Divergent* is set mostly in the Dauntless faction and compound which closely mirrors a school. Roberta

Seelinger Trites observes that "school settings exist in adolescent literature to socialize teenagers into accepting the inevitable power social institutions have over individuals in every aspect of their lives" (Trites 33). Indeed, the setting of a school establishes for the protagonists and readers who exactly holds power and what ideologies they must accept, what ideologies they can challenge and possibly alter. Dominant ideologies that are reinforced throughout *Divergent* include social power structures and compulsory heterosexuality. However, the social power that one may not expect *Divergent* to address is bullying, yet this first novel of *Divergent* especially engages in representations, causes, and effects of bullying that reinforce dominant patriarchal and heterosexual messages concerning gender, sex, and sexuality.

As much of the novel takes place in a school-like setting, the bullies echo the situations found in a school, particularly the group mentality. In schools there are both aggressive bullies and passive bullies, as described by Carol Hillsberg and Helene Spak:

> an aggressive bully is usually described as someone who is unable to deal with frustration. These individuals appear to be more inclined toward violence and belligerence than other children in the same age group. Passive bullies are those who team up with an aggressive bully but rarely instigate violence or intimidation themselves. Instead, a passive bully will participate in aggression toward weaker children, but he or she will continue to remain a follower of the more assertive bully [24].

Divergent has both kinds of bullies present within Dauntless: Eric and Peter are examples of aggressive bullies, while others such as Al and Molly are examples of passive bullies because they support Peter, allowing him to engage in aggressive, straight-forward acts of bullying while they watch and laugh. The several people supporting Peter in his bullying automatically form a group and soon become feared by Tris because she does not want to be caught alone and defenseless against them. The group mentality overpowers isolation and singularity because the single, sole person is unable to defend against the group of bullies, as evidenced in two key scenes with Tris and Peter's group. *Divergent* shows that the aggressive and passive bullies come together to form strong, formidable groups that will practice bullying by targeting Tris who is small and who is still constructing her gender and sexuality.

Bullying also occurs where there is an audience, because the bully desires others to witness how powerful he is and that he can dominate others. "Bullying seldom occurs in complete isolation, because the bully likes an audience for his/her exploits of intimidation" (Esch 380). This is shown repeatedly in *Divergent* when Peter taunts and harms Tris. Peter certainly illustrates the practice of isolation versus an audience and group when he taunts Tris when his friends are with him. He never bullies her when he is alone, but rather when he does have an audience. Often he is the primary bully, but occasionally his friends aid him in bullying her as well, such as the time when Peter has several of the other boys, including Tris's friend, Al, help him kidnap her, pick her up, and attempt to throw her into the chasm where she would surely die. Even though the degree in which the other teenagers will observe or participate in the bullying varies, the use of an audience contributes to the influence and power that the bully gains.

Gender and Sexuality

Bullying is traditionally viewed as a masculine act as the bully dominates the weak; as such, when masculinity is favored over femininity, bullying becomes pervasive, as is seen in the Dauntless faction. Jessie Klein reports that "in many studies, authors show that environments that value hypermasculinity—for instance, fraternities and male sports teams (especially football)—tend to breed inequalities that lead to violence against girls" (76). The Dauntless faction highlights male brutality and actions through the fighting and training that the transfers undergo. Tris and the other initiates learn the movements of combat individually, then they are paired up and must fight each other. The winner of the fight receives higher scores than the losers; and the initiates with the highest scores can become Dauntless members—those who do not score high enough become factionless, which means that they would no longer be in the Dauntless faction. In addition to making full use of their bodies in hand to hand combat, they also learn how to throw knives and how to use firearms. After some substantial training, they use paint guns and play capture the flag. For some young people, such a game with paint pellets may be considered fun and lighthearted, and they may not care who wins. However, in Dauntless, this capture-the-flag game simulates an actual battle as the initiates take it seriously despite there being no prize. One of the initiates asks what the prize is—what is the incentive to win. The Dauntless leaders and trainers, Eric and Four, answer that there is no tangible prize—only the pride of claiming victory. In a hypermasculine culture, the ability to claim victory is more than enough to satisfy as a prize because it would indicate that the victors—both male and female—have the drive, courage, and strength to overpower the weaker team. The privileging of masculinity automatically demeans femininity and anything else that is less than ubermasculine, including the feminine gender, female sexuality, and effeminate males.

A primary issue for young women—preteens and teenagers—is the balance between femininity and masculinity. Young women also experience objectification of their bodies as others will discuss and touch their bodies: forcing these young women to determine how they will perceive their femaleness and sexuality. Peter and his friends—both male and female—immediately begin making derogatory comments about Tris's body from the moment she enters the Dauntless faction. Klein observes that "in many environments, adults and students alike seem to assume that a girl's appearance—the way she dresses, her body type, or anything that makes her look 'different'—is fair game for commentary. The harassment isn't always explicitly sexual—any mention about a girl's appearance and body can be said to demonstrate dominance" (69). The young people in Dauntless comment and harass Tris on her body and her appearance. When Tris takes off her jacket before jumping off the edge of the building in order to enter the Dauntless compound, Peter and some of the boys joke by giving her conflicting directions: to take off her clothes or to keep them on. When she changes her clothing in the co-ed dorm, they tease her about seeing her body. The strongest indication of this harassment comes one day after Tris has taken a shower: in the bathroom, she begins to dress when she realizes that her trousers are so tight that she actually cannot fit into them. In order to get fully dressed, she enters the dorm to get more of her clothing, covering herself with her towel. In the dorm, she is surrounded by Peter and his friends who snag the towel away from her, revealing her bare bottom, and laughing as they see her scurry back into the bathroom, naked and mortified. They know that they have been successful in their jeering because she tries to escape from them and their bullying.

Another incident that traumatizes Tris occurs when Peter, his friends, and even Al (Tris's friend) kidnap her at night and try to throw her over the chasm, where she would surely die from hitting the rocks and rough water below. While Peter's goal is to physically eliminate her from Dauntless, before he does so, he has some fun with her by feeling her body, squeezing her breasts, and announcing to the other boys that he "found something." Although Tris is frightened of being beaten and possibly killed, she recognizes the sexual teasing and violation and feels humiliated that he has touched her without her consent. This scene conveys how abuse can influence a woman's perception of her body as Peter displays dominance over her body whereas she does not have the power to overcome him. This event, too, affects how she interacts later with Four: because one man already dominated her body physically and sexually, she fears allowing another man to do the same, even when she would give Four permission to touch her and even if she believes that she would be willing. She must come to terms with the feelings of dominance and submissiveness and understand for herself how she would perceive of her own body and how she would allow men, particularly her boyfriend Four, to treat her body.

Young women are expected to be feminine in their appearance and interactions with the opposite sex, yet they are also expected to put on masculinity as they establish their place in a school setting. Although Tris is in Dauntless and does everything she can to be tough so she can fit in with the faction, she also realizes that in order to be dauntless in a romantic relationship—to be daring as a woman in her body and sexuality—she must also be feminine. "Girls are in a new double bind. They are expected to be 'feminine'—demure and attracted and attractive to boys—but also 'masculine,' as the larger bully society demands—tough, hyperaggresive, excessively self-reliant, and able to fight for themselves if it comes to that" (98). Girls are expected to exert both feminine and masculine traits—a possibility, but one that can also lead to confusion and more bullying as she searches how best to go about acting feminine and displaying her masculinity.

Tris at first acts weaker and submissive when she is with Four, especially throughout the first novel. Her timidity with Four is due partly to being bullied by Peter and by witnessing the bullying actions that Four displays toward others. When Tris sees Four and how he treats the initiates, she perceives that he, too, has the potential to be a bully and a danger to her. Consequently, she at first distances herself from him. Yet as her instructor, he occasionally talks to her and he shows her the proper form for throwing punches, throwing knives, and firing guns. She sees him hold a loaded gun to Peter's head because Peter spoke out of turn; she witnesses as he threatens Christina if she speaks out of turn again; she sees him beat up the guys who kidnap her. Even though he appears to be gentler to her (she quickly enough believes that he likes her, so she develops a crush on him) she is still wary of him, his body, and his mind because she has seen his brutal and powerful side. One of the two most defining moments for Tris in terms of establishing Four's brutality comes when he throws knives at the target around her: she volunteers to take Al's place and so she must stand in front of the target unflinchingly as Four throws several knives at her. She believes that he will not miss or hurt her, yet the last knife nicks her ear, drawing blood, and Four admits that he cut her on purpose, supposedly in order to help her defiance and bravery impress Eric who is one of the few people who has the power to tell her stay or leave Dauntless.

The other most telling incident that causes Tris to be timid and uncertain of Four is her encounter with him in her fear landscape, which is a hallucination and test that imitates her fears. Her goal is to overcome her fears, and one of her fears includes being afraid of intimacy with a man, particularly Four. While she easily tells the imaginary Four that she refuses to have sex with him in a simulation, when she faces him in real life, she feels embarrassed to admit that she is afraid of him and what he could do to her. Even in her fear simulation, she reflects, "My fear is being with him. I have been wary of affection all my life.... This is the fear I have no solutions for—a boy I like, who wants to ... have sex with me?" (Roth 393). David Thompson observes that "students who did not fear bullying were more satisfied with life, had higher self-esteem, had greater feelings of personal control, felt fit, [and were] confident with the opposite sex" (72). Because Tris has experienced bullying directly from Peter and Al and indirectly from Four, she is not as confident as she desires to be with Four and with the opposite sex. She recognizes that this is one of the results from the bullying and intimidation she has experienced. Although she manages to overcome her fear of Four rather quickly by telling herself that she will be strong—dauntless—in her relationship with him, a reader may recognize that such a drastic change in action and attitude may not be possible for other young women as it may take longer for them to gain confidence with those of the opposite sex.

Tris gaining confidence in her gender and sexuality is a large part of her identity. Balaka Basu observes about the kidnapping scene and Tris's reactions to it that Tris is actually more concerned with her identity than with being harmed again by Peter and the others. Indeed, Tris is more preoccupied with her identity because her identity—as a faction member and an individual in general—includes her embodiment and portrayal of gender and sexuality. She must discover for herself what combination of gender traits and sexual actions she will promote within herself. She knows that once she determines and enacts her gender and sexuality, then she will be more confident in herself because she will know who and what she is, thereby disallowing others—especially the males—to decide for her.

As bullying for many young people is based on gender and sexuality, so too does it enter into romantic relationships, especially as the male and female counterparts determine how they will respond to each other and to those outside of their relationship. Jessie Klein writes about men and how they perceive their role in a romantic relationship: "Normalized masculinity encourages men to dominate women, to compete for particular women, and to 'protect' women who are perceived as 'belonging' to a particular man. Men are taught to perceive such challenges as threats to their sexual adequacy and then to restore their manhood with violence" (62). Four exhibits such domination and violence when he sees Peter and his friends bullying Tris by attempting to hang her over the chasm. Instead of simply fending them off and rescuing Tris, Four inflicts so much pain on them that he has to take one to the hospital before he returns and addresses Tris. He feels the need to protect her so strongly that he must severely injure the boys in order to prove to them that there is a man who cares about Tris and who has dominance and power over them. He uses his masculinity to claim his control over Tris, thereby removing their control over her.

Gay Bashing

Another kind of bullying related to gender and sexuality is based on same-sex sexualities, or seeming "gay." A young person may be bullied for being gay, though students—bullies, onlookers, and victims—clarify that "gay" does not necessarily mean that the victim is gay or claiming a different sexuality other than heterosexuality; rather "gay" and other terms related to gay bashing will be used for someone who seems different for any reason. Nevertheless, the term "gay bashing" certainly indicates that the taunting is pointed toward those who are not heterosexual. Klein describes gay bashing as including

> abuse against people who identify themselves as gay; it can also involve any abuse that is based upon its victims' perceived lack of hypermasculine qualities.... The perpetrators responded by picking up guns to prove their manhood using a time-honored method—extreme violence [Klein 82].

In a number of situations, it can be easy to classify the bullying as gay bashing; however, in other instances, it may be not as easy to label. In *Divergent*, there may not appear to be any gay bashing or anyone suffering from gay bashing, yet Al is an example of this kind of victimization. Tris describes Al as large and gentle: he dislikes fighting, and although he could easily overpower anyone who scrimmages against him, after he knocks out the first person, he feels so guilty that he then allows his opponents to overpower him. Then he lies on the floor and pretends to be knocked unconscious. While this logic works for Al and his friends, upon further examination, one can deduce that the Dauntless leader, Eric—one of the toughest men in the faction—knows exactly what Al is doing, yet in fact he does not stop him nor even bully him for it. Rather, Eric allows this situation of Al's gentleness and the Dauntless faction's brutality to play against each other, wearing down Al in his resolve to be gentle while being surrounded by so many vicious people.

An incident that solidifies Al's apathy and effeminacy occurs when he and the other Dauntless initiates are practicing throwing knives: everyone except Al is hitting the target. Eric tells Al to stand in front of the target and that Four would through knives at the target around him: if Al flinches, then he is out of Dauntless. Tris speaks up, asserting that anyone could stand in front of a target; and it is this verbal defense for him that leads into one of her bravest physical defenses for him: Eric tells her to take Al's place in front of the target as Four launches knives at her. She does so, proving, ultimately, that she has more masculinity in her than Al has in himself, and this knowledge is bitter as Al believes if a small girl like Tris can be hypermasculine, then there must be something wrong with him since he is a large male. Adding on to this, in another scene, although Tris does not overtly bully Al, she does reject him when he makes it clear to her that he likes her: he leans in to her, hoping to kiss her, yet she pulls away. She anticipates that her purposely putting distance between them will communicate to him that she does not like him in a romantic or sexual way, and she is pleased at her success, because she can tell that he has understood her message. Although Tris's reaction is not a bullying behavior, it does undermine Al's masculinity and it highlights to him his lack of masculine traits.

Thus, Al's ego is shattered as he recognizes that he lacks the masculinity necessary to make him an effective Dauntless male: he dislikes fighting, he lets Tris defend him, and he lets Tris reject him sexually. Thus, Al, whether or not he is gay, certainly feels the pressure to demonstrate his masculinity and "manhood using a time-honored method—extreme violence" (Klein 82). The violence he carries out is in conjunction with Peter who encourages Al to join him and the others in kidnapping Tris and hurting her. Peter, too, has observed that Al suffers from gendered stereotypes and so takes advantage by persuading Al that the way to demonstrate his masculinity is through violence. Klein writes about the results of gay bashing, a lack of hypermasculinity, and the need to prove masculinity in the teenage boys who have gone on shooting sprees in high schools and colleges (Columbine and Virginia Tech). Klein notes that in addition to the extreme violence used to establish their manhood and masculinity, many of the shooters also take their own lives. Al does the same as, several days later, he is found in the chasm, and it becomes clear to everyone that he committed suicide. David Thompson, Tiny Arora, and Sonia Sharp note that "bullying has been linked with low self-esteem, anxiety, impaired concentration, truancy, depression and suicidal thoughts" (71). Al certainly exemplifies these effects of bullying by having low self-esteem, anxiety, and suicidal thoughts. In a fixed message about gender and sexuality: because Tris overpowered him and escaped the attempted kidnapping and death that he participated in at the chasm, he throws himself into the chasm, because he lacks the male qualities he needs in order to be a man.

Reacting to Bullying

There are several reactions that a victim of bullying can take: one of which includes actually agreeing with the tormentor and not fighting back. The day after Peter and Al have kidnapped and beat up Tris, Four tells Tris to keep her head low and to pretend that they have hurt her and that she is scared of them. Esch observes that "one strategy that can be helpful in counteracting taunts is to 'agree' with the tormentor" (381). By agreeing with the tormentor, the bully may not know how to respond because usually they expect someone to be defensive. Indeed, Tris wants to be defensive and even to continue the struggle in order to prove that she is strong and that they have not defeated her. She dislikes Four's advice, but she takes it anyway, knowing that he is correct about Peter and his friends. She realizes that he will temporarily stop bothering her because he would believe that he had broken her spirit. So she keeps her head down as she walks through the cafeteria; in fact, she then admits to herself that she actually is in pain and that she probably would not have needed to pretend to be sore and defeated because she actually feels so. For Tris, her defeated actions and attitude are a combination of the physical and mental effects of being bullied and nearly dying in the process: she is physically defeated because of the cuts and bruises she has sustained, yet her spirit is also bruised because she must face the fact that two people in her own faction—Peter and Al—would actually harm her. Peter: she would expect him to commit such an act; on the other hand, she never would have imagined that Al would harm her since he was her friend. His kidnapping and beating her indicate to her that she cannot even trust a friend to defend her from bullying.

Another reaction to bullying—fighting back—may appear to be popular, and in some ways throughout *Divergent* it is used and it may even appear to be successful for the victim, yet researchers prove that retaliating is actually harmful. Esch recounts that "*Stop Bullying Now* (n.d.), The Safe Child program, and the American Academy of Child and Adolescent Psychiatry (2001) all concur that fighting or using physical force on a bully will not provide a positive solution for either the victim or the bully" (380). Although Tris keeps her head down and does not pick any more fights immediately following her kidnapping, she does retaliate in other instances. She usually does not strike immediately; instead, she waits for the perfect moment, which for her comes days after the original bullying event. For instance, Molly was one of Peter's friends who teased her about her body. The insults anger her, yet she does not immediately respond. Instead, she waits until the next time they are matched up to fight: this second scrimmage occurs after Molly has taunted Tris even more about her body and her family. With the physical and verbal taunts weighing on her, Tris in her anger retaliates and seriously hurts Molly, who lies on the floor, an image of Tris from before: bruised, bloody, and unconscious. Tris allows this anger and desire for fighting back to so consume her that Four must force her to stop beating Molly in order for Tris to exit from a bloodthirsty, kill or die, mindset.

Tris also fights back much later from the original times of bullying. Near the end of *Divergent*, she shoots Peter in the arm with her gun partly to force him to cooperate with her, but also to indicate to him that she is not as weak as he believes her to be and that she, too, can fight. Indeed, when Peter taunts her, asserting that she would not shoot him, she immediately does, proving to him that she knows how to use a gun and that she will use it, especially against someone who has repeatedly bullied her. Although this tactic works well for her: Peter is weakened due to the bullet and pain in his arm and he therefore helps her, she has issued a very plain, daring challenge to him that will entail that as long as she and Peter are in the same vicinity, she would have to be vigilant. Apparently, for Tris, this is a risk she is willing to take because she desires to establish herself as Dauntless, brave and strong—not someone who will cower at the sight of a bully but will stand up to them. In the process, she anticipates being able to stand strong against Peter and other bullies in order to protect the weak, mainly the Abnegation faction members, because they are weaker than she is and they need someone to fight for them: they need a bully to stand up to a bully.

Conclusion

The majority of the bullying in *Divergent* centers around dominant stereotypes of gender and sexuality, particularly favoring hypermasculinity. The American culture largely favors hypermasculinity and compulsory heterosexuality, resulting in the mixed messages sent to young women about sexualizing their appearance yet performing masculinity in public. The males in school settings are also encouraged to embrace hypermasculinity at any cost—even if it means bullying a friend—in order to establish their dominant gender and sexuality. The results of the various kinds of bullying shown throughout *Divergent* highlight the damages done through a bullying society: isolation, fear, an uncertain identity, and even suicide. Al's suicide is one of the most powerful events in the novel for Tris as she recognizes the impact and causes of his suicide.

In an interview with James Kidd, Veronica Roth states that when she wrote the *Divergent* trilogy, she stayed away from including political messages. If by political messages, she means Democrat versus Republican, then she is correct. However, this first novel of *Divergent* is replete with political and social messages about a bullying, hypermasculine, compulsory heterosexual society: if gender stereotypes and power structures do not change, then bullying will continue, and the results will be devastating as females will have to physically struggle for their gender and sexuality and as males will have to establish their dominance. Although Tris and several of the other characters may be divergent in various areas throughout the novel and trilogy, when it comes to bullying, they are anything but divergent as they succumb to and engage in a bullying society—a dystopia for sure.

Works Cited

Basu, Balaka. "What Faction Are You In? The Pleasure of Being Sorted in Veronica Roth's Divergent." *Contemporary Dystopian Fiction for Young Adults: Brave New Teenagers.* Eds. Balaka Basu, Katherine R. Broad, and Carrie Hintz. New York: Routledge, 2013. Print. 19–34.

Esch, Ginny. "Children's Literature: Perceptions of Bullying." *Childhood Education* 84.6 (2008): 379–382. Web. 8 Sept. 2014.

Hillsberg, Carol, and Helene Spak. "Young Adult Literature as the Centerpiece of an Anti-Bullying Program in Middle School." *Middle School Journal* 2006. Web.

Kidd, James. "'I don't want smut on the page': *Divergent* Author Veronica Roth on Sex and Teen Fiction." *The Independent*. Independent Print Ltd., Jan. 5, 2014. Web. 8 May 2014.
Klein, Jessie. *The Bully Society: School Shootings and the Crisis of Bullying in America's Schools*. New York: New York University Press, 2012. Print.
Roth, Veronica. *Allegiant*. New York: Katherine Tegen Books, 2013. Print.
_____. *Divergent*. New York: Katherine Tegen Books, 2011. Print.
_____. *Insurgent*. New York: Katherine Tegen Books, 2012. Print.
Thompson, David, Tiny Arora, and Sonia Sharp. *Bullying: Effective Strategies for Long-Term Improvement*. New York: Routledge, 2002. Print.
Trites, Roberta Seelinger. *Disturbing the Universe: Power and Repression in Adolescent Literature*. Iowa City: University of Iowa Press, 2000. Print.

The Post–9/11 John Wayne vs. Bullying

A Tale of a Schadenfreude Obsessed Culture

Kelly F. Franklin

The female presence within literature and films has become more powerful, literally and figuratively, within the last seven years; arguably, a response to the post–9/11 John Wayne[1] movement that the nation experienced in the early part of the 21st century. Suzanne Collins has been credited for revolutionizing the female heroine with her iconic, arrow-toting Katniss Everdeen—a character who rises above her post-apocalyptic society, redefines what it means to be female, and eventually wins her dystopia. Katniss gave birth, in a figurative sense, to a new era of female literary characters; young women who took power and wielded it for the good of others and themselves—an honorable notion to be sure. Revolutionary female characters have become so prominent in YAL that it begs the question, reminiscent of Paula Cole's famous song, "Where have all the cowboys gone?"

Naturally, male characters still exist in Young Adult Literature (YAL) only they, like female heroines, have changed as well. Males in YA are now more vulnerable, often outcasts, sensitive, and unsure. Typically, these male characters are supporting players—existing solely to provide backing for the lead female. Characters like Gus and Isaac from *The Fault in our Stars*; Peeta from *The Hunger Games*; and Four from *Divergent*, are integral to the novels they exist within simply because they support the female—a thought provoking and exciting gender role switch. Interestingly, male characters that serve as the central focus of YA novels still face adversity, but in a different sense. Katniss Everdeen and many female heroines are written fighting governmental oppression and traditional female roles. On the opposite side of the coin, audiences witness male heroes who are written to fight an even bigger foe: bullying. The modern John Wayne is no longer saving the day via vigilante justice; instead, male characters are shown surviving and rising above bullying situations, honorably attempting to fix a schadenfreude obsessed culture.

The Absolutely True Diary of a Part-Time Indian, published in 2007 by Sherman Alexie, provides readers with a post–9/11 male character. Though loosely based on his own life, and often considered metafictional, this book features a character who is deemed an Other by both his own culture and another. Bullied by both his own people, and by outsiders, Arnold Spirit, Jr. (Junior) comes of age while being repeatedly ridiculed. Eventually, he overcomes circumstance and behavior, ultimately leaving readers with the feeling that his future success is imminent. The publication of this beloved YA text, and specifically this male character, during the late 2000s is perfectly timed. Junior is the appropriate hero for this new generation of males coming of age in an era where feelings are championed, female characters have taken the reigns to defend/rebuild the world, and public embarrassment and bullying have become modes of entertainment.

The question "What does literature do?" evokes great debate within the English academic community; it challenges readers to make connections with character actions and real life results. The subtle answer to that question, in regard to YAL, is that literature is currently providing male readers of YAL with bullying survivors, in hopes of inspiring real life survivors of bullying with positive role models. Role models who take their experiences and react positively, rather than in detrimental violent behavior. Alexie's central character is a survivor whose struggles with bullying are relatable and realistic. Junior's path, struggles, and metamorphosis are inspiring. However, it is nearly impossible to prove that this text, this character, have changed lives. The notion that a strong fictional character could inspire youth to abstain from bullish behavior in a society rampant with YouTube follies and American Idol Auditions is noble, indeed. Fictional male heroes are winning the war on bullying in YAL, but the transmission of their message appears to be lost on the modern audience they are attempting to educate.

The Absolutely True Diary of a Part-Time Indian

Published in 2007, *The Absolutely True Diary of a Part-Time Indian* is the award winning story of Junior, a Native American boy growing up on a reservation in Washington State (referred to as the Rez throughout the text). Junior is born with a condition known as hydrocephalus, which he refers to as water on the brain. This condition results in him having an abnormally large head and a speech impediment, automatically singling him out as an Other[2] in his own community. Throughout the novel, Junior faces adversity as he deals with his depressed alcoholic parents, bullies on the reservation, and his own personal demons. As a result he becomes quick witted, sarcastic, a talented graphic artists, intelligent, and a star basketball player (an end result that even he did not see coming). In order to have a chance at a promising life outside of the Rez, a chance of a successful life at all, Junior leaves his hometown in order to attend an all–White school in a neighboring community called Reardon where he is still categorized as an Other. Though the book itself does not end in a traditional happy ending, readers come to the conclusion that Junior will lead a content life outside the Rez, and that there is a chance for him. At times violent, physically and verbally, this important YA text is relatable to anyone who has faced adversity. When given the opportunity, Alexie's book can be used to teach important lessons about identity, bullying, acceptance, and kindness.

Despite the fact that Junior and his story can be used as a teaching tool, this novel is often banned. Most recently, in June of 2014, this YA novel was once again challenged by a parent, Frankie Wood. Wood requested, in an official written complaint, that the book be banned from the Cedar Grove Middle School honors program because of "sexual behavior, vulgar language, racism and bullying" (Baird n. pag.). Thankfully, the committee voted to allow the text to remain a part of the program. Principal of Cedar Grove Middle School, Rhonda Benton, replied to Wood after an honors committee meeting discussing the merit of Alexie's text stating that *The Absolutely True Diary of a Part-Time Indian* definitely dealt with troubling matters; however, "the value of the text outweighed these concerns.... As stated by several committee members, the novel is a reflection of the real-life experiences of today's adolescents" (Baird n. pag.). Sadly, there are numerous public schools that do not have the same thoughts about the book as Cedar Grove Middle School, and despite the fact that Junior can serve as a powerful role model, and an example of the post–9/11 male, his story is often silenced.

In 2009, *The Horn Book Magazine* featured a speech given by Alexie, in response to his Fiction and Poetry Award, in which the author discusses in great length the positive effect his book has had on teenagers, as well as the knowledge he gleaned while promoting the novel:

> What I learned from my experience is that pretty much every teenager out there, regardless of class or race or culture or geography, feels pretty dang isolated and pretty dang misunderstood. And more than anything they feel this pressure—by their tribe, whatever their "tribe" is, by their class, by their families—to be a certain something [Alexie 26].

Historically, our society, and many cultures, categorize people and attempts to assign them identities, or as Alexie says mold them into a "certain something." Yet, few people actually fit these molds, which can make adolescence particularly painful. Junior's first day of school at Reardon provides readers with an immediate example of how Junior is seen by himself and society, "They stared at me, the Indian boy ... those white kids couldn't believe their eyes. They stared at me like I was Bigfoot or a UFO. What was I doing in Reardon, whose mascot was an Indian, thereby making me the only other Indian in town" (Alexie 56). When confronted with a real Native American the children at Reardon are somewhat taken aback; Arnold Spirit, Jr., looked nothing like the team mascot, his resemblance to the fighting Reardon savage was non-existent. Junior looked like an average kid from the poor side of town; he just happened to be Indian. Due to the color of his skin and inability to appear as expected, Junior becomes the perfect target for bullies.

In order to navigate the depressed climate of the Rez, as well as the elite atmosphere of his all-white school, Junior is forced to play many roles, explore new identities, reflect on actions/reactions, remain positive in a negative world, and deflect bullying hatred with humor. Alexie's Arnold Spirit, Jr. is awkwardly painful at times, and soul crushing, yet heartwarming:

> I get headaches because my eyes are, like enemies, you know, like they used to be married to each other but now hate each other's guts. And I started wearing glasses when I was three, so I ran around the rez looking like a three-year-old Indian grandpa. And, oh, I was skinny. I'd turn sideways and disappear [Alexie 3].

Junior's humor is his saving grace; it is his defense mechanism which helps him to process the name calling he receives on the Rez and in Reardon. When confronted with opportunities to be violent, Junior does not back down, but that does not mean he fails to feel remorse. Indeed, the words remorseful and reflective describe Junior perfectly. Throughout the text Alexie's central character responds to being bullied by friends, family, and high school students—attempting to understand his situation and behave appropriately. At one point during the novel Junior is bullied at his new school by a young man named Roger; Junior eventually has enough of being harassed and challenges the bully to a fight which results in a confusing exchange of glares, and Junior throwing a punch. Afterwards Junior laments:

> I didn't know what to say, so I just stood there red and mute like a stop sign. Roger and his friends disappeared. I felt like somebody had shoved me into a rocket ship and blasted me to a new planet. I was a freaky alien and there was absolutely no way to get home. I went home that night completely confused. And terrified [Alexie 65–66].

Distraught over his actions, and absolutely worried for his future, Junior talks to his grandmother about what had happened. She explains that he had challenged the Alpha Dog of the school, and that more than likely the bullying would subside now, but Junior is unsure. He nervously returns to school the following day ready for the bullying to continue. However, his grandmother's words prove to be correct. The bully Junior was nervous about confronting him again ends up talking to Junior instead of fighting him, resulting in Junior feeling accepted at Reardon. However, his actions fall short in winning over Penelope, the object of his affection. In fact, the young lady pretends to not know him at all (Alexie 65–67). By providing this exchange, Alexie discounts the vigilante justice that Junior dispenses. He is no hero; he simply is a young man that reacted violently to bullying, and this does not win him the girl. As such, Junior evaluates his actions realizing that violence although at times seemingly justifiable, is not the answer to solving problems.

Schadenfreude and the Entertainment of the Masses

Though deemed comic relief, many moments in the book can be considered self-defacing as Junior draws caricatures of himself; or, at least how he thinks people view him, often represented as a gawky, nerdy, small, unimportant person. As a reader it is difficult not to laugh at the way Junior depicts himself. Of course, this laughter is not meant to be hurtful because the scenes are intended to be humorous. By writing in this manner Alexie is able to subtly bring to the forefront a human characteristic that explains why bullying will undoubtedly never subside—humiliation. The human race is often entertained by the misfortunes and miseries of others, a notion known as Schadenfreude.

Schadenfreude can be defined as "the malicious enjoyment of the misfortunes of others" (Hu n. pag.). Though it sounds especially malevolent, most people experience feelings of Schadenfreude in their own daily lives, but especially while watching television. Producers who seek to entice audiences create TV programs that cater to this human characteristic, particularly reality TV shows. Competition style reality programming typically features try-outs or auditions, where supposedly average people attempt to catapult themselves into stardom. *American Idol*, one of the longest running-reality TV programs, is famous for its auditions. A series that features episodes where young people sing off-tune, dramatically so, judges conceal pained faces, and audiences laugh hysterically at the misfortune of others. Indeed, it has been argued that "humiliation is the unifying principle behind a successful reality show" (Wulf par. 2). The psychology behind this behavior can be explained simply—people want to be better than other people. Witnessing a person fail, in a spectacular way, allows viewers to feel better about themselves and think, "Well, at least I don't sing that badly" or "I would never behave in that way." As such, Schadenfreude ultimately allows people to feel better about themselves because of the embarrassment of others, a notion eerily similar to bullying.

Although modern reality TV is typically credited with transporting Schadenfreude to television programming, its first appearance can be directly linked to a classic and beloved family show: *Candid Camera*. According to John Wulf, "When Alan Funt debuted *Candid Camera* in 1948, the show displayed everyday Americans caught in embarrassing moments. These moments brought laughter to a postwar nation and were an amusing part of entertainment" (par. 1). *Candid Camera* has historically been thought of as good natured, wholesome, and light hearted humor; families would watch this program together and laugh. *America's Funniest Home Video's* is a modern incarnation of Alan Funt's program attempting to make light of embarrassing situations in order to create family entertainment.

Sadly, the majority of reality programming is created to humiliate. In fact, the more humiliating it is the better, and often the more popular among viewers. Families also watch many of these programs together, they laugh together, and witness moments where experts critique amateurs in extremely brash and hurtful methods. Such was the case in Season 6 of *American Idol* auditions when Simon Cowell made hurtful comments in regard to the audition of Kenneth Briggs, a hopeful contender with Aarskog's Syndrome.[3] After watching Briggs perform, Simon stated, "You look a little odd. Your dancing is terrible, the singing was horrendous and you look like one of those creatures that live in the jungle with those massive eyes—a bush baby" (Wulf n. pag.). Naturally, Briggs suffered hurt feelings, but much of the nation laughed. Shortly after the broadcast Briggs' family issued a statement expressing the hurt that Kenneth felt, Cowell failed to apologize.

As television has become a staple in most American homes, many children are raised watching programs that feature Schadenfreude. Thus, bullying has become a subliminal part of everyday life. Perhaps people do not realize that they are taking part in bullying behavior when they laugh at the misfortune of others. Arguably, most people would never behave in that way in public toward another person. However, when children witness their parents laughing at people on television the idea of doing so themselves begins to form. Indeed, many behaviors are learned because of parental actions. Monitoring, or censoring, programming is one way of an attempt to thwart the influence of bad behavior; however, this censoring limits itself to vulgar language and inappropriate visuals. It does nothing to control Schadenfreude. As such, youth viewing broadcasts today are indoctrinated into a psyche of bullying without realizing it—laughing at the expense of others to feel good about themselves for entertainment.

Naturally, Schadenfreude transcends TV and can be witnessed on the Internet. Sites like YouTube, Facebook, and Twitter are all forums for public bullying. In these instances people are allowed to bully others solely with words, hiding behind the perceived safety of social media. Although this may sound less violent than physical bullying, it can spread rampantly. It is not uncommon to find an embarrassing picture of a person quickly turned into a meme and then spread throughout the social network. Typically, people do not think about who was in the embarrassing picture, they just continue to share the humorous meme, failing to realize that the picture was a real person, who more than likely currently exists. A real person with feelings, but all of that is lost on a quick laugh spread through cyberspace.

Internet bullying has become a monster in and of itself within the past five years. Cyberbullying can and has ended in suicide—a devastating fact. According to the CDC:

> Suicide is the third leading cause of death among young people with approximately 4,400 deaths every year. The CDC estimates that there are at least 100 suicide attempts for every suicide among young people. More than 14 percent of high school students have considered suicide and nearly 7 percent have

attempted it, that is why you will, sadly, read about cyberbullying cases in the media now more than ever [Six Unforgettable n. pag.].

Though cyberbullying is currently at the forefront in the media, arguably because of the presence social media has in the lives of many modern Americans, bullying still occurs face-to-face in schools throughout the country. Elementary, middle, and high schools are no stranger to bullying seminars where people are encouraged to be kind to one another, to treat each other with respect, and stop the bullying of others. Despite these frequent seminars and anti-bullying activities, bullying appears to be a larger problem in schools now than it ever has been in the past. According to the National Center for Educational Statistics, "Nearly 1 in 3 students (27.8%) report being bullied during the school year … 19.6% report being bullied at school … 14.8% reported being bullied online" (Bullying Statistics n. pag.). These statistics continue to rise every year, resulting in more programs introduced into schools about tolerance, acceptance, and social justice; yet, the bullying continues.

Arguably, reality TV, YouTube, and Schadenfreude are to blame for the surge in bullying behaviors. True, people have always experienced the notion of Schadenfreude. However, within the last fourteen years it has been broadcast to families the world over—becoming a part of enjoyable family time. Naturally, it would be hard for children to judge this bad behavior when they witness their parents enjoying it, often delighting in it with their parents. Separating what is right from what is humorous can be a daunting task for children. Perhaps most parents do not realize that they are championing bullying when watching programs designed to seduce by Schadenfreude which means the rate of bullying will not decrease.

The Post–9/11 Hero and Bullying

While male superheroes are battling supernatural foes onscreen, realistic male heroes are attempting to defeat bullying in YAL. Characters like Arnold Spirit Junior are not typically thought of as heroic. Junior describes himself as a gangly nerd. Audiences view Junior as an awkward boy longing for acceptance from his different discourse communities. Indeed, audiences laugh at Junior, it is near impossible to stifle laughter when reading Alexie's novel. However, these audiences are not truly laughing at Junior. Instead they are responding to the humorous way in which he processes his emotions. Throughout the novel Junior draws images of himself, his best friend, his love interest, his parents and typically with comedic flair. However, never once do readers find themselves rejoicing in Junior's misery; readers empathize with Junior, they want him to be happy, and are thrilled when he succeeds. Alexie is able to garner this response from his readers because he did not write this book to humiliate anyone, but rather to tell the story of someone who was frequently humiliated. *The Absolutely True Diary of a Part-Time Indian* is the poignant story of a young man who rises above circumstances that most readers can relate to and be educated by.

The irony is not lost on the fact that Arnold Spirit Junior, a native American character, represents a modern John Wayne all American Cowboy figure, a new version of the post–9/11 male hero. He embodies the characteristics that contemporary young men are now being championed for, including sensitivity, egoless, a friend to many, unsure of himself, intelligent, fair, quick witted, and athletic. He does not resemble a Clint Eastwood, but instead is closer to a Rick Moranis. Yet he, and other male characters like him published post–9/11, typically triumph in their novels. Nancy Farmer's *The House of the Scorpion* and *The Lord of Opium*, both published post–9/11, feature a male character known as Mateo Alacran who was bullied by both family and non–family members. The bullying that Mateo endures both defines and inspires him. Readers become enraged at the way Mateo is treated, hoping that he will somehow evade his terrible circumstances. In Farmer's novels Mateo toes the line between responding violently to his bullying and responding in a peaceful manner. Eventually he overcomes the human desire for vigilante justice and chooses right over wrong, thus becoming a positive symbol of bullying survivorship.

Male heroes that react positively to bullying are warranted as well as needed in a society heavily laden with reactionary violence. According to the article "School Bullying: Why Quick Fixes Do Not Prevent School Failure," bullying is an issue of critical concern in many schools across the United States, as studies have shown that many school shootings are the result of bullying (Casebeer 165). The Columbine, Colorado, school shooting has been considered one of the most brutal school shootings in United States history, and the initial investigative findings directly linked the massacre to bullying (Bentley n. pag.). However, recent studies have concluded that the young men both suffered from social disorders; indeed, they had been bullied or picked on, but did not directly lash out at those who had been teasing them. Instead their reactions were heightened due to the mental disorders they suffered from, resulting in the young men taking their frustrations out on a grand traumatic scale. Yet, the notion still persists that bullying has a great deal to do with how and why the tragedy at Columbine occurred (Bentley n. pag.).

Anti-bullying assemblies are held at elementary, middle, and high schools throughout the country on a semi-annual basis. Today's youth are constantly bombarded with anti-bullying propaganda by way of interactive role playing, songs, and testimonials. Many students return home from these assemblies wearing stickers pledging to stand up to bullies. The youth of today are proactively being made aware of the dangers of bullying; yet, the behaviors persist. Although much of the fault lies within the human characteristic of Schadenfreude and modern entertainment, blame in the failure to truly educate about bullying can directly be placed on people who ban books like *The Absolutely True Diary of a Part-Time Indian*. In Alexie's text, young readers are given the opportunity to laugh and cry alongside a bullying victim. These young adults can vicariously experience the same emotions that Junior does, and perhaps feel as if someone else understands.

The notion of instruct and delight is not new to YAL, as many books written within the genre are created with this ideology. Sadly, some parents do not view these texts as the portals for discussion that they are and side to ban them before any conversation or lesson can be learned. Books like *Forever* by Judy Blume provide a platform for conversations about sex; the book itself, though no prize winning literature like Alexie's, deals with tough topics in a way that is inviting and entertaining. These types of books, which toe the line of what is considered ethical, and are read by young adults with more fervor than any pamphlet or text book. Sometimes these books are so beloved that they are passed to others, in hopes that the book can help that person too: "When I read *The Absolutely True Diary of a Part-Time Indian* I finally felt like I wasn't alone. Like, someone else knew what it was like ... to be picked on by everyone. To not fit in. This book made me feel like I belonged. That I was okay" (Sharp n. pag.). Ashton Sharp, a high school senior, shared this book with many people after she had finished reading it, as it had helped her to process her own traumatic bullying events. Instead of banning this book, it would be a bold move to pair it with anti-bullying propaganda as a way to instruct and delight youth rather than continue to provide them with reinvented versions of the same material.

Arnold Spirit Junior may not be the strong John Wayne cowboy type many people think of when envisioning a hero. He is not the hero that will save the day guns blazing, but he is a hero who does stand up for what is right in a just and contemplative way. Junior is representative of what young men are becoming today, as gender roles become redefined. Many life lessons can be gleaned from Alexie's text; indeed, it is a story rich in "and the moral to the story is" scenarios. Ultimately, the novel allows readers to experience life through the eyes of an Other. Indeed, adolescence itself is ripe with moments such as this, a time when young adults feel as if they have to fit in and are often ridiculed if they do not. YAL has been battling fantastical dystopic conditions for the past eight years, and no doubt will continue to do so for the foreseeable future. Indeed, adolescence itself can be compared to a dystopia where there is a controlling force, high technology, power struggles, and often a love story. It is relevant that this subgenre would be so popular in YAL, and even more relevant that young women, whose roles are often assigned in real life, are the heroines of these novels, winning their dystopias. YAL has also been waging its own war against bullying, another theme rampant in adolescence, only with young vulnerable, sensitive men leading the charge, showing that men do not have to react violently and can learn to get along with one another through conversation rather than belittling and fighting.

Anti-bullying pamphlets, Readers Theater, and propaganda are no match for the constant barrage of Schadenfreude that youth are exposed to today. An afternoon assembly of fun activities may reach a few students, but in a larger sense this type of educating seems to be falling short. As such, educators and parents need to be willing to allow young adults to read books like *Part-Time Indian*, to not be afraid of the vulgarity within the story, but to instead learn from it. The post–9/11 male hero is ready to save the day, if only parents and educators will let him.

Notes

1. The John Wayne movement can be described as a response that a culture experiences post-tragedy—in other words, the need of a strong male hero to save the day feeling. Typically, females are seen in more traditional roles when this happens and popular culture becomes ripe with strong male characters

2. "The Other is an individual who is perceived by the group as not belonging, as being different in some fundamental way. Any stranger becomes the Other. The group sees itself as the norm and judges those who do not meet that norm (that is, who are different in any way) as the Other. Perceived as lacking essential characteristics possessed by the group, the Other is almost always seen as a lesser or inferior being and is treated accordingly. The Other in a society may have few or no legal rights, may be characterized as less intelligent or as immoral, and may even be regarded as sub-human" (The Other n. pag.).

3. A rare genetic disorder that effects the height, physical features, skeleton, and muscles of a person.

Works Cited

Alexie, Sherman. *The Absolutely True Diary of a Part-Time Indian.* New York: Little, Brown, 2007.

———. "Fiction and Poetry Award Winner." *The Horn Book Magazine* 85.1 (2009): 25–28. *MasterFILE Premier.* Web. 30 Nov. 2014.

Baird, Pressley. "Brunswick School Officials to Keep Challenged Book in Curriculum, Library." *The Star-News* (2014): n.p. *Regional Business News.* Web. 30 Nov. 2014.

Bentley, Lynn. "Bullying and Rampage School Shootings." *The New Bullying* (2012): n.p. *Michigan State University School of Journalism.* Web. 1 Dec. 2014.

"Bullying Statistics." *PACER's National Bullying Prevention Center,* PACER Center (2013): n.p. Web. 1 Dec. 2014.

Casebeer, Cindy M. "School Bullying: Why Quick Fixes Do Not Prevent School Failure." *Preventing School Failure* 56.3 (2012): 165–171. *Academic Search Elite.* Web. 6 Dec. 2014.

Hu, Jane. "A Joyful and Malicious History of Schadenfreude." *The Awl.com,* The Awl. 10 Oct. 2011. n.p. Web. 4 Deb. 2014.

Sharp, Ashton. Personal interview. 21 Nov. 2014.

"Six Unforgettable Cyberbullying Cases." *NoBullying.com,* NoBullying.com. 23 Apr. 2013. Web. 4 Dec. 2014.

Wulf, Jon. "A Critical Guide to Reality Television." *Ethics Debasement and Evaluation* (n.d.): n.p. *Academic Search Elite.* Web. 4 Deb. 2014.

About the Contributors

Eduardo **Barros-Grela** is an associate professor in the Department of English at A Coruna University (Spain), where he teaches American studies and cultural studies. His academic interests include posthuman aesthetics, *in*organic bodies and spaces, visual studies, and the dialectics of representation and performance. Recent publications include studies of spaces of violence in the areas of American studies, contemporary film, ecocriticism and literature.

Nina Marie **Bone** is a member of the English faculty at the Saginaw Chippewa Tribal College in Mount Pleasant, Michigan. She received a master's degree from the University of Texas–Pan America. Her research focused on young adult anti-bullying novels and she continues helping young adults create positive relationships through books.

Kasey **Butcher** is a doctoral candidate at Miami University, where she studies girlhood and cultural citizenship in American literature and human rights rhetoric. In addition to teaching first-year composition and American literature courses, she has also published essays about high achieving girls on *Glee* and *Veronica Mars*, as well as depictions of girlhood and violence on the U.S.-Mexico border.

Mary-Lynn **Chambers** has taught English in Virginia and North Carolina at community colleges and universities. Her instructional focus is composition, with a research focus in online education at HBCU schools. She enjoys interacting with her students and inspiring them to write better, think more critically, and love literature.

Kelly F. **Franklin** is a full-time member of the English faculty at Southwestern Community College in Creston, Iowa. Much of her research is centered on role performance in young adult literature—particularly post–9/11 female character depiction in popular culture, specifically in *The Walking Dead*. She also writes for *www.nerdsandnomsense.com*, and her own blog entitled Threat Level Violet.

Tamara **Girardi** is an English instructor for Harrisburg Area Community College's Virtual Learning program. Her primary research interests are creative writing studies, online pedagogy and learning environments, popular culture, Twitter and Facebook as learning tools, and young adult literature.

Kylo-Patrick R. **Hart** is chair of the Department of Film, Television and Digital Media at Texas Christian University. He is the author or editor of several books about media, including *The AIDS Movie: Representing a Pandemic in Film and Television*; *Film and Sexual Politics*; *Film and Television Stardom*; *Images for a Generation Doomed: The Films and Career of Gregg Araki*; and *Queer Males in Contemporary Cinema: Becoming Visible*.

Kulwinder P. **Kaur** is a professor of psychology and chair of the institutional review board at Elizabeth City State University. She has published a book chapter and research articles in addition to book reviews and funded grant projects. She has varied research interests including student-related issues such as bullying, HIV prevention, classroom etiquettes, psychoanalysis of literature, and health disparities.

Katherine **Lashley** is a Ph.D. candidate in English at Morgan State University. Her dissertation analyzes the themes of gender, disability, and social class in young adult dystopias, including *The Hunger Games* by Suzanne Collins and *Divergent* by Veronica Roth. She teaches first-year writing courses at Towson University and Harford Community College.

Chantelle **MacPhee** is an academic chair at Miami Dade College West. Her research interests include British literature, Harry Potter, William Shakespeare, William Blake and eighteenth-century visual and verbal representations of Shakespeare.

Fernando Gabriel **Pagnoni Berns** of the Universidad de Buenos Aires (UBA)—Facultad de Filosofía y Letras (Argentina) teaches seminars on American horror cinema and Euro horror. He is director of a research group on horror cinema, "Grite," and has published essays in the books *Undead in the West*; *To See the Saw Movies: Essays on Torture Porn and Post 9/11 Horror*; and *Reading Richard Matheson: A Critical Survey*, among others.

Canela Ailen **Rodriguez Fontao** holds a degree in arts from the Facultad de Filosofía y Letras, Universidad de Buenos Aires (Argentina). She is a member of the research group oncinema CIyNE and Grite and has published articles on cinema and television in publications as *lafuga* and in books such as *Cine y Revolución en America Latina*, edited by Ana Laura Lusnich. She is a lecturer specializing in horror TV and cinema.

Abigail G. **Scheg** is an assistant professor of English at Elizabeth City State University and a dissertation chair for Northcentral University and Grand Canyon University. She researches, publishes, and makes presentations at conferences in the areas of online pedagogy, composition, distance education, and popular culture.

Don **Tresca** has a master's degree in English from California State University, Sacramento, where he specialized in 20th century American literature and film studies. He has previously published essays on a wide variety of pop culture subjects, including the works of Joss Whedon, J. K. Rowling, Stephen King, and Clint Eastwood.

Mariana S. **Zárate** is a graduate in arts at the Universidad de Buenos Aires (Argentina) and a member of the research group in horror cinema, "Grite." She lectures on Argentine cinema and conducts research on Argentine horror films of the last decade as a marginal expression.

Index

abjection 131, 138–142
absenteeism 114
The Absolutely True Diary of a Part-Time Indian 11, 176–178, 180
abused 78
accomplishments 78
accountability 79
Adler, Max 109
administrator 72, 74, 76, 79
African American 6, 66, 67, 77, 118
aggression 14, 16, 22, 31, 65, 67, 68, 85, 117–122, 125–127, 154; *see also* passive aggression; relational aggression
Alexie, Sherman 11, 177–179, 183–185
alienation 73
American Idol 181
anal intercourse 107
anger 74
anti-bullying 2, 5–6, 22–23, 29, 35–36, 55–59, 62, 80, 88–90
anxiety 68, 69, 74
appropriate 65, 70
Asperger syndrome 21
assault 111
assertiveness 76
audience 97
Autism Spectrum Disorders 21

The Big Bang Theory 4
Blubber 58
Brainstorm 75
Bully (video game) 5
Burke, Michael 103
The Burning 134

Canada 66, 79
Candid Camera 181
Carrie (film) 8, 10, 117, 121, 130, 131, 135–137, 139–140, 142, 152–161
Carrie (novel) 152
castration 108
class 98, 119, 125–126

clique 121–123, 126–127
coach 77
Colfer, Chris 109
Collins, Suzanne 176
Columbine 157–159
coming out 113
community 68
confidence 66, 76, 77, 78, 79
confidentiality 75
covert 69, 70, 71, 72, 75
Criss, Darren 110
Cruel Intentions 121
cyberbullying 13, 19–21, 30, 36–37, 75, 82–90, 182, 183

DARE 65
De Palma, Brian 153–156
depression 21, 74, 114
deviant 132–135, 137
Divergent 2, 10
dystopia 176, 184–186

educators 77, 78, 79, 80
emotion 57, 73, 76, 78, 80
encouragement 78
ethnicities 68
Everdeen, Katniss 176
expulsion 111

family 67, 76
Farmer, Nancy 185
father 66
fellatio 104, 107
female objectification 167–168
femininity 117–120, 153
film 67, 71, 79, 126
The Final 141–142
Friday Night Lights 117, 123–125
future 77, 78, 79

gang 66, 67, 68, 77
gender 20–23, 65, 117–120, 122–123, 176, 177

Glee 7, 103, 109–115
golden snitch 9, 147
Gossip Girl 117, 120, 125
Grease 121
Guiry, Tom 104

healing 77, 79, 80
Heathers 117, 120–121
helplessness 114
hierarchy 117–120, 125
high school 66, 71, 73
Hirsch, Emile 104
homophobia 109, 111, 170
horror films 8, 130–131, 138–139, 142
The House Bunny 126
The Hunger Games 2, 6, 91

identity 67, 77, 78
Inge, William 108
intervention 115
intimidation 65, 69, 73

Jawbreaker 117, 121–122
Jenkins, Richard 104

Karate Kid 6, 71, 73, 78
King, Stephen 152–154
Kristeva, Julia 138

language 57–59, 61, 63
latent homosexuality 103, 110
Law and Order: Special Victims Unit 6, 82–90
LGBT 21
A Little Raw on Monday Mornings 56
loneliness 114

makeover 121, 127
male bonding 106
Malfoy, Draco 1, 144
masculinity 106, 166, 171
Mean Girls 73, 117, 119–120, 122, 126–127
mentor 66, 78, 79, 80
Michele, Lea 111
middle school 66, 68, 69
Middleton, Kate 113
mobbing 131–135, 137
Monteith, Cory 111
mourning 105
The Mudge Boy 7, 103–109, 110, 113–115
Murphy, Ryan 113

name-calling 114
Napoleon Dynamite 4
Never Been Kissed 121

Odd Girl Out 117, 122, 127
Olweus, Dan 13, 14, 16, 18–19, 132
O'Malley, Mike 111
Otherness 131–142

parents 6, 72, 75–79, 82–90
Parents, Family and Friends of Lesbians and Gays (PFLAG) 112
passive aggression 117–123, 126–128
physical 4, 16, 30–32, 65, 67, 69, 72, 75, 80, 85, 109–111, 113, 114
Pittsburgh Public Schools 36–37
post 9/11 176–178, 183, 186
Potter, Harry 2, 144
praise 66, 77, 78, 79
Precious 67, 73, 77
pregnancy 83–88
Pretty Little Liars 117, 119, 126–127
Prince, Phoebe 119
Prom Night 133

Queen Bees and Wannabes 117, 120, 122, 127
queerness 7, 103–115, 132, 135
Quidditch 9, 145–146

race 16, 118
The Real World 29–31
Reality TV 4, 30–39, 181–183
relational aggression 16, 112–121, 122–123, 126–128
Remember the Titans 73
Renault, Jerry 5, 56–57, 60–63
representation 103
revenge 72, 130, 132–134, 140
Reviving Ophelia 119
Rivera, Naya 112
role model 66
Rosemont, Romy 111

The Sand Lot 73
Schadenfreude 11, 177, 180–183, 186
Sedgwick, Eve Kosofsky 103
self-concept 114
self-defense 67, 77
self-esteem 66, 68, 69, 74, 78
self-loathing 107
Seth's Law 23
sexual orientation 21, 103, 105, 108, 109, 112, 114
sexuality 21, 67, 73, 123–125, 127
She's All That 121
shootings 1, 65, 72, 152, 154
slasher 131–135, 142
small town life 108
social media 20
suicide 20, 29, 83, 112, 113, 114

teachers 73–79
Terror Train 133
Tormented 140, 142
Twilight 2

Ushkowitz, Jenna 109

verbal abuse 16, 109, 111–112
Veronica Mars 117, 126
victim-bully 74
video game 5, 32
vigils 5, 56, 62

Voldemort 145

weirdness 106
white 6, 66, 71
wife beating 104
Williams, Tennessee 108
workplace bullying 22, 97

young adult literature 2, 5, 177–179, 183–186

zero tolerance 30, 65, 110

www.ingramcontent.com/pod-product-compliance
Lightning Source LLC
Chambersburg PA
CBHW061348300426
44116CB00011B/2041